Mental Health Systems and Policy in Low- and Middle-Income Countries

Series Editor

S. M. Yasir Arafat, Bangladesh Specialized Hospital, Dhaka, Bangladesh

This series of books explores critical dimensions of mental health and psychology in low- and middle-income countries (LMICs), where the majority of people with mental illness live but access to care and research remains limited. Despite a significant disease burden, mental health services in LMICs face challenges such as inadequate infrastructure, workforce shortages, stigma, and high treatment gaps. These volumes aim to address these gaps by presenting culturally relevant, evidence-based insights and practical solutions tailored to resource-constrained settings.

Covering topics such as mental health services, epidemiology, social psychiatry, addiction, suicide prevention, psychiatric nursing, and the impact of climate change, migration, and disasters, the series integrates global perspectives with local realities. Each book emphasizes innovative interventions, policy recommendations, and strategies for improving mental health literacy and reducing stigma. Contributions from LMIC-based clinicians and researchers ensure authentic, context-specific knowledge.

Designed for academics, practitioners, policymakers, and students, this series provides a comprehensive platform for advancing research, informing practice, and supporting capacity building. By addressing underexplored areas and fostering inclusive discourse, it seeks to improve mental health outcomes and promote sustainable development across diverse LMIC settings.

S. M. Yasir Arafat
Editor

Suicidal Behavior in Bangladesh

Epidemiology, Risk Factors, and Prevention

Second Edition

Springer

Editor
S. M. Yasir Arafat
Bangladesh Specialized Hospital
Dhaka, Bangladesh

ISSN 3120-4376 ISSN 3120-4384 (electronic)
Mental Health Systems and Policy in Low- and Middle-Income Countries
ISBN 978-981-95-8320-1 ISBN 978-981-95-8321-8 (eBook)
https://doi.org/10.1007/978-981-95-8321-8

This Springer imprint is published by the registered company Springer Nature Singapore Pte Ltd.
The registered company address is: 152 Beach Road, #21-01/04 Gateway East, Singapore 189721, Singapore

To my beloved wife, Asma Khatun

Preface

Suicidal behavior is a major, however, under-researched public health problem in Bangladesh. The country still lacks a national suicide surveillance system and a national suicide prevention strategy. Therefore, access to quality suicide data for policymaking is a fundamental challenge. There are wide variations in the suicide rate as per different studies and international reports. Additionally, there are strong possibilities of under-reporting of suicidal behavior in the country. Suicide attempt is a criminal offense in the legal system of the country, which certainly hinders the disclosure of the behavior. A high level of stigma, a low level of suicide literacy, an enduring culture, a Muslim majority religious background, and criminality badge affect suicide prevention initiatives in Bangladesh. Fortunately, an increased number of studies are coming out in the current decade exploring multiple aspects of suicidal behavior, indicating that social factors have a prominent role than the mental disorder, which is a noticeable prospect in the country. Nevertheless, there is no book on suicide and suicidal behavior in Bangladesh, neither in English nor in Bangla. Therefore, this book aimed to present a comprehensive outlook on suicidal behavior in the country based on existing evidence and expertise covering epidemiology, concerns of quality data of suicidal behavior, local culture, forensic aspects, health and mental health care, media and suicide, crisis management system, family dynamics and suicidal behavior, socio-ecological perspectives, non-suicidal self-injury (NSSI), law and policies on suicide prevention, suicide prevention status, and status of suicide research in the country. This edition adds some chapters and widens the focus from suicide to suicidal behavior after the addition of details of suicidal thoughts, plans, and attempts. It also includes NSSI to cover every aspect of self-harm behavior, socio-ecological analysis, law and policy aspects of suicide prevention, and suicide literacy and stigma towards suicide in Bangladesh. This book is the first of its kind to address multiple aspects of suicidal behavior in the country. It would be a useful resource for academics, researchers, policymakers, as well as non-governmental and voluntary organizations interested in suicide prevention in the country. It highlights the research gaps and recommendations for the national suicide prevention strategy in Bangladesh.

Dhaka, Bangladesh S. M. Yasir Arafat

Contents

About the Editor

S. M. Yasir Arafat is currently working as an Associate Consultant of Psychiatry at Bangladesh Specialized Hospital, Dhaka, Bangladesh. He is an Associate Professor of Frontier University Garowe, Somalia, an Associate Fellow of the Bangladesh Academy of Sciences, and a Senior Research Fellow of the Biomedical Research Foundation, Bangladesh. He was affiliated with the University of Bristol, UK, as a Visiting Senior Research Associate (August 2021–2023) and an Honorary Research Fellow with Dnet (October 2023–2025). He completed his MD in Psychiatry from Bangabandhu Sheikh Mujib Medical University, Dhaka, and his MBBS from the Dhaka Medical College, Bangladesh. He also did an MPH in Health Economics and an MBA in Marketing. Dr. Arafat has (co)authored more than 400 peer-reviewed articles and more than 50 book chapters, and (co)edited more than 15 books with Springer. He is the lead editor of the book series *South Asian Perspectives in Mental Health and Psychology* with Springer. He has been included in the global 2% researcher list in 2021–2023, and 2025. He is an editorial member of more than 10 leading journals in mental health, published by Elsevier, Wiley, Springer, and Routledge. His research focused on mental health, suicidal behavior, psychometrics, panic buying, and psycho-sexual disorders.

List of Figures

List of Tables

Chapter 1
Data Is Silent, Epidemiology Is Blur: Suicidal Behavior in Bangladesh—What Is Known and What Needs to Improve

S. M. Yasir Arafat and Russell Kabir

1 Introduction

Bangladesh has been one of the fastest-growing economies in the world over the past decade (World Bank, 2024). Like many other developing nations, Bangladesh is also experiencing enormous political, environmental, and social challenges within itself. The most significant challenge is the country's large population. Dhaka, the capital, is the sixth most densely populated city in the world, with around 29,069 people per square kilometer (World Atlas, 2025).

Although the public health scenario has improved remarkably in Bangladesh over the last 30 years, the country still faces significant health challenges, and there are still numerous health issues that its health care system has yet to handle successfully (Muhammad et al., 2017). Suicidal behavior is one of them. Suicide is a complex phenomenon and is considered a major public health problem. Not only demographic factors but also an amalgam of psychological, social, biological, cultural, and environmental factors push an individual to die by suicide (Zalsman et al., 2016). Effective suicide prevention warrants good empirical studies, and epidemiological data help us to identify the population at risk; this, in turn, can be used to reinforce decision-making (Fairchild et al., 2018). Against this backdrop, this chapter aims to explore the epidemiological aspects of suicidal behavior in Bangladesh and evaluate the quality of suicide data in the country.

S. M. Y. Arafat (✉)
Department of Psychiatry, Bangladesh Specialized Hospital, Dhaka, Bangladesh

Department of Public and Community Health, Faculty of Medicine and Health Sciences, Frontier University Garowe, Garowe, Somalia

R. Kabir
School of Allied Health, Anglia Ruskin University, Essex, UK

S. M. Y. Arafat (ed.), *Suicidal Behavior in Bangladesh*, Mental Health Systems and Policy in Low- and Middle-Income Countries,
https://doi.org/10.1007/978-981-95-8321-8_1

2 Epidemiology

2.1 Rate

2.1.1 Suicide

Bangladesh has no central suicide database or national suicide surveillance system (Arafat, 2017, 2019a, 2025a). To the best of our knowledge, no nationwide study has been conducted to assess the burden of suicide in the country in different age groups. There are wide variations among the rates published in World Health Organization (WHO) reports, nongovernmental organization data, and empirical studies. Above all, there are concerns about underreporting and misclassification of suicides that hide the real gravity of the problem. The WHO publishes suicide rates periodically using a modelling approach. We mention the WHO-published suicide rates in Bangladesh in 2012, 2016, 2019, and 2025 in Table 1.1.

Surprisingly, the data revealed that Bangladesh is relatively prosperous in suicide reduction without any visible efforts or preventive measures from the government. In 2012, the suicide rate for both sexes was 7.8/100,000, while it was 6.1/100,00 in 2016 and 3.9/100,000 in 2019. Another surprising finding is that the rate was higher in females until 2016, but the recently published 2019 data showed that males died more than females, as shown in Table 1.1. WHO (2014) reported that the age-standardized suicide rate for both sexes was 7.8/100,000, for males was 7.3/100,000, and for females 8.2/100,000. A community-based survey conducted by Feroz and his colleagues identified that the rate of suicide attempts was 281.8 per 100,000 and the rate of suicide was 128.8 per 100,000, which seems to be significantly higher in comparison to the WHO reports (Feroz et al., 2012). Another WHO report mentioned that the suicide rate was 14.7 per 100,000 population, which was found by

Table 1.1 Suicide rate in Bangladesh according to WHO reports

Year	Sex	Number of suicides	Crude suicide rate (per 100,000)	Age-standardized suicide rate (per 100,000)
2012	Total	10,167	6.6	7.8
	Female	5773	7.6	8.7
	Male	4394	5.6	6.8
2016	Total	9544	5.9	6.1
	Female	5666	7.0	6.7
	Male	3878	4.7	5.5
2019	Total	5998	3.7	3.9
	Female	1331	1.7	1.7
	Male	4667	5.7	6.0
	Total	4714	2.8	2.9
2021	Female	1701	2	1.9
	Male	3013	3.6	3.9

Adapted from: WHO (2014, 2017, 2021, 2025)

the *Bangladesh Health and Injury Survey 2016* (World Health Organization, 2022). Another community-based study with 20-year duration conducted in the South-East part of the country from 1983 to 2002 identified the suicide rate of 39.6 per 100,000 population (ICDDR,B, 2003). Mashreky and his colleagues interviewed 819,429 community populations from 12 different districts of Bangladesh in 2003 and found the rate of suicide was 7.3 per 100,000 population (Mashreky et al., 2013). Another rate was revealed from police data from 1996 to 2014, which revealed the rate of unnatural death was 10.4 per 100,000 population; among them, hanging and pesticide poisoning accounted for 6.5 per 100,000 population (Chowdhury et al., 2018). The unnatural deaths include hanging, pesticide/medication poisoning, road traffic, railway, and waterway accidents, fall from height, construction injury, snake bite, drowning, electrocution, thunderbolt injury, and burn-related deaths (Chowdhury et al., 2018). Another report published in 1998 found that the suicide rate among young populations was 30 per 100,000 population living in the rural part of Bangladesh (Ruzicka, 1998, cited in Begum et al., 2017a). A recent study in the *Jhenaidah* district of Bangladesh assessed 3152 suicide data of an NGO (*Societies for Voluntary Activities (SOVA*) from 2010 to 2018 (Khan et al., 2020). The study found the suicide rate was 20.6/100,000 in *Jhenaidah* (Khan et al., 2020). Available evidence suggests that suicide happens more in the peripheral districts and rural parts, mentioning *Chuadanga*, *Jenaidah*, *Kustia*, *Meherpur*, *Jashore*, and *Chandpur* (Arafat, 2019a). However, caution is warranted to consider the areas with high rates, as we do not have any countrywide data, and the rate varies widely.

2.1.2 Suicidal Behavior

In recent years, studies have been coming out assessing suicidal behavior among specific cohorts, like among students (Arafat et al., 2024a; Marthoenis & Arafat, 2022), nurses (Arafat et al., 2021a), Imams (Arafat et al., 2024b), cancer patients (Emi et al., 2025), adolescents (Begum et al., 2017a), older adults (Wahlin et al., 2015; Arafat & Mazumdar, 2025), and gays (Mozumder et al., 2023). One study assessed suicidal behavior in Jhenaidah between 2010 and 2018, with 22,675 suicide attempts, and found that the rate of suicide attempts was 136.35/100,000 (Khan et al., 2020). Another community-based study in Chuadanga found the rate of suicide attempts was 281.8 per 100,000 (Feroz et al., 2012). One recent meta-analysis found that the rate of suicide attempts was 4.25%, with a higher prevalence among females and an increase in the second half of the decade (Shuvo et al., 2024).

One nationwide study assessed suicidal behavior among youths (10–24 years) among 1744 participants using the Bangla *SUPRE-MISS* questionnaire. It found the prevalence of suicidal idea, plan, and attempt was 4.7%, 1.5%, and 1.5%, respectively. Females had significantly higher rates than males, and these rates were significantly higher in urban areas (National Institute of Mental Health, 2021). Multiple studies have been published assessing suicidal behavior among students. One meta-analysis analysed 12 studies among students and found the rate of suicidal ideation, plan, and attempt was 13%, 8%, and 4%, respectively, in a year (Arafat et al.,

2024a). A nationwide study among the general population is warranted to understand the burden. One recent meta-analysis found that the prevalence of suicidal thoughts, plans, and attempts was 24.2%, 5.6%, and 7%, respectively, in lifetime. The prevalence of thoughts, plans, and attempts was 15%, 5.2%, and 3.9%, respectively, in a year, and the prevalence of thoughts was 6.7% in a month (Arafat et al., 2025a). The analysis found that the prevalence of lifetime suicidal thoughts has increased by 0.4% per year over the years. The prevalence of suicidal thoughts was significantly higher among students during their lifetime, 30.9% (95% CI: 18.6–46.6%); in a year, 15.6% (95% CI: 11.7–20.6%); and in a month, 9.7% (95% CI: 6.7–13.8%). The prevalence of suicidal plans was also higher among students during their lifetime, 11.2% (95% CI: 5.2–22.3%), and in a year, 7.3% (95% CI: 6.7–8.1%). The rate of lifetime suicide attempts (9.2%, 95% CI: 6.7–12.5%) was higher among students compared to others (Arafat et al., 2025a).

2.2 Gender Distribution

In Bangladesh, it has been shown that females are dying more by suicide in the available literature, which is opposite to the Western country distribution (Arafat, 2019a, 2019b; Bachmann, 2018; Jordans et al., 2014; Shahnaz et al., 2017). Several empirical studies revealed this female predominance in Bangladesh (see Ahmad & Hossain, 2010; Reza et al., 2014; Feroz et al., 2012; Talukder et al., 2014; Ali et al., 2014; Shah et al., 2018; Shah et al., 2017; Arafat et al., 2018; Qusar et al., 2010; Khan et al., 2020; Mashreky et al., 2013). We speculate that patriarchal societal norms, perceived passive gender roles, early marriage, low empowerment, comparatively lower educational attainment, forceful marriage, and lack of economic freedom could be the potential reasons for this high rate of suicide in females (Reza et al., 2014; Feroz et al., 2012; Arafat, 2017; Arafat, 2019a). However, further studies are warranted to identify the precise explanations of this female dominance in suicide in Bangladesh. The latest systematic review assessing suicidal behavior revealed no variations based on gender (Arafat et al., 2025a).

2.3 Age Distribution

Arafat (2017) cited that the younger generation of Bangladesh is dying more by suicide than other age groups. Suicides are noted from 8 years to 78 years old. We identified only one study revealing the highest rate of suicide among the older age group (Mashreky et al., 2013). Several other studies identified that the third decade (20–29 years) of life is the most risky period for suicide in Bangladesh (see Arafat, 2017; Arafat, 2019a; Feroz et al., 2012; Ali et al., 2014; Choudhury et al., 2013; Hossain et al., 2012; Sarkar et al., 2013; Talukder et al., 2014; Begum et al., 2017b; Ahmad & Hossain, 2010; Shah et al., 2017). Loss of life during this decade creates an immense social burden. This is the time of life when people start to contribute to society and their families. Many of the deceased have little kids and spouses. Therefore, it causes a huge burden on society. The recent trend of increased suicides among adolescent students in Bangladesh is a major matter of concern. It is important to note that all the studies assessed a group of populations in a specific period of time. To get a clearer picture, there is a need for nationwide long-term follow-up studies.

2.4 *Risk Factors for Suicide*

Assessment of risk factors for suicidal behavior is a neglected area in Bangladesh. The first case-control study was published in 2014 by Reza and his colleagues. It found several risk factors, including love affair problems, discord with relatives, economic hardship, academic failure, long-term disability, chronic diseases, past suicidal attempts, familial conflict, sleep disturbance, and substance abuse (Reza et al., 2014). The study included samples of both fatal and nonfatal attempts. Nevertheless, it did not clearly indicate the number of suicides and self-harm cases. The only case-control psychological autopsy study revealed existing mental illness, past suicidal attempts, immediate life events, physical disability, physical abuse, social isolation, unemployment, substance abuse, and encounter with sexual abuse as notable risk factors for suicides (Arafat et al., 2021b, Box 1). It also revealed that individuals with psychiatric disorders are 15 times more likely to die by suicide, and individuals who experienced sexual abuse are 12 times more likely to die by suicide. A separate analysis revealed different characteristics of suicide with and without mental illness. It was noted that psychiatric disorders were more common in suicides among males, adults, and deceased living alone (Arafat et al., 2021c). In 2021, Arafat and colleagues, in their psychological autopsy study, reported that social risk factors such as life events, physical and sexual abuse, employment, and social isolation are playing a more influential role than clinical risk factors like psychiatric disorders (Arafat et al., 2021d). Arafat and Khan (2021) shared that there is a close relationship between psychosexual issues and suicides in Bangladesh due to socio-cultural effects. About 47% of the suicides are taking place concerning sexual and marital matters, such as extramarital relationships (12%), premarital love relationships (12%), sexual abuse (6%), and forced marriage (2%) (Arafat & Khan, 2021). Li et al. (2021) analyzed that younger women within 1 year of pregnancy are more vulnerable to die by suicide. Age, education, employment, living with parents, and ownership are also reported as risk factors by Begum et al. (2017a, 2017b), and they found that adolescents who live with other people than their parents and are unemployed have a higher risk of dying by suicide (Begum et al., 2017a). Shah et al. (2017) found that conflict within the family (34.3%) and sexual harassment and problems in the relationship (10.3%) as major factors for suicide attempts. Also, Arafat (2017) highlighted in his review that a quarrel between husband and wife is a common risk factor for suicide in Bangladesh. Another research by Arafat et al.

(2018) found that affair-related issue (14.3%) is a major contributor to suicides. Research by Khan et al. (2020) concluded that married women between the ages of 15 and 29 who have experienced physical and sexual abuse and who live in rural regions are the group most at risk for engaging in suicidal behavior. Sharmin Salam et al. (2017) identified that married adolescents are 22 times more likely to attempt suicide than never-married people in Bangladesh.

Suicide is extremely multifactorial. A higher prevalence of psychiatric disorders is noted in Western countries, while in Bangladesh, along with mental illness, life events closely related to family members (family discord, disapproval of affair marriage) and psycho-sexual events (extra-marital affair, sexual harassment) play a significant role in suicides (see Feroz et al., 2012; Reza et al., 2014; Arafat, 2017, Arafat, 2019a; Ali et al., 2014; Hossain et al., 2012; Talukder et al., 2014; Ahmad & Hossain, 2010; Arafat & Khan 2021; Shahanaz et al., 2017; Shah et al., 2017; Arafat et al., 2018, 2024c, 2025b). According to the empirical studies from the aforementioned review, married women and adolescents between the ages of 12 and 29 who live in rural areas and who are subjected to physical and sexual abuse by their husbands and their families are significantly more likely to die by suicide, attempt suicide, or have suicidal thoughts.

Mashreky and his colleagues found more suicides in rural areas in comparison to the urban parts of Bangladesh. Repeated countrywide studies are warranted to get the picture more precisely. The reasons for higher suicide rates in the rural areas of Bangladesh are lack of literacy and failure to overcome poverty (Mashreky et al., 2013). Several studies noted that suicide is common more among married persons in comparison to never-married persons (Feroz et al., 2012; Ali et al., 2014; Ahmad & Hossain, 2010). Marriage is found as a protective factor against suicide in Western countries, which is the opposite in Bangladesh and other South Asian countries (Arafat et al., 2023a). We speculate several possibilities, such as early marriage, economic dependency on parents, and less freedom in choosing partners (Arafat, 2017).

Box 1 Important Risk Factors for Suicide in Bangladesh

1. Psychiatric disorders: depression, personality disorder, substance (Yaba) abuse
2. Adverse life events: Premarital affair and marriage, extra-marital affair and sex, premarital pregnancy, academic failure, marital discord, familial disharmony
3. Previous suicide attempt
4. Sexual abuse
5. Social isolation
6. Unemployment
7. Domestic violence
8. Academic failure
9. Demanding behavior

2.5 *Methods of Suicide*

The common methods of suicide in Bangladesh include hanging, pesticide poisoning, road traffic, railway accidents, falling from a height, drowning, electrocution, firearms, cut injury, and burning (Arafat, 2019a, 2017; Chowdhury et al., 2018). Hanging and poisoning are the two prominent methods of suicide in Bangladesh. A recent, systematic review identified that hanging was the most commonly used method in Bangladesh from 2011 to 2020 (Arafat et al., 2021e). Earlier studies conducted in rural samples found poisoning as the most common method, while recent studies found hanging as the most common method (Chowdhury et al., 2018; Arafat, 2019a; Mashreky et al., 2013; Shahnaz et al., 2017; Arafat et al., 2021e; Halim et al., 2010). The ban of class I pesticides in the year 2000 could be an important factor in Bangladesh (Chowdhury et al., 2018). Police data from 1996 to 2014 revealed that pesticide poisoning was the most common method (37.1%) of suicide, followed by hanging (30.5%) (Chowdhury et al., 2018). Other studies found hanging as the most common method of suicide (see Sharmin Salam et al., 2017; Shah et al., 2017; Arafat et al., 2018; Feroz et al., 2012; Arafat et al., 2021b; Ali et al., 2014; Hossain et al., 2012). The method of suicide among different cohorts is yet to be revealed. One study collected data from news reports of suicide among physicians and police and found that police used firearms and doctors used overdose. The difference was statistically significant (Arafat et al., 2025c).

2.6 *Rare Suicide Events in Bangladesh*

2.6.1 Protest Suicide

Sometimes, suicide is a tactic of persuasion (Biggs, 2013). Suicide protest is noted when someone selects suicide as a form of tactic to obtain their argument against potent challenges (Tilly, 2013). In the first week of July 2022, a 50-year-old businessman from Kushtia, Bangladesh, attempted suicide in front of the National Press Club (NPC) at Dhaka by setting himself on fire (Correspondence, 2022). He suffered 90% on his body and died the next day in a specialized burn hospital. He died suicide as he couldn't get hold of his 1.2 crore taka ($1.3 million) that he had lent to the owner of a company (Correspondence, 2022). He arranged a human chain in front of the NPC a few days earlier as a method of protest, but it did not help him get his money back from the borrower.

In the last week of October 2022, a 35-year-old mother of three children (3,10, and 16 years old) from Narayanganj attempted suicide by setting herself and the children on fire in front of NPC, Dhaka (Representatives, 2022). The family died by suicide because a local, politically influential person was trying to evict them from their home. The lady tried to seek help from all sections of society, but failed to resolve the issue (Representative, 2022). They took sedative pills before pouring kerosene on their body to set fire.

Bangladesh is facing an adverse political situation and financial problems due to price hikes and loss of jobs, which has been complicated further by the COVID-19 pandemic and the Russia–Ukraine war. Two incidents have occurred recently where the victims were the prey of social injustice, and as a method of protest, they attempted self-destruction. The cases indicate some wider social factors of suicide prevention in Bangladesh. It indicates the role of social justice in suicide prevention. Both the attempts happened in a nationally focused place, that is, the National Press Club, and in both of these cases, the method used for dying was burning. We have discussed such attempts in Chap. 8 of this book (Arafat et al., 2026).

2.6.2 Group Suicide

In 2007, nine family members died by suicide in Mymensingh, which was attributed to shared delusion (Selim, 2010). The father of that family was the primary motivating person for that event.

2.6.3 Suicidal Behavior Among Prisoners

There is lack of academic attention to the study of self-harm and suicidal behavior among prisoners in Bangladesh (Arafat & Kar, 2025) despite a high burden of mental disorders. There is no publicly available data on self-harm and suicide in the prisons in Bangladesh; only limited information is available in the news reports.

One study assessed 20 suicides among prisoners and revealed that 90% of the deceased were ≤ 40 years old, 95% of suicides happened among males, and 90% of them died by hanging, where a towel (gamsa) was frequently used for hanging (Arafat, 2025b).

2.6.4 Suicide in Facebook Live

In recent years, suicides have been noticed on Facebook Live, and/or people have died by suicide after posting a Facebook post (Soron & Islam, 2020; Islam et al., 2021). The gender of the deceased, the methods of suicide attempt, and the risk factors distribution match the usual pattern in the country. It poses a prevention challenge in the country.

2.6.5 Filicide-Extended Suicide

These events are noted in Bangladesh among the low socioeconomic class and associated with social factors such as poverty and relationship issues (Arafat et al., 2025d). These events happen within the family, and many times, the death of the whole family. Isolated filicide cases have also been reported in the country, where socioeconomic factors were revealed as a significant factor (Arafat et al., 2023b, 2025e).

3 Suicide Data in Bangladesh

According to a WHO (2014) report, among 183 countries, only 80 countries had good quality suicide data, while suicides from the other 103 countries were calculated by a modelling approach that covered 61% of total deaths by suicide. Good quality suicide data are more pertinent in high-income countries than in countries with low income (WHO, 2014, 2025). The report revealed that 50 high-income countries with good quality suicide data covered 98% of suicides in high-income group countries, whereas the remaining 37 low- and middle-income countries (LMICs) covered only 22% of suicides that happened in LMICs in 2012 (WHO, 2014). Ritchie et al. (2015) mentioned that data on suicides are flawed due to the frequency and reliability of vital registrations of data in many countries. Generally, the estimated suicide rates from the WHO member states are based on modelling assumptions. Also, the inaccurate official figures are submitted to the WHO by its member states as they do not have a rigorous suicide registration system. Furthermore, suicidal behavior is considered an illegal act in some member states, resulting in underreporting and misclassification of suicide-related data. One previous study identified that Islamic countries record more "other violent death" than the United Kingdom, indicating the misclassification (Pritchard & Amanullah, 2007). Another recent study compared the suicide data of Muslim countries with the Western ones and identified the possibility of underreporting of suicide (Pritchard et al., 2020).

Bangladesh is a country with an LMIC background where more than 90% of the population is Muslim. Suicide is prohibited in Islam, and it is a criminal offence in the country. Mental health literacy here is supposedly poor, and studies identified a low suicide literacy and high stigma toward suicide (Arafat et al., 2021b, 2022a; Sharmin Salam et al., 2017; Shahnaz et al., 2017). All these reasons contribute to the possible underreporting and misclassification of suicides and suicidal behavior. We mention some possible areas of postmortem examination and possible caveats of underreporting during the forensic examination in Chap. 2 (Bose & Arafat, 2026). We also discuss help-seeking and the health services for suicidal behavior in Chap. 3 (Arafat, 2026). Additionally, due to low mental health and suicide literacy, family members usually make homicidal claims when death happens in the in-laws' environment without considering mental illness, personality traits, and life events. They usually consider suicide a monocausal outcome. It is important to note that, currently, we do not know the exact proportion of underreporting and misclassification of suicides in Bangladesh.

Bangladesh does not have a national suicide surveillance and nationwide epidemiological study of suicide and suicidal behavior (Arafat et al., 2021f; Arafat, 2017, 2019a). The WHO (2014) mentioned the quality of suicide data for Bangladesh as category 4 (i.e., death registration data are unavailable or unusable due to quality issues). As a result, there are variations in suicide rates in Bangladesh based on WHO reports, NGO data, and empirical studies. Furthermore, the quality of suicide data has always been challenged in Bangladesh due to possible underreporting and misclassification resulting from low mental health and suicide literacy, criminalized legal status, and high stigma (Arafat, 2025a).

The lack of a nationally reliable source of suicide data impedes research and policymaking in Bangladesh (Arafat, 2017). Available evidence suggests that the majority of the suicide data are collected from police, records available in forensic medicine departments (which only includes data of deceased whose medico-legal autopsy is performed), some court reports, and a few epidemiological studies conducted in specific areas and/or in specific populations such as adolescents or pregnant women (Arafat, 2017; Feroz et al., 2012). Recently, data collected from newspaper reports have been used in some publications (Shah et al., 2017; Arafat et al., 2018).

4 Current Challenges and Ways Forward

4.1 Current Challenges

Lack of quality suicide data Is one of the prime challenges in Bangladesh because it affects all aspects of suicide prevention. Collecting data on a sensitive subject like suicide due to confidentiality issues in a conservative Islamic country, where it is criminal, is challenging. Given that a substantial number of risk factors are connected to recent, very emotional occurrences, next-of-kins are reluctant to talk about those (Arafat, 2021a). The lack of quality data and adequate empirical studies could be attributed to some extent to this social barrier in Bangladesh. There is inadequate empirical large-scale nationwide research on suicide and its risk factors in Bangladesh, even though an increased number of articles are coming out in recent years (Arafat et al., 2021f). Another fundamental issue that should be mentioned here is that the recent suicide-related publications are performed by collecting data from print and online media report analysis (Arafat et al., 2021f). Media reports could be a source of data; however, it is necessary to consider the epidemiological aspects of any entity. There are several reasons behind that, such as not all suicides are published in the media, and the data collection method for preparing a media report is not scientific. Certainly, all suicides are being reported in newspapers, especially suicides in rural areas. Crime reporters are not efficient and interested in bringing out the mental health–related factors. Suicide is a complex, multifactorial outcome. Previous studies identified that the quality of suicide reporting in both online and print newspapers is poor compared to the WHO media guidelines (Arafat et al., 2019, 2020). One study conducted in India comparing the media reporting with epidemiological data identified that there are significant discrepancies between suicide metrics in the community population and the reports collected from the media (Armstrong et al., 2019). Additionally, no nationwide, longitudinal, and interventional research activities were undertaken in the last decade, and lack of research funds for researchers to conduct empirical research on suicide (Arafat et al., 2021f).

Poor mental health and suicide literacy, high stigma, and criminalized status of suicidal behavior fundamentally affect suicide research, help-seeking, and suicide prevention in Bangladesh (Arafat et al., 2022a). Currently, there are no specialized clinical services for suicidal behavior (Arafat, 2024). The relationship between mental illness and suicidal behaviors is documented in the country as well as other parts of the world (Arafat et al., 2021b; Zalsman et al., 2016). The psychological autopsy study identified that 86% of the suicides were not in contact with any mental health care setting, which may be attributed to the aforementioned aspects (Arafat et al., 2021d). The same study also identified that psychiatric illnesses were more common among suicides living in upper and middle socioeconomic conditions than among the deceased living in lower socioeconomic conditions (Arafat et al., 2021c). This can also be attributed to the fact that upper and middle-class people may have better mental health and suicide literacy, so that they can identify the illness.

4.2 Way Forward

There is no alternative to a national suicide surveillance system, which should be an immediate priority in Bangladesh. An enduring monitoring system would ensure the quality of suicide data at the community level. Standard quality suicide data would help suicide prevention in all aspects. In the absence of a national suicide surveillance system, data from the police could be an important source despite its limitations (Arafat, 2025a). Due to the legal structure, the police have the list of suicides in the country. However, some initiatives are needed to publish the data periodically and publicly, as well as to improve the data quality.

There is a paucity of suicide related research in Bangladesh, and inadequate activities around suicide prevention are the major obstacles to implementing suicide prevention programs in Bangladesh. More empirical research activities and multilateral collaborative research in Bangladesh should be undertaken, and the emphasis should be on identifying the risk and protective factors for suicidal behavior in Bangladesh. Suicide decriminalization should be given immediate priority; this has already been accomplished in several industrialized nations, including those neighboring and Muslim-majority countries in South Asia, such as India and Pakistan. Soron (2019) recommended decriminalizing suicide in Bangladesh; authorities need to ensure that they do not punish people for attempting suicide. Society and the state should provide adequate support systems to people experiencing mental distress. Policymakers should obtain different strategies that can provide expeditious support to accomplish the sustainable development goal of suicide reduction (Arafat, 2025c).

Additional multidisciplinary research is required to pinpoint the risk factors and their connections to the biopsychosocial aspects of suicide that already prevail, as well as to develop the ideal, culturally specific preventive plan that makes the most use of the resources to deal. Following WHO recommendations, a national suicide prevention program should be implemented to get the attention of local, regional, and international stakeholders (World Health Organization, 2018; Arafat, 2021b). Suicide is also often associated with an act of hopelessness, rage, and fleeing away from unbearable pain due to disturbances within the family system, personal loss, and lack of social support, and the importance of family roles cannot be avoided for suicide prevention (Arafat et al., 2022b).

5 Conclusion

This chapter draws attention to the epidemiological metrics of suicidal behavior and the quality and sources of data in Bangladesh. For a national suicide prevention strategy, the country needs further epidemiological studies on suicide to identify the national rate of suicide. Prevention strategies could prioritize young adults, females, students, and housewives. Increasing mental health and suicide literacy would help in all aspects, including conducting epidemiological studies. Reducing stigma and decriminalization of suicide will encourage the sufferer to seek medical and/or psychiatric care. The psychiatric services should be expanded for suicidal behavior across the country. Along with other prevention strategies, gate-keeper training and involving the family members could be tested in Bangladesh, as a significant proportion of suicides are closely associated with family-related events. Immediate steps should be taken to establish a source of quality suicide data, because without quality data, there is a poor chance of having a successful suicide prevention strategy in the country.

References

Ahmad, M., & Hossain, M. Z. (2010). Hanging as a method of suicide: Retrospective analysis of postmortem cases. *Journal of Armed Forces Medical College, Bangladesh, 6*(2), 37–39. https://doi.org/10.3329/jafmc.v6i2.7273

Ali, E., Maksud, M., Zubyra, S. J., Hossain, M. S., Debnath, P. R., Alam, A., & Chakrabarty, P. K. (2014). Suicide by hanging: A study of 334 cases. *Bangladesh Medical Journal, 43*(2), 90–93. https://doi.org/10.3329/bmj.v43i2.21390

Arafat, S. M. Y. (2026). Mental health and suicidal behavior in Bangladesh. In S. Y. Arafat (Ed.), *Suicidal behavior in Bangladesh*. Springer. https://doi.org/10.1007/978-981-95-8321-8_3

Arafat, S. M. Y., Amin, R., & Lester, D. (2026). Suicide after an immediate negative life event: Protest, defeat, bargain, or impulse? In S. Y. Arafat (Ed.), *Suicidal behavior in Bangladesh*. Springer. https://doi.org/10.1007/978-981-95-8321-8_8

Arafat, S. Y. (2025a). Suicide is criminal, data is silent: Reimagining suicide surveillance in Bangladesh—from police reports to public health action. *International Journal of Mental Health and Addiction*, 1–3. https://doi.org/10.1007/s11469-025-01514-1

Arafat, S. M. Y. (2025b). Prison suicide in Bangladesh: A news content analysis. *Health Science Reports, 8*(6), e70951. https://doi.org/10.1002/hsr2.70951

Arafat, S. M. Y. (2025c). Suicide prevention in Bangladesh: Critical analysis of mental health law, policy and strategy. *BJPsych International, 22*(4), 138–141. https://doi.org/10.1192/bji.2025.10042

Arafat, S. M. Y., & Mazumdar, A. H. (2025). Geriatric psychiatry in Bangladesh: Current status and ways ahead. *Geriatric Psychiatry in South Asia, South Asian Perspectives in Mental Health and Psychology*. https://doi.org/10.1007/978-981-96-7469-5_2

Arafat, S. M. Y., & Kar, S. K. (2025). Self-harm and suicidal behavior among prisoners in South Asia: A narrative review. *Health Science Reports, 8*(4), e70695. https://doi.org/10.1002/hsr2.70695

Arafat, S. M. Y., Baminiwatta, A., Amin, R., Akter, H., & Kabir, R. (2025a). Prevalence of suicidal behavior in Bangladesh: A systematic review and meta-analysis. *Health Science Reports, 8*, e71200. https://doi.org/10.1002/hsr2.71200

Arafat, S. M. Y., Mali, B., & Mazumder, A. H. (2025b). Nonsuicidal self-injury in Bangladesh: A narrative review. *Health Science Reports, 8*(5), e70790. https://doi.org/10.1002/hsr2.70790

Arafat, S. M. Y., Mozaffor, M., & Kibria, M. G. (2025c). Method of suicide among police and physicians in Bangladesh. *Geopsychiatry, 2*, 100029. https://doi.org/10.1016/j.geopsy.2025.100029

Arafat, S. M. Y., Hossain, S., & Mali, B. (2025d). Filicide-extended suicide in Bangladesh: A socio-demographic analysis from media reports. *South East Asian Journal of Suicide Prevention, 2*(1) Retrieved from https://seajsp.qvjournal.com/index.php/about/article/view/9

Arafat, S. M. Y., Mourin, C., & Khan, S. T. (2025e). Maternal filicide in Bangladesh: Cases and areas of prevention. *Asian Journal of Psychiatry*, 104740. https://doi.org/10.1016/j.ajp.2025.104740

Arafat, S. M. Y., Baminiwatta, A., Menon, V., Sharma, P., Htay, M. N. N., Akter, H., Marthoenis, M., & Dorji, C. (2024a). Prevalence of suicidal behavior among students in South-East Asia: A systematic review and meta-analysis. *Archives of Suicide Research, 28*(1), 50–70. https://doi.org/10.1080/13811118.2023.2176272

Arafat, S. M. Y., Islam, M. K., Khan, M. A. S., & Amin, R. (2024b). The perception of imams (Islamic religious leaders) on the legal status and decriminalization of suicide attempts in Bangladesh: A cross-sectional study. *Global Psychiatry Achieves, 7*(1), 7–12. https://doi.org/10.52095/gpa.2023.7115.1077

Arafat, S. M. Y., Shormi, F. R., & Kibria, M. G. (2024c). Psychiatric disorder and life-event in self harm: A cross-sectional study among clinical population in Bangladesh. *Heliyon, 10*(19), e38627. https://doi.org/10.1016/j.heliyon.2024.e38627

Arafat, S. M. Y. (2024). Suicidal behavior and suicide prevention in Bangladesh. In S. M. Y. Arafat (Ed.), *Mental health in Bangladesh*. Springer. https://doi.org/10.1007/978-981-97-0610-5_11

Arafat, S. M. Y., Menon, V., Khan, M. A. S., Htay, M. N. N., Singh, R., Biyyala, D., Krishnamoorthy, Y., & Mynampally, K. (2023a). Marital status and suicidal behavior in South Asia: A systematic review and meta-analysis. *Health Science Reports, 6*(12), e1781. https://doi.org/10.1002/hsr2.1781

Arafat, S. M. Y., Monira, S., & Lily, S. A. (2023b). Filicide in Bangladesh: A case indicating the need for psychosocial support among mothers during peripartum. *Journal of General and Family Medicine, 24*(4), 254–256. https://doi.org/10.1002/jgf2.624

Arafat, S., Hussain, F., Hossain, M. F., Islam, M. A., & Menon, V. (2022a). Literacy and stigma of suicide in Bangladesh: Scales validation and status assessment among university students. *Brain and Behavior, 12*(1), e2432. https://doi.org/10.1002/brb3.2432

Arafat, S., Saleem, T., Edwards, T. M., Ali, S. A., & Khan, M. M. (2022b). Suicide prevention in Bangladesh: The role of family. *Brain and Behavior, 12*(5), e2562. https://doi.org/10.1002/brb3.2562

Arafat, S., & Khan, M. M. (2021). Sexual violence and suicide in Bangladesh. *Health Science Reports, 4*(2), e269. https://doi.org/10.1002/hsr2.269

Arafat, S. (2021a). Challenges of conducting psychological autopsy study in Bangladesh: Data enumerator's view. *Asian Journal of Psychiatry, 63*, 102760. https://doi.org/10.1016/j.ajp.2021.102760

Arafat, S. M. Y. (2021b). Formulation of national suicide prevention strategy of Bangladesh: The readiness assessment. *Journal of Public Health (Oxford, England), 43*(1), e131–e132. https://doi.org/10.1093/pubmed/fdaa117

Arafat, S. M., Laila, Z. D., Akter, H., Mali, B., Chowdhury, M. H., & Morshed, N. M. (2021a). Suicidal behaviors among Bangladeshi nurses: A cross-sectional study in a tertiary care hospital. *Mymensingh Medical Journal, 30*(2), 426–431.

Arafat, S., Mohit, M. A., Mullick, M., Kabir, R., & Khan, M. M. (2021b). Risk factors for suicide in Bangladesh: Case-control psychological autopsy study. *BJPsych Open, 7*(1), e18. https://doi.org/10.1192/bjo.2020.152

Arafat, S., Mohit, M. A., Mullick, M., Khan, M., & Khan, M. M. (2021c). Suicide with and without mental disorders: Findings from psychological autopsy study in Bangladesh. *Asian Journal of Psychiatry, 61*, 102690. https://doi.org/10.1016/j.ajp.2021.102690

Arafat, S., Khan, M., Knipe, D., & Khan, M. M. (2021d). Population attributable fractions of clinical and social risk factors for suicide in Bangladesh: Finding from a case-control psychological autopsy study. *Brain and Behavior, 11*(12), e2409. https://doi.org/10.1002/brb3.2409

Arafat, S., Ali, S. A., Menon, V., Hussain, F., Ansari, D. S., Baminiwatta, A., Saleem, T., Singh, R., Varadharajan, N., Biyyala, D., Kar, S. K., & Khan, M. M. (2021e). Suicide methods in South Asia over two decades (2001-2020). *The International Journal of Social Psychiatry, 67*(7), 920–934. https://doi.org/10.1177/00207640211015700

Arafat, S. M. Y., Hussain, F., Jakaria, K. M., Itu, Z. T., & Islam, M. (2021f). Empirical studies on suicide in Bangladesh in a decade (2011–2020). *Global Psychiatry, 4*(1), 109–122. https://doi.org/10.52095/gp.2021.10692

Arafat, S. M. Y., Khan, M. M., Niederkrotenthaler, T., Ueda, M., & Armstrong, G. (2020). Assessing the quality of media reporting of suicide deaths in Bangladesh against World Health Organization guidelines. *Crisis, 41*(1), 47–53. https://doi.org/10.1027/0227-5910/a000603

Arafat, S. M. Y., Mali, B., & Akter, H. (2019). Quality of online news reporting of suicidal behavior in Bangladesh against World Health Organization guidelines. *Asian Journal of Psychiatry, 40*, 126–129. https://doi.org/10.1016/j.ajp.2018.10.010

Arafat, S. M. Y. (2019a). Current challenges of suicide and future directions of management in Bangladesh: A systematic review. *Global Psychiatry, 2*(1), 9–20. https://doi.org/10.2478/gp-2019-0001

Arafat, S. (2019b). Females are dying more than males by suicide in Bangladesh. *Asian Journal of Psychiatry, 40*, 124–125. https://doi.org/10.1016/j.ajp.2018.10.014

Arafat, S., Mali, B., & Akter, H. (2018). Demography and risk factors of suicidal behavior in Bangladesh: A retrospective online news content analysis. *Asian Journal of Psychiatry, 36*, 96–99. https://doi.org/10.1016/j.ajp.2018.07.008

Arafat, S. M. Y. (2017). Suicide in Bangladesh: A mini review. *Journal of Behavioral Health, 6*(1), 66–69. https://doi.org/10.5455/jbh.20160904090206

Armstrong, G., Vijayakumar, L., Pirkis, J., Jayaseelan, M., Cherian, A., Soerensen, J. B., Arya, V., & Niederkrotenthaler, T. (2019). Mass media representation of suicide in a high suicide state in India: An epidemiological comparison with suicide deaths in the population. *BMJ Open, 9*(7), e030836. https://doi.org/10.1136/bmjopen-2019-030836

Bachmann, S. (2018). Epidemiology of suicide and the psychiatric perspective. *International Journal of Environmental Research and Public Health, 15*(7), 1425. https://doi.org/10.3390/ijerph15071425

Begum, A., Rahman, A. F., Rahman, A., Soares, J., Reza Khankeh, H., & Macassa, G. (2017a). Prevalence of suicide ideation among adolescents and young adults in rural Bangladesh. *International Journal of Mental Health, 46*(3), 177–187. https://doi.org/10.1080/00207411.2017.1304074

Begum, A., Khan, N. T., Shafiuzzaman, A., Shahid, F., Anam, A. A., Ahmed, K. S., Begum, R. A., & Fahmi, S. (2017b). Suicidal death due to hanging. *Delta Medical College Journal, 5*(2), 89–93. https://doi.org/10.3329/dmcj.v5i2.33347

Biggs, M. (2013). How repertoires evolve: The diffusion of suicide protest in the Twentieth Century. *Mobilization: An International Quarterly, 18*(4), 407–428. https://doi.org/10.17813/maiq.18.4.njnu779530x55082

Bose, P. K., & Arafat, S. M. Y. (2026). Forensic medicine, post-mortem and suicide in Bangladesh. In S. M. Y. Arafat (Ed.), *Suicidal behavior in Bangladesh*. Springer. https://doi.org/10.1007/978-981-95-8321-8_2

Choudhury, M. H., Rahman, M. M., Hossain, M. G., Tabassum, N., & Islam, M. R. (2013). Trends of suicidal death at a tertiary care hospital in Bangladesh. *Journal of Shaheed Suhrawardy Medical College, 5*(1), 28–30.

Chowdhury, F. R., Dewan, G., Verma, V. R., Knipe, D. W., Isha, I. T., Faiz, M. A., Gunnell, D. J., & Eddleston, M. (2018). Bans of WHO class I pesticides in Bangladesh-suicide prevention without hampering agricultural output. *International Journal of Epidemiology, 47*(1), 175–184. https://doi.org/10.1093/ije/dyx157

Correspondent, S. (2022) Businessman who set himself on fire in front of press club dies, Prothomalo. Prothomalo. Available at: https://en.prothomalo.com/bangladesh/businessman-who-set-himself-on-fire-in-front-of-press-club-dies. Accessed November 14, 2022.

Emi, M. Y., Imran, S. M., Adib, A. A., Al Mamun, F., Mamun, M. A., Islam, F., & Roy, N. (2025). Prevalence and associated risk factors of suicidal behaviors among cancer patients in a tertiary care hospital in Bangladesh. *Scientific Reports, 15*(1), 7055. https://doi.org/10.1038/s41598-024-84731-3

Fairchild, G., Tasseff, B., Khalsa, H., Generous, N., Daughton, A. R., Velappan, N., Priedhorsky, R., & Deshpande, A. (2018). Epidemiological data challenges: Planning for a more robust future through data standards. *Frontiers in Public Health, 6*, 336. https://doi.org/10.3389/fpubh.2018.00336

Feroz, A., Islam, S. N., Reza, S., Rahman, A. M., Sen, J., Mowla, M., & Rahman, M. R. (2012). A community survey on the prevalence of suicidal attempts and deaths in a selected rural area of Bangladesh. *Journal of Medicine, 13*(1), 3–9. https://doi.org/10.3329/jom.v13i1.10042

Jordans, M. J., Kaufman, A., Brenman, N. F., Adhikari, R. P., Luitel, N. P., Tol, W. A., & Komproe, I. (2014). Suicide in South Asia: A scoping review. *BMC Psychiatry, 14*, 358. https://doi.org/10.1186/s12888-014-0358-9

Halim, K. S., Khondker, L., Wahab, M. A., Nargis, F., & Khan, S. I. (2010). Various factors of attempted suicide in a selected area of Naogaon district. *Mymensingh Medical Journal, 19*(2), 244–249.

Hossain, M., Rahman, Z., & Akhter, S. (2012). Suicidal death autopsy analysis at Dhaka medical college. *Bangladesh Medical Journal, 40*(1), 18–21. https://doi.org/10.3329/bmj.v40i1.9957

ICDDR,B. (2003). Mortality due to suicide in rural Bangladesh [Bangla]. *Health and Science Bulletin, 1*(5), 7–10. http://dspace.icddrb.org/jspui/bitstream/123456789/4810/1/2003-ICDDRBHealthScienceBulletin-Vol1%285%29-Bangla.pdf. Accessed on October 7, 2022

Islam, M. R., Qusar, M. S., & Islam, M. S. (2021). Suicide after Facebook posts—an unnoticed departure of life in Bangladesh. *Emerging Trends in Drugs, Addictions, and Health, 1*, 100005. https://doi.org/10.1016/j.etdah.2021.100005

Khan, A. R., Ratele, K., Arendse, N., Islam, M. Z., & Dery, I. (2020). Suicide and attempted suicide in Jhenaidah District, Bangladesh, 2010-2018. *Crisis, 41*(4), 304–312. https://doi.org/10.1027/0227-5910/a000631

Li, J., Imam, S. Z., Jing, Z., Wang, Y., & Zhou, C. (2021). Suicide attempt and its associated factors amongst women who were pregnant as adolescents in Bangladesh: A cross-sectional study. *Reproductive Health, 18*(1), 71. https://doi.org/10.1186/s12978-021-01127-6

Marthoenis, M., & Arafat, S. M. Y. (2022). Rate and associated factors of suicidal behavior among adolescents in Bangladesh and Indonesia: Global school-based student health survey data analysis. *Scientifica, 2022*, 8625345. https://doi.org/10.1155/2022/8625345

Mashreky, S. R., Rahman, F., & Rahman, A. (2013). Suicide kills more than 10,000 people every year in Bangladesh. *Archives of Suicide Research, 17*(4), 387–396. https://doi.org/10.1080/13811118.2013.801809

Mozumder, M. K., Jasmine, U. H., Haque, M. A., & Haque, S. (2023). Mental health and suicide risk among homosexual males in Bangladesh. *PLoS One, 18*(8), e0289597. https://doi.org/10.1371/journal.pone.0289597

Muhammad, F., Chowdhury, M., Arifuzzaman, M., & Chowdhury, A. A. (2017). Public health problems in Bangladesh: Issues and challenges. *South East Asia Journal of Public Health, 6*(2), 11–16. https://doi.org/10.3329/seajph.v6i2.31830

National Institute of Mental Health. (2021). Epidemiology of suicide and suicidal behavior among youth and adolescents in Bangladesh. (Project Report).

Pritchard, C., & Amanullah, S. (2007). An analysis of suicide and undetermined deaths in 17 predominantly Islamic countries contrasted with the UK. *Psychological Medicine, 37*(3), 421–430. https://doi.org/10.1017/S0033291706009159

Pritchard, C., Iqbal, W., & Dray, R. (2020). Undetermined and accidental mortality rates as possible sources of underreported suicides: Population-based study comparing Islamic countries and traditionally religious Western countries. *BJPsych Open, 6*(4), e56. https://doi.org/10.1192/bjo.2020.38

Qusar, M. S., Morshed, N. M., Azad, M. A. K., Kader, M. A., Shams, S. F., Ahmed, M. F., Haque, M. M. M., Uddin, M. A., & Shahid, S. F. B. (2010). Psychiatric morbidity among suicide attempters who needed ICU intervention. *Bangabandhu Sheikh Mujib Medical University Journal, 2*(2), 73–77. https://doi.org/10.3329/bsmmuj.v2i2.4761

Reza, A. S., Feroz, A. H. M., Islam, S. N., Karim, M. N., Rabbani, M. G., Shah Alam, M., Rahman, M. M., Rahman, M. R., Ahmed, H. U., Bhowmik, A. D., Khan, M. Z. R., Sarkar, M., Alam, M. T., & Jalal Uddin, M. M. (2014). Risk factors of suicide and Para suicide in rural Bangladesh. *Journal of Medicine, 14*(2), 123–129. https://doi.org/10.3329/jom.v14i2.19653

Representative, U. (2022) Woman's bid to commit suicide at Press Club: AL leader sent to jail. Daily Obsrver. Available at: https://observerbd.com/news.php?id=390631. Accessed: November 14, 2022.

Ritchie, H., Roser M., & Ortiz-Ospina, E. (2015). Suicide. [online] Available at https://ourworldindata.org/suicide. Accessed on October 4, 2022.

Ruzicka, L. T. (1998). Suicide in countries and areas of the ESCAP region. *Asia-Pacific Population Journal, 13*(4), 55–74.

Sarkar, D., Shaheduzzaman, M., Hossain, M. I., Ahmed, M., Mohammad, N., & Basher, A. (2013). Spectrum of acute pharmaceutical and chemical poisoning in northern Bangladesh. *Asia Pacific Journal of Medical Toxicology, 2*(1), 2–5.

Selim, N. (2010). An extraordinary truth? The Ādam "suicide" notes from Bangladesh. *Mental Health, Religion and Culture, 13*(3), 223–244. https://doi.org/10.1080/13674670903061230

Shah, M., Ahmed, S., & Arafat, S. (2017). Demography and risk factors of suicide in Bangladesh: A six-month paper content analysis. *Psychiatry Journal, 2017*, 3047025. https://doi.org/10.1155/2017/3047025

Shah, M., Sajib, M., & Arafat, S. (2018). Demography and risk factor of suicidal behavior in Bangladesh: A cross-sectional observation from patients attending a suicide prevention clinic of Bangladesh. *Asian Journal of Psychiatry, 35*, 4–5. https://doi.org/10.1016/j.ajp.2018.04.035

Shahnaz, A., Bagley, C., Simkhada, P., & Kadri, S. (2017). Suicidal behaviour in Bangladesh: A scoping literature review and a proposed public health prevention model. *Open Journal of Social Sciences, 5*(07), 254. https://doi.org/10.4236/jss.2017.57016

Sharmin Salam, S., Alonge, O., Islam, M. I., Hoque, D., Wadhwaniya, S., UlBaset, M. K., Mashreky, S. R., & El Arifeen, S. (2017). The burden of suicide in rural Bangladesh: Magnitude and risk factors. *International Journal of Environmental Research and Public Health, 14*(9), 1032. https://doi.org/10.3390/ijerph14091032

Shuvo, T. A., Hossain, K., & Dey, D. R. (2024). Suicide attempts in Bangladesh: Prevalence, trends, and disparities. *Journal of Medicine, Surgery and Public Health*, 100170. https://doi.org/10.1016/j.glmedi.2024.100170

Soron, T. R. (2019). Decriminalizing suicide in Bangladesh. *Asian Journal of Psychiatry, 39*, 91–92. https://doi.org/10.1016/j.ajp.2018.12.012

Soron, T. R., & Shariful Islam, S. M. (2020). Suicide on Facebook-the tales of unnoticed departure in Bangladesh. *Global mental health (Cambridge, England), 7*, e12. https://doi.org/10.1017/gmh.2020.5

Talukder, N., Karim, K. A., Chowdhury, T., Habib, A., Chowdhury, A. M., & Perveen, K. (2014). Study of autopsy based suicidal hanging. *Bangladesh Journal of Physiology and Pharmacology, 30*(2), 14–17. https://doi.org/10.3329/bjpp.v30i2.22677

World Bank. (2024). The World Bank in Bangladesh [Online] Available at: https://www.worldbank.org/en/country/bangladesh/overview. Accessed on May 24, 2025.

Tilly, C. (2013) Contentious performances.: Cambridge University Press.

Wahlin, Å., Palmer, K., Sternäng, O., Hamadani, J. D., & Kabir, Z. N. (2015). Prevalence of depressive symptoms and suicidal thoughts among elderly persons in rural Bangladesh. *International Psychogeriatrics, 27*(12), 1999–2008. https://doi.org/10.1017/S104161021500109X

World Health Organization. (2014). Preventing suicide: a global imperative. WHO: Geneva, Switzerland.https://apps.who.int/iris/handle/10665/131056. Accessed on July 15, 2022.

World Health Organization. (2017). *Depression and other common mental disorders: Global health estimates* (No. WHO/MSD/MER/2017.2). World Health Organization.https://apps.who.int/iris/handle/10665/254610. Accessed on October 7, 2022.

World Health Organization. (2021). *Suicide worldwide in 2019: Global health estimates.* WHO: Geneva, Switzerland. Available online: https://www.who.int/publications/i/item/9789240026643. Accessed on September 15, 2021.

World Health Organization. (2022). *Addressing mental health in Bangladesh.* Retrieved June 28, 2025, from https://www.who.int/publications/i/item/9789290210146.

World Health Organization. (2025). *Suicide worldwide in 2021: Global health estimates.* World Health Organization https://www.who.int/publications/i/item/9789240110069. Accessed on October 18, 2025.

World Atlas. (2025). The world's most densely populated cities. [online] Available at: https://www.worldatlas.com/articles/the-world-s-most-densely-populated-cities.html. Accessed on May 24, 2025.

World Health Organization. (2018). National suicide prevention strategies: Progress, examples and indicators. Geneva. https://apps.who.int/iris/bitstream/handle/10665/279765/9789241515016-eng.pdf.

Zalsman, G., Hawton, K., Wasserman, D., van Heeringen, K., Arensman, E., Sarchiapone, M., Carli, V., Höschl, C., Barzilay, R., Balazs, J., Purebl, G., Kahn, J. P., Sáiz, P. A., Lipsicas, C. B., Bobes, J., Cozman, D., Hegerl, U., & Zohar, J. (2016). Suicide prevention strategies revisited: 10-year systematic review. *The Lancet Psychiatry, 3*(7), 646–659. https://doi.org/10.1016/S2215-0366(16)30030-X

Chapter 2
Forensic Medicine, Postmortem, and Suicide in Bangladesh

Palash Kumar Bose and S. M. Yasir Arafat

1 Introduction

Suicide is a global public health crisis influenced by religion, culture, the social class of an individual, and the income of the country. According to the World Health Organization (WHO), more than 700,000 deaths occurred due to suicide in 2019 in the world, with an age-standardized rate of 9.0 per 100,000 population (WHO, 2021). Additionally, about 10–20 suicide attempts happen for each suicide (WHO, 2014). It is the third leading cause of death among individuals aged 15–29 years (WHO, 2025). About three-fourths (73%) of the global suicides happen in low- and middle-income countries (LMICs) (WHO, 2025). In the case of Bangladesh, the suicide rate widely varies among published articles, such as WHO reports, NGO data, and police reports, as the country is yet to establish a standard suicide reporting and surveillance system (Arafat, 2019). The WHO report published in 2021 estimated the age-standardized rate of suicide in Bangladesh as 3.9 per 100,000 population (WHO, 2021). In the majority of cases, people rely on data available from the police, which seems to be an underestimation of actual rates. At the same time, we do not know the exact proportion of underestimation. The detailed epidemiology of suicide in Bangladesh is discussed in Chap. 1 of this book (Arafat & Kabir, 2026).

P. K. Bose
Department of Forensic Medicine and Toxicology, Enam Medical College, Dhaka, Bangladesh

S. M. Y. Arafat (✉)
Department of Psychiatry, Bangladesh Specialized Hospital, Dhaka, Bangladesh

Department of Public and Community Health, Faculty of Medicine and Health Sciences, Frontier University Garowe, Garowe, Somalia

S. M. Y. Arafat (ed.), *Suicidal Behavior in Bangladesh*, Mental Health Systems and Policy in Low- and Middle-Income Countries,
https://doi.org/10.1007/978-981-95-8321-8_2

Bangladesh is a Muslim-majority country located in South Asia with about 170 million people; among them, more than 90% are Muslims (Bangladesh Bureau of Statistics, 2024). Suicide is prohibited in Islam, and it is a criminal offence in the legal system of the country. As per the current legal structure of the country, any unnatural death should be reported to the nearby police station. Subsequently, a postmortem or medicolegal autopsy is conducted to ascertain the manner of death, that is, suicide or other unnatural deaths like accident or homicide. At this point, a significant portion of unnatural deaths is kept away from the medicolegal autopsy to avoid the legal procedure, disfiguration of the deceased body, and the potential harassment of police due to the criminal legal identity (Rahman et al., 2010).

2 Process of Suicide Declaration in Bangladesh

As per the legal directives, a medicolegal autopsy procedure should be performed in case of any unnatural death, as we mentioned earlier. The autopsy procedure is maintained by the local police station. Therefore, any unnatural death should be reported to the police. In Bangladesh, postmortems are performed under the provisions of three laws: (i) *The Penal Code* (1860), (ii) *The Code of Criminal Procedure* (1898), and (iii) *The Evidence Act* (1872) (Islam & Islam, 2003). The Code of Criminal Procedures, 1898 (Act No. V of 1898, 174(1) part V Chap. XIV) describes the acts of the response of police regarding suicide, accidental death, or homicide. 174(1) (a) describes the response of police in case of death by suicide; 174(1) (b) and (c) describe the duties of police in case of homicidal, accidental, or suspicious deaths (Code of Criminal Procedure, 1898). As per the legal directives, a police officer working at least at the rank of subinspector of the concerned police station, in the presence of two or more witnesses (usually neighbors), shall make an investigation and prepare an inquest (preliminary investigation conducted by a police officer into the cause of death; *surathal* in Bangla) report regarding the apparent cause of death, unless otherwise directed by any rule where magistrate investigation is necessary. On the other hand, section 176(1) describes inquiry should be performed by a magistrate into the cause of death in case of death in the custody of the police and in any other case mentioned in 174(1) (a) (b) and (c) (Code of Criminal Procedure, 1898). The magistrate inquiry is performed in exchange for or accompanied by a police investigation. That means, the process of suicide declaration follows the law-enacted proceedings. The police are the authority that should carry out the declaration of suicide, primarily by visiting the scene of the crime and preparing an inquest report, which is to be confirmed by autopsy. In case of death by suicide in a hospital, a police case should be filed and the death certificate and the dead body should be handed over to the police. Subsequently, the deceased body is sent for medicolegal autopsy to nearby establishments where forensic morgues are available (Islam & Islam, 2003). But if a person dies in the custody of police, whether it is a natural or unnatural death, an inquest report is prepared by the magistrate, and then the body is sent for autopsy. A copy of the inquest report and challan

(Government gazetted, tabulated form no. 5371) should be sent along with the dead body. On completing the medicolegal autopsy, the physician prepares an autopsy report (form no 5372) with a carbon copy. The handwritten copy of the postmortem is sent to the police to be produced in the concerned court. The carbon copy is kept in the forensic medicine department or the records of the district hospital. After completion of the postmortem, the dead body is handed over to the family members to perform the rituals before burial. Based on the inquest report, the postmortem report, and information obtained from the police investigation, the *manner* of death, whether it is natural or unnatural (suicidal, homicidal, or accidental), is finally decided by the legal bodies instead of the doctors (Islam & Islam, 2003). Sometimes, the family members try to take the dead body without performing an autopsy by submitting an application to the legal authority (Additional District Magistrate), mentioning that they don't have any complaint against anyone and will not file any case. In some other cases, such as a definite road traffic accident, the police may hand over the body to the family members. It is important to note that ideally, all unnatural deaths should undergo a medicolegal autopsy as per the law of the country. Therefore, according to the code of criminal procedure in Bangladesh, the declaration of suicide, whether it occurs at home or in a hospital, rests with the police (Arafat, 2025).

Manner of death means the circumstances that cause the person to die. It can be better understood if the circumstantial evidence, crime scene investigation, and information from the first-hand witness, family, and friends are available and cooperative. Such information helps the autopsy surgeon a lot during the time of autopsy to collect evidence from the body for related investigations, viscera for chemical analysis, and finally to prepare an opinion regarding cause, mode, and manner of death. In the case of hospital death, the treatment papers help the forensic pathologists to gather information related to the death. Inference from circumstantial and supportive evidence and information and autopsy findings, the opinion regarding the manner of death can be given. However, it is important to note that medicolegal autopsy, along with all the necessary investigations, such as microscopic examination, laboratory investigation, chemical analysis of viscera, and other related investigations (if done), may fail to provide an inference regarding the cause and manner of death (Rahman & Ahmad, 1994). This is called a negative autopsy, which is about 2–5% of all deaths brought to the morgue. Postmortem reports don't mention the manner of death in the case of poisoning, falling from a height, jumping in front of moving objects, railway accident, electrocution, burning, or drowning. In the above cases, the manner of death is confirmed by police investigation.

3 Current Status of Postmortem Facilities in Bangladesh

The word "postmortem" is derived from the words "post," which means "after," and "mortem," which means "death." It is also called "autopsy," which is derived from the *Greek* words *autopsia*. "Autos" means "self" and "opis" means "view." So autopsy means "the act of seeing for oneself." The other name of autopsy is necropsy. Autopsy is the scientific dissection of a dead body in order to ascertain the cause of death. The procedure should be conducted in a systematic and scientific manner with standard facilities for the related investigations. Inadequate facilities and poorly or untrained manpower would fail in revealing the fact.

There are eight divisions and 64 districts in Bangladesh. In the 64 districts, there are 37 public medical colleges. Among these medical colleges, 19 are conducting autopsies under the department of *Forensic Medicine and Toxicology (FMT)* as they have morgues to keep dead bodies (Table 2.1). Other newly established medical colleges are yet to be prepared for medicolegal autopsy, though FMT departments have been established without a morgue facility. Third-year medical students of these medical colleges have to visit the district hospital morgue for the purpose of hands-on training on medicolegal autopsy. Autopsies are conducted in public medical colleges having morgue facilities by the department of FMT. In other settings where there are no public medical colleges or morgue facilities, autopsies are performed by doctors who are working under the responsibility of the district hospital superintendent (previously under the civil surgeon). Especially, residential medical officers (RMOs) in the district hospitals perform autopsy. Unfortunately, it has observed that the physicians working in the district hospitals who perform postmortem lack the necessary expertise to conduct the medicolegal autopsy (Rahman et al., 2010). Usually, they are working in other disciplines of medical science and are called on to conduct postmortems. Therefore, the whole procedure is more dependent on the morgue attendants rather than the field experts. Moreover, there are no independent forensic, pathology, and toxicology labs supporting the process of medicolegal autopsies in medical colleges and district-level hospitals of Bangladesh. There was a chemical examiner's office established in Dhaka, the capital city. Therefore, all the viscera/samples were to be sent to Dhaka (Rahman et al., 2010). Recently, two other chemical examiner labs in two other cities have been established. Autopsies are conducted during daylight hours in Bangladesh. Usually, no autopsy is carried out if a dead body comes after 5 pm, and only in certain cases, if the state higher authority gives any special direction, can autopsy be done at night. For example, an incident occurred in 2009, notoriously known as "Bangladesh Rifles (BDR) Massacre," in which 57 army officers, including BDR director-general, were brutally killed at theBDR headquarters (now known as BGB, Border Guard Bangladesh) by a group of rebellious BDR soldiers. In that case, postmortem examinations were carried out at night. But normally, when a body comes after 5 pm (scarcity of daylight), the dead body is received by the morgue attendant, papers are prepared, and the body is kept in a refrigerator/freezer to be autopsied the next day. Usually, the freezing facilities are available in the morgues of medical college hospitals only. In most district hospital morgues, this facility is currently not available, and in these facilities, postmortem examination is carried out the next day as early as possible, and the body is handed over to the police for the purpose of burial.

As far as chemical labs are concerned, there are currently three labs working in Bangladesh: in Dhaka (the capital city), Chattogram, and Rajashahi. Previously, there was only one chemical lab, in Dhaka (Rahman et al., 2010). The second

Table 2.1 List of public medical colleges in Bangladesh having facilities for medicolegal autopsy

SL	Name of public medical college	District	Division	Medico-legal activities[a]
1	*Patuakhali Medical College*	Patuakhali	Barisal	Not yet
2	*Sher-e-Bangla Medical College*	Barisal		Yes
3	*Noakhali Medical College*	Noakhali	Chattogram	Not yet
4	*Chandpur Medical College*	Chandpur		Not yet
5	*Chattogram Medical College*	Chattogram		Yes
6	*Cox's Bazar Medical College*	Cox's Bazar		Not yet
7	*Cumilla Medical College*	Cumilla		Yes
8	*Rangamati Medical College*	Rangamati		Not yet
9	*Faridpur Medical College*	Faridpur	Dhaka	Yes
10	*Manikganj Medical College*	Manikganj		Yes
11	*Dhaka Medical College*	Dhaka		Yes
12	*Mugda Medical College*	Dhaka		Not yet
13	*Shaheed Suhrawardy Medical College*	Dhaka		Yes
14	*Shaheed Tajuddin Ahmad Medical College*	Gazipur		Yes
15	*Shahid Syed Nazrul Islam Medical College*	Kishoreganj		Not yet
16	*Tangail Medical College*	Tangail		Not yet
17	*Gopalganj Medical College*	Gopalganj		Not yet
18	*Sir Salimullah Medical College*	Dhaka		Yes
19	*Jashore Medical College*	Jashore	Khulna	Yes
20	*Khulna Medical College*	Khulna		Yes
21	*Kushtia Medical College*	Kushtia		Not yet
22	*Magura Medical College*	Magura		Not yet
23	*Satkhira Medical College*	Satkhira		Not yet
24	*Mymensingh Medical College*	Mymensing	Mymensing	Yes
25	*Netrokona Medical College*	Netrokona		Not yet
26	*Jamalpur Medical College*	Jamalpur		Yes
27	*Naogaon Medical College*	Naogaon	Rajshahi	Not yet
28	*Pabna Medical College*	Pabna		Yes
29	*Rajshahi Medical College*	Rajshahi		Yes
30	*Shirajganj Medical College*	Shirajganj		Not yet
31	*Shaheed Ziaur Rahman Medical College*	Bogura (Bogra)		Yes
32	*Dinajpur Medical College*	Dinajpur	Rangpur	Yes
33	*Nilphamari Medical College*	Nilphmari		Not yet
34	*Rangpur Medical College*	Rangpur		Yes
35	*Sunamganj Medical College*	Sunamganj	Sylhet	Not yet
36	*Habiganj Medical College*	Habiganj		Not yet
37	*Sylhet MAG Osmani Medical College*	Sylhet		Yes

[a] Till June 27, 2025

chemical analysis lab was established in Chattogram, a port and divisional city of Bangladesh. In January 2020, a third forensic laboratory, including a chemical lab, was established in Rajshahi, a divisional city of Bangladesh, by the *Criminal Investigation Department (CID)*. Due to the expansion of chemical labs, chemical examiner reports are now available earlier compared with the past. Along with the chemical labs, two DNA labs are also functioning at Dhaka for identification of criminals, fixation of paternity and maternity, and establishment of identity related to DNA test. One is the National Forensic DNA Profiling Laboratory (NFDPL), the first forensic DNA profiling lab, established in 2006 at the Nuclear Medicine building of *Dhaka Medical College*. The second DNA testing lab runs under the Bangladesh Police, namely the Forensic DNA Laboratory of Bangladesh Police, under CID, Dhaka. It started its journey as a project in 2011, and finally, after completing all the validation processes, it started case sample examination in 2014. To broaden the services all over Bangladesh, the government set up a separate DNA Laboratory Management Department by a gazette notification on August 9, 2020. After the gazette notification, divisional DNA screening laboratories have now been established and running in *Rajshahi*, *Sylhet*, *Barishal*, *Khulna*, *Rangpur*, and *Faridpur*. These six centers collect and preserve DNA samples and send them to NFDPL.

In the case of autopsy and medicolegal works, where any test is required to confirm the cause of death, forensic experts have to take help from the chemical examiner's office and the DNA Lab, along with other departments, such as radiology and imaging, microbiology, pathology, etc., which work independently. Notably, due to the various departments having poor collaboration and coordination, final reports by the forensic experts submitted to the legal authority are time-consuming and delayed.

It is an unfortunate reality that there is scarcity of forensic experts in Bangladesh due to its job pattern, work environment, and benefit package. According to the Director General of the Health Education Department Statistics (August 02, 2022), only 22 forensic experts are now working all over Bangladesh, with a vacancy of 65 posts. There are 103 posts for lectures. Among them, 58 are filled and 45 are vacant. Due to the shortage of data for 2025, exact figures are unavailable. But the overall scenario represents that there is a significant shortage of forensic experts in Bangladesh. Despite this shortage of manpower, very few doctors show interest in building a career in this field due to various reasons. Sometimes they have to perform these medicolegal works under undue pressure from different corners for favor. This creates a psychological burden, as well as a feeling of lack of safety for a new doctor starting to work in this field. Nonetheless, they have to perform all sorts of medicolegal work, including autopsy, without additional payment. On the other hand, they have to produce evidence as expert witness in the court of law and travel frequently to the different districts of Bangladesh. This goes on even after retirement from government service till death, which may contribute as a demotivating factor. Surprisingly, after retirement from government services, they have to continue working without any remuneration, and even the travel expenses are delayed. In an unfortunate condition, it may even be unpaid. During the time of cross-examination by the lawyers, forensic experts face unwanted questions with no link to the case. These sorts of questions are felt as humiliating by the young doctors, especially the female doctors. As a result, young doctors prefer avoiding these unexpected situations. Besides bearing these pressures, the forensic pathologists, who are working in the public medical college, have to maintain academic activities such as teaching and conducting exams. Additionally, the doctors are more oriented toward private clinical practice, which is a source of additional income, which is an important reason for showing low interest in a forensic medicine career. Moreover, there is no post for forensic pathologist at the district level. So there are unmet needs for creating the positions in the district hospitals as well as to fill up the present vacancies in the FMT department of public medical colleges based on the workload and responsibilities. Moreover, there are chances of creating new positions for forensic experts in the medical colleges according to the rules and regulations formulated by the *Bangladesh Medical and Dental Council (BMDC).*

It is a bitter truth we can admit simply in a way that when there is a scarcity of forensic experts, the mortuary facilities will also be far behind the standard level in the morgues of medical colleges as well as in the district hospitals in Bangladesh, except a few (Islam & Islam, 2003). The poor and neglected conditions of dead bodies have been identified as a result of mishaps (Bose et al., 2021a). Cases of necrophilia have been reported in the morgues of Shaheed Suhrawardy Medical College, Chattogram Medical College, and Mymensigh Medical College, perhaps due to poor privacy of dead bodies and wide access to them by morgue assistants (Hossain & Arafat, 2026; Bose et al., 2021a). If we consider the standard morgue facility, we can point out the mortuary facilities ensured and recommended by the National Pathology Accreditation Advisory Council, Commonwealth of Australia. It is important for the safety of the autopsy surgeon and assistants working in the mortuary (Australian Government Department of Health, 2013). The council depicts autopsy as a level 1, level 2, level 3 facility and high-risk autopsy, which should be maintained for setting up a mortuary that comprises an autopsy theatre, change room, and observation area. A level 1 facility indicates a mortuary where an autopsy suite is not available. At this level, postmortems are conducted by external examinations with or without radiological support and percutaneous needle sampling. The level 2 facility contains an autopsy suite where infrastructure or manpower for high-risk autopsies is not available. The next level (level 3) facility contains a mortuary with an autopsy suite, along with infrastructure and expertise to conduct high-risk postmortems. The autopsies with the risk of hazards from infections, chemicals, and biological or radiation matters are considered high-risk postmortems. Sirohiwal et al. mentioned the minimum facilities of mortuaries, indicating the arrangements for receiving the deceased bodies, conducting postmortems, transferring the bodies after the medicolegal examination, a postmortem observation gallery, and some other basic needs for an office (Sirohiwal et al., 2011). The mortuaries should be well-equipped to ensure the smooth functioning of the team. It also describes the design of a mortuary for a secondary, tertiary-level mortuary complex and miscellaneous requirements (Sirohiwal et al., 2011). If we give the example of the *Dhaka Medical College* morgue, the country's most familiar and reliable hospital, the autopsy is still done with ancient equipment, such as a hammer, chisel, knife, etc. As a result, it is time-consuming to complete an autopsy and hand over the bodies to the police and finally to the relatives of the victims.

4 Current Challenges and Way Forward

The law in our country, which started over 160 years ago during the British regime considers suicidal attempt a criminal offence. The legal aspects of suicidal behavior have been discussed later in this book in Chap. 10 (Arafat, 2026). It is clear that criminalizing suicidal attempts is not a way to mitigate the problems. Rather, the law is deterring people from seeking consultation and even from escaping from the hospital without fulfilling the course of treatment just to avoid legal problems. So we will have to think again and again to prevent suicide or suicidal attempts. Current criminal legal status hinders people from disclosing suicidal behavior and help-seeking, which in turn increases the risk for further attempts and death by suicide. Therefore, attempting suicide should be decriminalized. That will help the victim seek necessary help for the management of further suicidal attempts without any fear of imprisonment and social stigma. However, it is yet to receive adequate attention in the country.

There is lack of modern mortuary and forensic experts in Bangladesh. Without modern facilities and experts, it is difficult to give an opinion on any unnatural deaths, especially in cases of advanced decomposed, mutilated, and burnt bodies, where there is effacement of identities. Recently, we noticed that it took about a week to identify a body with a cut throat wound due to LSD intoxication (Bose et al., 2021b). The traditional ways of performing an autopsy in cases of unnatural deaths should be upgraded. The forensic expert should be continuously trained. For instance, the traditional procedure of dissecting the dead body for confirmation of death in case of suicide can also be performed by psychological autopsy. That is to ask the relatives, friends, or roommates who were in close contact with the deceased about the habits, history of taking antidepressant or antipsychotic medications, suicidal thoughts, failure or frustration etc., regarding any issue without dissecting the body. These will help us to follow the trend and pattern of suicide, which in turn will facilitate the formulation of suicide prevention. But in any doubtful cases, we can dissect the body as well. Furthermore, related laboratory investigations, such as toxicological, histopathological, and radiological facilities, should be set up under the forensic departments in order to avoid undue delay in giving an opinion. In district hospitals, forensic consultants must be appointed to perform an autopsy. Rahman and his colleagues recommended setting up of medical examiner's system through international support, which could be tested in the country to assess its suitability in the current decades (Rahman et al., 2010).

The number of forensic medicine experts needs to be increased, and decentralizing the services may help the health and judicial systems manage the autopsy cases with limited resources. Without adequately trained experts and supporting staff, further expansion and upgradation of forensic services cannot be expected. Adequate facilities should be ensured in such a pattern that young doctors spontaneously choose their careers in forensic medicine. Second, in addition to forensic medicine, adequate opportunities for forensic psychiatrists would expand the services. Adequate training (both national and international) should be arranged to ensure the continuous progression of expertise.

Morgue staff (well known as Dom in Bangla) plays a vital role in medicolegal autopsy. They are engaged in receiving the dead body, dissection, preservation of viscera, reconstruction, and, finally, handing over the body to the legal authority. Surprisingly, they are generationally engaged in this profession; the legacy started from their families. But nowadays, they are not well trained as professionals. They learn to handle autopsy cases by watching their family members perform the procedure, though they need to be scientifically well-trained. That is why there is lack of well-trained mortuary staff. Moreover, their salary and remuneration are so undervalued. Which is unacceptable. If we want to take initiatives for upgrading forensic medicine, we will have to have a holistic approach, like morgue attendants should be properly trained to ensure full monetary benefit packages.

Suicide prevention is everyone's business (World Health Organization, 2014). Currently, the scattered and scant prevention strategies are not harmonized in Bangladesh (Arafat & Khan, 2019; Arafat, 2018). Enduring liaisons between mental health professionals, forensic experts, journalists, and legal bodies are warranted to change the legal status, raise awareness, and improve the medicolegal decisions.

5 Conclusion

There are undeniable roles of forensic medicine, forensic psychiatry, and legal bodies in suicide prevention that should not be an exception in Bangladesh. Death declaration, identification of suicides, and crafting laws and regulations affect help-seeking behavior and suicide prevention. Immediate initiatives are warranted to change the criminal status of suicidal behavior in Bangladesh. Additionally, both qualitative and quantitative improvement of forensic services should be prioritized. Adequate measures should be made to reduce the postmortem dropouts so that the underestimation of suicide could be resolved. There is no alternative to an enduring collaboration among forensic medicine, psychiatry, police, media, and other stakeholders.

References

Arafat, S. M. Y., & Kabir, R. (2026). Data is silent, epidemiology is blur: Suicidal behavior in Bangladesh-what is known and what needs to improve. In S. M. Y. Arafat (Ed.), *Suicidal behavior in Bangladesh*. Springer. https://doi.org/10.1007/978-981-95-8321-8_1

Arafat, S. M. Y. (2026). Law, policy, and strategies on suicide prevention in Bangladesh. In S. M. Y. Arafat (Ed.), *Suicidal behavior in Bangladesh.* Springer. https://doi.org/10.1007/978-981-95-8321-8_10
Arafat, S. M. Y. (2025). Suicide prevention in Bangladesh: The role of police. *The Lancet. Psychiatry, 12*(3), 173. https://doi.org/10.1016/S2215-0366(24)00443-7
Arafat, S. M. Y. (2019). Current challenges of suicide and future directions of management in Bangladesh: A systematic review. *Global Psychiatry, 2*(1), 9–20. https://doi.org/10.2478/gp-2019-0001
Arafat, S., & Khan, S. T. (2019). Suicide prevention in Bangladesh: Only decriminalization would not be beneficial in an expected fashion. *Asian Journal of Psychiatry, 42*, 22–23. https://doi.org/10.1016/j.ajp.2019.03.027
Arafat, S. M. Y. (2018). Suicide prevention activities in Bangladesh. *Asian Journal of Psychiatry, 36*, 38. https://doi.org/10.1016/j.ajp.2018.06.009
Australian Government Department of Health. (2013). Requirements for the facilities and operation of mortuaries. https://www1.health.gov.au/internet/main/publishing.nsf/Content/health-npaac-docs-mortuari.htm. Accessed on July 29, 2022.
Bangladesh Bureau of Statistics. (2024). Population & Housing Census 2022. https://bbs.gov.bd/site/page/47856ad0-7e1c-4aab-bd78-892733bc06eb/Population-&-Housing. Accessed on June 23, 2025.
Bose, P. K., Arafat, S. Y., Shoib, S., & Reza, A. S. (2021a). Necrophilia in a forensic morgue staff in Bangladesh: Forensic psychiatric challenges and implications. *Journal of Affective Disorders Reports, 5*, 100158. https://doi.org/10.1016/j.jadr.2021.100158
Bose, P. K., Ray, D., Biswas, P., & Arafat, S. (2021b). Suicidal cut-throat wound during LSD intoxication. *Clinical Case Reports, 9*(11), e05100. https://doi.org/10.1002/ccr3.5100
Code of Criminal Procedure. (1898). Laws of Bangladesh. Act No. V of 1898 chapter XIV. Available online: http://bdlaws.minlaw.gov.bd/act-75.html. Accessed on July 25, 2022.
Hossain, S., & Arafat, S. M. Y. (2026). Necrophilia among forensic morgue staff in Bangladesh: Three cases and the enduring concern. *Ethics, Medicine and Public Health, 34*, 101216. https://doi.org/10.1016/j.jadr.2021.100158
Islam, M. N., & Islam, M. N. (2003). Forensic medicine in Bangladesh. *Legal Medicine (Tokyo, Japan), 5*(Suppl 1), S357–S359. https://doi.org/10.1016/s1344-6223(02)00132-3
Rahman, K., Osman, M., & Mahmud, S. (2010). Forensic medicine: Bangladesh perspective. *Journal of Dhaka Medical College, 19*(1), 61–64. https://doi.org/10.3329/jdmc.v19i1.6255
Rahman, M., & Ahmad, Z. K. (1994). Determination of negative autopsy rate at Sir Salimullah Medical College, Dhaka. *Bangladesh Medical Research Council Bulletin, 20*(1), 21–23.
Sirohiwal, B. L., Paliwal, P. K., Sharma, L., & Chawla, H. (2011). Design and layout of mortuary complex for a medical college and peripheral hospitals. *Journal of Forensic Research, 2*(6), 102. https://doi.org/10.4172/2157-7145.1000102e
World Health Organization. (2025). Suicide; WHO: Geneva, Switzerland. Available online: https://www.who.int/news-room/fact-sheets/detail/suicide. Accessed on June 27, 2025.
World Health Organization. (2021). *Suicide worldwide in 2019: Global health estimates.* WHO. https://www.who.int/publications/i/item/9789240026643. Accessed on September 18, 2025
World Health Organization. (2014). *Preventing suicide: A global imperative.* WHO. https://apps.who.int/iris/handle/10665/131056. Accessed on July 15, 2022

Chapter 3
Mental Health and Suicidal Behavior in Bangladesh

S. M. Yasir Arafat

1 Introduction

Suicidal behavior is a global public health issue that is not an exception for Bangladesh (World Health Organization, 2021). A total of 727,000 people die by suicide in the world in a year; 73% of the suicides happened in low- and middle-income countries (LMICs) (World Health Organization, 2025). Many more people attempt suicide. It is still mysterious to know the suicide pathway in a definitive fashion. Suicide is an outcome of a complex interaction between several factors, like gene–environment interaction, proximal–distal factor interaction, and biopsychosocial interaction (Zalsman et al., 2016; World Health Organization, 2014). Among several factors, psychiatric disorder has been considered an important risk factor for suicide across the world, with some variations in rate (Zalsman et al., 2016; Cho et al., 2016). Current evidence supports that about 90% of suicides have at least one psychiatric illness in Western countries (Zalsman et al., 2016). However, recent repeated autopsy studies from eastern countries such as China, India, and Bangladesh revealed a lower rate of mental illness among suicides (Zalsman et al., 2016; Cho et al., 2016; Milner et al., 2013; Arafat et al., 2022a). One systematic review concluded that the prevalence of mental illness is possibly lower in LMICs (Knipe et al., 2019). Another recent meta-analysis replicates the lower prevalence of depressive disorder in suicides and suicidal behavior in South Asian countries (Arafat et al., 2022b). It revealed the pooled prevalence of depression was 37.3% in suicide and 32.7% in nonfatal suicide attempts (Arafat et al., 2022b).

S. M. Y. Arafat (✉)
Department of Psychiatry, Bangladesh Specialized Hospital, Dhaka, Bangladesh

Department of Public and Community Health, Faculty of Medicine and Health Sciences, Frontier University Garowe, Garowe, Somalia

S. M. Y. Arafat (ed.), *Suicidal Behavior in Bangladesh*, Mental Health Systems and Policy in Low- and Middle-Income Countries,
https://doi.org/10.1007/978-981-95-8321-8_3

Bangladesh is an LMIC located in South Asia with potential economic growth in recent decades. It has an area of 147,570 square kilometers and about 170 million populations substantiating it one of the highest densely populated states in the world (Bangladesh Bureau of Statistics, 2024). Among the population, more than 90% are Muslims. Suicide is prohibited in Islam, and it is considered a criminal offence in the country (Arafat et al., 2022c). Bangladesh is enjoying a demographic dividend from its huge young population which makes its prolific economic growth despite huge corruption and money laundering to Western countries. The country has lifted from the low-income to the lower-middle-income group in recent years. At the same time, it is facing a double burden of diseases, with a gradual inclination toward noncommunicable diseases. Currently, more than 60% of the disease burden is incurred by noncommunicable diseases (Ahmed, 2018). Mental disorders are one of the major burdens after cardiovascular diseases, diabetes mellitus, chronic respiratory diseases, and malignancy (Ahmed, 2018). The latest nation-wide mental health survey of Bangladesh, conducted by the *National Institute of Mental Health (NIMH)*, the *Ministry of Health*, and *World Health Organization* (WHO) in 2018–2019, revealed that the prevalence of psychiatric disorders was 18.7% (95% CI: 17.4–20.0%), which was 16.1% in 2003–2005 (Alam et al., 2024; Mazumder, 2024; Firoz et al., 2006). Among the disorders, the highest prevalence was noted for depression (6.7%), followed by anxiety disorders (4.7%), somatic symptoms and related disorders (2.3%), and psychotic disorders (1%) (Alam et al., 2024). The study identified a treatment gap of 91% among the adult populations of Bangladesh (Ministry of Health & Family Welfare, 2021). A significant portion of the patients visit traditional healers (Samans, Kabiraz, etc.) and nonmedical health professionals before seeing mental health professionals (Giasuddin et al., 2012; Nuri et al., 2018). Studies identified that less than 30% of the patients visit mental health professionals at their first point of contact for mental health care (Arafat et al., 2024a; Giasuddin et al., 2012; Nuri et al., 2018). Another important aspect of health services should be mentioned regarding the high out-of-pocket expenses for the treatment of mental illness in Bangladesh. I couldn't find any specific study on the out-of-pocket expenses of psychiatric disorders in the country. However, available studies identified that the out-of-pocket expenses on overall health revealed more than 70% in Bangladesh (World Bank, 2022). Being a densely populated country with a low health budget, double disease burden, low mental health literacy, high stigma, and attribution of mental illness to super-natural power like jinn, overall mental health care is grossly underprioritized, especially for the community people of Bangladesh. As a result, the association between suicide and psychiatric disorders is yet to be adequately established.

2 Epidemiology of Suicidal Behavior in Bangladesh

We discuss the epidemiology of suicidal behavior in detail in Chap. 1 of this book (Arafat & Kabir, 2026). Here we mention some details to maintain the context. At the same time, I was careful in reducing the repetitions. Suicidal behavior is an underresearched problem in Bangladesh. The country still lacks a suicide surveillance system and any national suicide prevention initiative (Arafat, 2017). The rate of suicide varies among the empirical studies and WHO reports (Arafat, 2019a). The latest (2025) WHO report revealed the suicide rate was 2.9 per 100,000 population in 2021, which was 3.9 in 2019, 6.1 in 2016, and 7.8 per 100,000 in 2000. The total number of suicides was 4714, 5998, 9544, and 10,167 in 2021, 2019, 2016, and 2012, respectively (WHO, 2014, 2019, 2021, 2025). The statistics indicate a decline in suicide rates and numbers in the last decade. However, the empirical studies revealed different rates in regard to the WHO estimates and even vary among the studies (Arafat, 2019a). Nation-wide studies are warranted to determine the prevalence rates.

The first nationwide epidemiological study among adolescents and youths on suicidal behavior was completed in 2021 by NIMH (Dhaka), WHO (Bangladesh), and Non-Communicable Diseases Control, *Ministry of Health, Bangladesh* (NIMH, 2021). The study utilized the adapted Bangla WHO multisite intervention study on suicidal behaviors *SUPRE-MISS*, among 1744 participants aged 10–24 years. It found the rates of suicidal ideation, planning, and attempt to be 4.7%, 1.5%, and 1.5%, respectively. The rate was significantly higher among females and urban populations. Several aspects should be considered while considering the rates, such as sources of data, concerns of underreporting and misclassification, and methods of data recording in the context of countries like Bangladesh.

There is an extreme dearth of research estimating the prevalence rate of self-harm in the country. The rate of nonsuicidal self-injury (NSSI) was 17% among university students and 40.2% among gays. Self-cutting (39%) was the most common method of NSSI in the country. It revealed a similar pattern of associated factors mentioned as family and marital conflict, premarital and extramarital relationships, and adverse life events (Arafat et al., 2025).

Hanging is the commonest method of suicide, followed by poisoning (Arafat et al., 2021a). Females die more than males, and the majority of the suicides occur among persons under the age of 30 years (Arafat, 2019b). Familial discord, marital disharmony, psychiatric disorders, immediate life events, past suicide attempt, sexual violence, unemployment, and social isolation were identified as the major risk factors for suicide in Bangladesh (Arafat, 2017, 2019a; Arafat et al., 2021b, 2024b; Feroz et al., 2012; Reza et al., 2014; Salam et al., 2017; Shahnaz et al., 2017). However, social factors have a dominant role over clinical factors in Bangladesh (Arafat et al., 2021c). One analysis identified that if the life events could be prevented, about 86% of suicides would be prevented, which was about 50% for psychiatric disorders (Arafat et al., 2021c).

3 Psychiatric Disorders in Suicide and Self-Harm in Bangladesh

3.1 Psychiatric Disorder in Suicide in Bangladesh

The assessment of the prevalence and role of psychiatric disorders in suicide and suicidal behavior is grossly understudied in Bangladesh. Only one case-control psychological autopsy study was conducted in an urban setting, that is, Dhaka city, the capital of the country, which was published in 2020 (Arafat et al., 2021b). The study identified that 61% of the suicides had at least one mental illness. Among them, major depressive disorder was the most prevalent diagnosis (44%), followed by personality disorder (14%), amphetamine (yaba) use disorder (9%), acute stress disorder (4%), adjustment disorder (3%), and schizophrenia (1%) (Arafat et al., 2021b). The study also identified comorbidities of psychiatric disorders, personality disorders, and substance use disorders among suicide deceased. Among the suicides, only 13% were previously diagnosed and being treated, and only one suicide with depression was regular and compliant with the psychiatrist. Among the 13 previously identified cases, five had depressive disorder, seven had substance use disorder, and the remaining one was psychotic (Arafat et al., 2021b). The study identified that the service gap was 87%. It also revealed that only 14% had past suicidal attempts (Arafat et al., 2021b). This is perhaps the only systematized attempt to assess the psychiatric disorders among suicides where the psychiatric diagnoses were assessed by the *Structured Clinical Interview for DSM-IV Axis I Disorders* (SCID-I) (First et al., 1996) and the *Structured Clinical Interview for DSM-IV Personality Disorders* (SCID-II) (First et al., 1994). A different analysis of the same data by comparing suicides with and without mental disorders revealed some additional interesting findings (Arafat et al., 2021d). Mental illness was significantly higher among the suicides that occurred in adulthood than adolescence, among males than females, and among socially isolated persons than those who were living with family (Arafat et al., 2021d). The analysis indicates that 70% of the depressive disorder cases were males, and 70% of the adults had psychiatric disorders, while it was 36% among suicides by adolescents. Significantly higher age was noted among the suicides with mental disorders than suicides without mental illness. All the suicides with acute stress disorder were developed among females in response to sexual harassment (Arafat et al., 2021d). Interestingly, psychiatric disorders were significantly higher in middle and upper socioeconomic classes and persons living in a parental house or had house ownership harassment (Arafat et al., 2021d). In summary, psychiatric disorders were more common among suicides of adult age, males, living alone, and having a middle- and upper-class environment. The findings clearly indicate a lower rate of mental illness among the suicides in Bangladesh in comparison to Western countries. Additionally, it draws our attention toward the social factors and life events such as marital discord, familial disharmony, sexual harassment, and premarital and extramarital relationships in attributing and preventing suicides. However, poor mental health and suicide literacy could be important reasons for this low attribution.

3.2 *Psychiatric Disorder in Self-Harm/Nonfatal Attempt in Bangladesh*

Assessment of psychiatric morbidity in suicidal behaviors has been poorly prioritized in Bangladesh. Available studies indicate the rate is 45–71% (Arafat et al., 2024a, 2025; Uddin et al., 2019; Islam et al., 2019; Roy et al., 2016; Reza et al., 2014; Qusar et al., 2010). The latest study assessed psychiatric disorders among 100 patients with self-harm by SCID-I and SCID-II (Arafat et al., 2024a, 2024b). It revealed that the prevalence of psychiatric disorders was 71%. Depression (19%) and adjustment disorder (11%) were the common disorders (Arafat et al., 2024a, 2024b). A study of 51 patients with NSSI in Chattagram (Chittagong) revealed that 45% of the patients had a psychiatric disorder, which was assigned by clinical interviews conducted by psychiatrists (Uddin et al., 2019). Among the disorders, depressive disorder was found in 23.5%, followed by borderline personality disorder (BPD) (11.8%), and schizophrenia (5.9%) (Uddin et al., 2019). Another study in Comilla (Cumilla) Medical College determined that the prevalence of psychiatric disorders was 65% (Islam et al., 2019). Islam and his colleagues interviewed 120 patients with suicidal behavior using the *Composite International Diagnostic Interview* (CIDI), and diagnoses were assessed as per the DSM-5 classification (Islam et al., 2019). They identified BPD as the topmost psychiatric morbidity, which was found in 16.7%, and depression was found in 7.5% of patients (Islam et al., 2019). In one study conducted at *Rangpur Medical College* in 2017, among 101 clinical patients who presented with nonfatal attempts were assessed for psychiatric morbidity where the diagnosis was assigned clinically by the *Diagnostic and Statistical Manual of Mental Disorders* (DSM-IV-TR) (American Psychiatric Association, 2000; Roy et al., 2016). The study revealed that 65% of the patients with nonfatal attempts had psychiatric disorders, where depressive disorder was the highest (18%), followed by conversion disorder (12%), psychotic disorder (12%), bipolar disorder (6%), and substance abuse disorder (4%) (Roy et al., 2016). Another case-control study published in 2013 assessed psychiatric morbidity by SCID-I in the rural part of Bangladesh (Chuadanga) among 113 respondents with suicidal behavior (Reza et al., 2014). The study revealed that psychiatric morbidity was 58.5% (Reza et al., 2014). However, it didn't categorize the respondents based on suicidal behavior, that is, how many were suicides and how many had only nonfatal attempts. Additionally, it was not demarcated whether the interview was conducted by a psychiatrist or any other well-trained clinician (Reza et al., 2014). A study conducted in 2008 in 44 admitted patients in the intensive care unit (ICU) after a nonfatal attempt assessed psychiatric morbidity by clinical interview, and diagnoses were confirmed as per DSM-IV criteria (Qusar et al., 2010). It identified that about 59% ($n = 26$) of the participants had psychiatric disorders; among them, depressive disorder was the highest morbidity and was identified in 25% of the cases followed by personality disorder (9.1%), psychosis (9.1%), obsessive-compulsive disorder (4.5%), substance-related disorder (4.5%), and acute stress disorder (4.5%) (Qusar et al., 2010). It is important to note that these 44 cases are supposed to have severe intent and clinical outcomes as they were collected after a life-threatening attempt and admitted into the ICU. Therefore, the rate of morbidity among less severe attempters may not be the same. It is important to note that the prevalence has been calculated irrespective of the assessment of intent, whether suicidal or nonsuicidal self-harm. Interestingly, the studies revealed a low rate of mental illness (45%, 58.5% vs 59% and 65%) both in the community (Reza et al., 2014) and clinical sample (Uddin et al., 2019; Islam et al., 2019; Roy et al., 2016; Qusar et al., 2010; Arafat et al., 2024a, 2024b).

4 Psychiatric Services for Suicidal and Self-Harm Behavior

Whatever the service burden, there is extreme insufficiency and inadequate readiness for the provision of evidence-based services for suicide and self-harm in Bangladesh. The autopsy study identified that the unidentified mental health need was 87% (Arafat et al., 2021b). The latest mental health survey conducted in 2018–2019 identified the treatment gap for psychiatric disorders at 91% (Ministry of Health & Family Welfare, 2021). After the service gaps, let us check the service delivery pattern of the health system in Bangladesh. The criminal legal status creates an additional burden for service provision as well as service receiving for nonfatal attempts. As patients with self-harm and suicidal behavior have been considered as police cases, a seal is stamped on the hospital file of the patients mentioning "police case." This stamping is supposed to create a further psychological burden in addition to the primary distress. Private hospitals are reluctant to provide services, and usually, they refer such patients to the public hospitals to avoid unwanted legal hazards. Generally, such patients are treated in the public hospitals, starting from Upazila Health Complex to District (Sadar hospital in Bangla) and then medical college hospitals. These hospitals have a separate corner for stomach wash for patients with poisoning and medication overdose. After that, they are grossly neglected, as in most cases, they are kept on the floor of the hospital veranda. In the general hospital settings, patients with suicidal behavior have been treated by medicine specialists in the majority of situations. There is almost no privacy and psychological support, and even such patients are not being referred to a psychiatrist for evaluation of suicidal intent, mental health status, and tailored need for psychological support. Due to these reasons, patients with NSSI do not take medical advice unless an emergency arises. Sometimes, public hospitals are located far away from the living place, and for hospitalization, patients have to travel a long distance, which may be an important cause of mortality (Verma et al., 2017). If we look into available human resources for service provision, we can see that there are about 350 psychiatrists in Bangladesh, and every year about 10–20 psychiatrists are coming out, including the MCPS, FCPS, MD

Psychiatry, and MD Child and Adolescent Psychiatry (Arafat et al., 2024b; WHO, 2020). The country has 0.17 psychiatrists, 0.43 mental health nurses, and 0.35 psychologists per 100,000 population, respectively (WHO, 2020). If we calculate the proportion with the prevalence of the latest national mental health survey, I find that only one psychiatrist is available for 110,000 patients, considering the prevalence (18.7%) and the availability of psychiatrists (0.17 per 100,000) (Arafat et al., 2024b). The situation is further complicated by the inequitable distribution of mental health professionals. Most of the psychiatrists are located in the city, and the majority of the psychiatrists live in Dhaka (the capital city). Only about 0.5% of the total country budget has been allocated for mental health, and the total mental health expenditure is about 9 Taka (0.1 USD) for an individual (WHO, 2022). Only two specialized service centers have been identified in the country; both of them are located in Dhaka city. The first Suicide Prevention Clinic (SPC) was started at the psychiatry department of Bangabandhu Sheikh Mujib Medical University (BSMMU, currently, it is Bangladesh Medical University). It was started in September 2016, aiming at providing a specialized service to patients with active suicidal ideation or previous suicide/self-harm attempts. The clinic works at weekly two-hour basis in the outpatient department (OPD) services, only on Saturday from 11.00 a.m. to 1.00 p.m. (Arafat, 2018). Prof. Mohsin Ali Shah, professor of psychiatry, started the services in the country. The clinic maintains follow-up by making phone calls to the service recipients to ascertain whether attempts are made. Reports from the clinic revealed that about two-thirds of the patients were aged under 25 years, 70% were females, and depressive disorder was the most common psychiatric morbidity (Shah et al., 2018). Unfortunately, it has ceased after the COVID-19 pandemic (Arafat, 2024).

The second SPC was started at the department of psychiatry of Enam Medical College and Hospital (EMCH), a private medical college in Dhaka, by Dr. S. M. Yasir Arafat, a disciple of Prof. Mohsin Ali Shah. The service hour is extended from 9 a.m. to 5 p.m. on working days. It started in October 2021 and ceased in November 2023 (Arafat, 2024). Any other specialized clinical services for suicide prevention have not been identified in Bangladesh. The patients presenting at the SPC of BSMMU are mostly referred by the psychiatry OPD, while the SPC of EMCH gets patients by self self-referred due to some awareness materials like banners containing basic information on suicide and self-harm. A mental health OPD is available at 72 hospitals countrywide (WHO, 2022). However, it is questionable whether any mental health specialist is available in all the centers, except the medical colleges. Even general physicians having training in mental health would be difficult to find in every centre at the primary care level of Bangladesh. Therefore, it is unexpected that these centres would be able to handle suicide and suicidal behaviour efficiently. It is important to note that none of the persons in the SPCs has any formal training on suicide and suicide prevention, except for their academic background.

5 Current Challenges and Way Forward for Suicide Prevention

Detailed suicide prevention activities have been discussed in Chap. 14 of this book by Hoque and Arafat (2026). Here, I have tried to mention the prevention activities closely associated with mental health. Criminal legal status, low quality data, inadequate services, high out-of-pocket expense, low mental health and suicide literacy, low research, lack of national data bases and suicide surveillance system, nonexistence of intersectoral collaboration, inadequate funds, unavailability of professional training, lack of national suicide prevention strategies are the potential challenges of suicide and self-harm prevention in Bangladesh (Arafat, 2025a). Self-harm behavior is a covert problem in Bangladesh. Usually, young child(ren) hide(s) it from their parents. Parents are not aware at such a stage to consider it as a mental health issue due to high-level stigma and low mental health literacy. There is an extreme dearth of health services having adequate training and expertise to deal with the problems. The problem is yet to get the political attention to have any health policy and visible prevention activities. The Mental Health Act of Bangladesh was passed in 2018 and contains nothing about suicide prevention (Mental Health Act, 2018; Arafat, 2025b).

There is no alternative to raising awareness among the service providers first and then among the general population, indicating that suicide is preventable and a past attempt is the strongest risk factor for suicide (WHO, 2025). Adequate mental health services should be ensured throughout the country with proper psychological support readily available. Periodic training for human resources working in suicide prevention should be ensured. General physicians should be adequately trained to identify the warning signs of suicide, depression, and substance abuse (Arafat & Kabir, 2017). Enduring collaboration is necessary between the mental health professionals, media personnel, crisis service centers, and forensic experts. Decriminalization of suicide would help people to disclose suicidal behavior and hospitals to provide necessary services to the needy people (Soron, 2019). Initiating the school mental health programs and ensuring the gate-keeper training of teachers to identify the signs of depression, substance misuse, and suicidal behavior could be a potential area in the country (Zalsman et al., 2016). There is a dire need for research in suicide and suicide prevention to identify the role of psychiatric disorders in suicide, as well as to test any culture-sensitive suicide prevention strategies.

6 Conclusions

Mental health and mental illness are closely associated with suicide and suicidal behavior in Bangladesh, as in other parts of the world, even though the available rate is lower when compared to Western countries. However, neither the mental health care providers nor the service receivers are ready in either way to deal with suicidal behavior in psychiatric care. Low mental health and suicide literacy, high stigma toward suicide and mental health services, lack of service outlets, and awareness could be the potential factors. There is no alternative to raising awareness about suicide prevention among all the stakeholders in the country. Urgent attention of policymakers and responsible authorities is warranted to address the service care of patients and their family members with suicidal and self-harm behavior, as well as to train the service providers. Academic institutions should prioritize suicide prevention research to find out the risk factors for suicide in the country. And finally, the implementation of the research findings into the policy should start in Bangladesh.

References

Ahmed. (2018). Non-communicable diseases and their prevention: A global, regional and Bangladesh perspective. *National Bulletin of Public Health (NBPH), 1*(3), 2–4.

Alam, M. F., Ahmed, H. U., Alam, M. T., Sarkar, M., Khan, N. M., Uddin, M. J., & Sarkar, A. A. (2024). Community prevalence of psychiatric disorders: Findings from a nationwide survey in Bangladesh. *Asian Journal of Psychiatry, 92*, 103897. https://doi.org/10.1016/j.ajp.2023.103897

American Psychiatric Association. (2000). *Diagnostic and statistical manual of mental disorders* (4th ed, text revision ed.). American Psychiatric Association.

Arafat, S. M. Y., & Kabir, R. (2026). Data is silent, epidemiology is blur: Suicidal behavior in Bangladesh-what is known and what needs to improve. In S. M. Y. Arafat (Ed.), *Suicidal behavior in Bangladesh*. Springer. https://doi.org/10.1007/978-981-95-8321-8_1

Arafat, S. M. Y. (2025a). Suicide prevention in Bangladesh: The role of police. *The Lancet. Psychiatry, 12*(3), 173. https://doi.org/10.1016/S2215-0366(24)00443-7

Arafat, S. M. Y. (2025b). Suicide prevention in Bangladesh: Critical analysis of mental health law, policy and strategy. *BJPsych International, 22*(4), 138–141. https://doi.org/10.1192/bji.2025.10042

Arafat, S. M. Y., Mali, B., & Mazumder, A. H. (2025). Nonsuicidal self-injury in Bangladesh: A narrative review. *Health Science Reports, 8*(5), e70790. https://doi.org/10.1002/hsr2.70790

Arafat, S. M. Y., Giasuddin, N. A., & Mazumder, A. H. (2024a). Access to mental health care in Bangladesh—current status, potential challenges, and ways out. In S. M. Y. Arafat & S. K. Kar (Eds.), *Access to mental health care in South Asia*. Springer. https://doi.org/10.1007/978-981-99-9153-2_3

Arafat, S. M. Y., Shormi, F. R., & Kibria, M. G. (2024b). Psychiatric disorder and life-event in self harm: A cross-sectional study among clinical population in Bangladesh. *Heliyon, 10*(19), e38627. https://doi.org/10.1016/j.heliyon.2024.e38627

Arafat, S. M. Y. (2024). Suicidal behavior and suicide prevention in Bangladesh. In S. M. Y. Arafat (Ed.), *Mental health in Bangladesh*. Springer. https://doi.org/10.1007/978-981-97-0610-5_11

Arafat, S., Menon, V., Varadharajan, N., & Kar, S. K. (2022a). Psychological autopsy studies of suicide in South East Asia. *Indian Journal of Psychological Medicine, 44*(1), 4–9. https://doi.org/10.1177/02537176211033643

Arafat, S. M. Y., Saleem, T., Menon, V., Ali, S A.-e.-Z., Baminiwatta, A., Kar, S. K., Akter, H., & Singh, R. (2022b). Depression and suicidal behavior in South Asia: A systematic review and meta-analysis. *Global Mental Health, 9*, 181–192. https://doi.org/10.1017/gmh.2022.20

Arafat, S. M. Y., Marthoenis, M., Khan, M. M., & Rezaeian, M. (2022c). Association between suicide rate and human development index, income, and the political system in 46 Muslim-majority countries: An ecological study. *European Journal of Investigation in Health, Psychology and Education., 12*(7), 754–764. https://doi.org/10.3390/ejihpe12070055

Arafat, S., Ali, S. A., Menon, V., Hussain, F., Ansari, D. S., Baminiwatta, A., Saleem, T., Singh, R., Varadharajan, N., Biyyala, D., Kar, S. K., & Khan, M. M. (2021a). Suicide methods in South Asia over two decades (2001-2020). *The International Journal of Social Psychiatry, 67*(7), 920–934. https://doi.org/10.1177/00207640211015700

Arafat, S., Mohit, M. A., Mullick, M., Kabir, R., & Khan, M. M. (2021b). Risk factors for suicide in Bangladesh: Case-control psychological autopsy study. *BJPsych Open, 7*(1), e18. https://doi.org/10.1192/bjo.2020.152

Arafat, S., Mohit, M. A., Mullick, M., Khan, M., & Khan, M. M. (2021c). Suicide with and without mental disorders: Findings from psychological autopsy study in Bangladesh. *Asian Journal of Psychiatry, 61*, 102690. https://doi.org/10.1016/j.ajp.2021.102690

Arafat, S., Khan, M., Knipe, D., & Khan, M. M. (2021d). Population attributable fractions of clinical and social risk factors for suicide in Bangladesh: Finding from a case-control psychological autopsy study. *Brain and Behavior, 11*(12), e2409. https://doi.org/10.1002/brb3.2409

Arafat, S. M. Y. (2019a). Current challenges of suicide and future directions of management in Bangladesh: A systematic review. *Global Psychiatry, 2*(1), 9–20. https://doi.org/10.2478/gp-2019-0001

Arafat, S. M. Y. (2019b). Females are dying more than males by suicide in Bangladesh. *Asian Journal of Psychiatry, 40*, 124–125. https://doi.org/10.1016/j.ajp.2018.10.014

Arafat, S. M. Y. (2018). Suicide prevention activities in Bangladesh. *Asian Journal of Psychiatry, 36*, 38. https://doi.org/10.1016/j.ajp.2018.06.009

Arafat, S. Y., & Kabir, R. (2017). Suicide prevention strategies: Which one to consider? *South East Asia Journal of Public Health, 7*(1), 1–5. https://doi.org/10.3329/seajph.v7i1.34671

Arafat, S. M. Y. (2017). Suicide in Bangladesh: A mini review. *Journal of Behavioral Health, 6*(1), 66–69. https://doi.org/10.5455/jbh.20160904090206

Bangladesh Bureau of Statistics. (2024). *Population & Housing Census*, 2022. https://bbs.gov.bd/site/page/47856ad0-7e1c-4aab-bd78-892733bc06eb/Population-&-Housing. Accessed on May 23, 2025

Cho, S. E., Na, K. S., Cho, S. J., Im, J. S., & Kang, S. G. (2016). Geographical and temporal variations in the prevalence of mental disorders in suicide: Systematic review and meta-analysis. *Journal of Affective Disorders, 190*, 704–713. https://doi.org/10.1016/j.jad.2015.11.008

First, M. B., Spitzer, R. L., Gibbon, M., Williams, J. B., & Benjamin, L. (1994). *Structured clinical interview for DSM-IV Axis II personality disorders*. Biometrics Research Department, New York State Psychiatric Institute.

First, M. B., Spitzer, R. L., Gibbon, M., & Williams, J. B. (1996). *Structured clinical interview for DSM-IV Axis I disorders*. Biometrics Research Department, New York State Psychiatric Institute.

Feroz, A., Islam, S. N., Reza, S., Rahman, A. M., Sen, J., Mowla, M., & Rahman, M. R. (2012). A community survey on the prevalence of suicidal attempts and deaths in a selected rural area of Bangladesh. *Journal of Medicine, 13*(1), 3–9. https://doi.org/10.3329/jom.v13i1.10042

Firoz, A. H. M., Karim, M. E., Alam, M. F., Rahman, A. H. M. M., & Zaman, M. M. (2006). Prevalence, medical care, awareness and attitude towards mental illness in Bangladesh. *Bangladesh Journal Psychiatry, 20*(1), 9–32.

Giasuddin, N. A., Chowdhury, N. F., Hashimoto, N., Fujisawa, D., & Waheed, S. (2012). Pathways to psychiatric care in Bangladesh. *Social Psychiatry and Psychiatric Epidemiology, 47*(1), 129–136. https://doi.org/10.1007/s00127-010-0315-y

Hoque, M. B., & Arafat, S. M. Y. (2026). Suicidal behavior in Bangladesh: The preventive measures. In S. Y. Arafat (Ed.), *Suicidal behavior in Bangladesh*. Springer. https://doi.org/10.1007/978-981-95-8321-8_14

Islam, M. S., Mamun, S. A. A., Haque, M. M., Mohammad Khan, N., Rashid, M. H. A., Sinha, R. K., Abedin, M. F., & Uddin, M. N. (2019). Psychiatric disorders among suicidal behavior patients attending mental health facilities: A descriptive cross sectional study. *Journal of*

Bangladesh College of Physicians and Surgeons, 37(3), 130–134. https://doi.org/10.3329/jbcps.v37i3.41735

Knipe, D., Williams, A. J., Hannam-Swain, S., Upton, S., Brown, K., Bandara, P., Chang, S. S., & Kapur, N. (2019). Psychiatric morbidity and suicidal behaviour in low- and middle-income countries: A systematic review and meta-analysis. *PLoS Medicine, 16*(10), e1002905. https://doi.org/10.1371/journal.pmed.1002905

Mazumder, A. H. (2024). Epidemiology and burden of mental disorders in Bangladesh. In S. M. Y. Arafat (Ed.), *Mental health in Bangladesh.* Springer. https://doi.org/10.1007/978-981-97-0610-5_2

Mental Health Act. (2018). Bangladesh. [Online]. Accessed on December 12, 2018. Available from https://legislativediv.gov.bd/site/page/3c13bbde-76b4-41fc-89cab738dd04a0bb.

Milner, A., Sveticic, J., & De Leo, D. (2013). Suicide in the absence of mental disorder? A review of psychological autopsy studies across countries. *The International Journal of Social Psychiatry, 59*(6), 545–554. https://doi.org/10.1177/0020764012444259

Ministry of Health & Family Welfare. (2021). National Mental Health Survey 2019. Retrieved May 23, 2025, from http://nimh.gov.bd/wp-content/uploads/2021/11/Mental-Health-Survey-Report.pdf.

National Institute of Mental Health. (2021). Epidemiology of suicide and suicidal behavior among youth and adolescents in Bangladesh. (Project Report).

Nuri, N. N., Sarker, M., Ahmed, H. U., Hossain, M. D., Beiersmann, C., & Jahn, A. (2018). Pathways to care of patients with mental health problems in Bangladesh. *International Journal of Mental Health Systems, 12*, 39. https://doi.org/10.1186/s13033-018-0218-y

Qusar, M. S., Morshed, N. M., Azad, M. A. K., Kader, M. A., Shams, S. F., Ahmed, M. F., Haque, M. M. M., Uddin, M. A., & Shahid, S. F. B. (2010). Psychiatric morbidity among suicide attempters who needed ICU intervention. *Bangabandhu Sheikh Mujib Medical University Journal, 2*(2), 73–77. https://doi.org/10.3329/bsmmuj.v2i2.4761

Reza, A. S., Feroz, A. H. M., Islam, S. N., Karim, M. N., Rabbani, M. G., Shah Alam, M., Rahman, M. M., Rahman, M. R., Ahmed, H. U., Bhowmik, A. D., Khan, M. Z. R., Sarkar, M., Alam, M. T., & Jalal Uddin, M. M. (2014). Risk factors of suicide and Para suicide in rural Bangladesh. *Journal of Medicine, 14*(2), 123–129. https://doi.org/10.3329/jom.v14i2.19653

Roy, J., Al Adiluzzaman, M. A. F., Hasan, M. T., Roy, D. D., Qusar, M. S., Shah, M. M. A., & Arafat, S. Y. (2016). Socio-demographic profile and psychiatric morbidities of suicide attempters: A cross-sectional observation in a tertiary care hospital of Bangladesh. *Bangladesh Journal of Psychiatry, 30*(2), 36–40. https://doi.org/10.3329/bjpsy.v30i2.45363

Shahnaz, A., Bagley, C., Simkhada, P., & Kadri, S. (2017). Suicidal behaviour in Bangladesh: A scoping literature review and a proposed public health prevention model. *Open Journal of Social Sciences, 5*, 254–282. https://doi.org/10.4236/jss.2017.57016

Shah, M., Sajib, M., & Arafat, S. (2018). Demography and risk factor of suicidal behavior in Bangladesh: A cross-sectional observation from patients attending a suicide prevention clinic of Bangladesh. *Asian Journal of Psychiatry, 35*, 4–5. https://doi.org/10.1016/j.ajp.2018.04.035

Salam, S. S., Alonge, O., Islam, M. I., Hoque, D., Wadhwaniya, S., UlBaset, M. K., Mashreky, S. R., & El Arifeen, S. (2017). The burden of suicide in rural Bangladesh: Magnitude and risk factors. *International Journal of Environmental Research and Public Health, 14*(9), 1032. https://doi.org/10.3390/ijerph14091032

Soron, T. R. (2019). Decriminalizing suicide in Bangladesh. *Asian Journal of Psychiatry, 39*, 91–92. https://doi.org/10.1016/j.ajp.2018.12.012

World Bank. (2022). Out-of-pocket expenditure (% of current health expenditure)—Bangladesh. https://data.worldbank.org/indicator/SH.XPD.OOPC.CH.ZS?locations=BD. Last Accessed on September 21, 2022.

Uddin, M. G., Biswas, R. S. R., & Mamun, S. M. H. (2019). Sociodemographic profile and intention of deliberate self-harm among patients admitted in a tertiary care hospital, Chittagong, Bangladesh. *Journal of the Scientific Society, 46*(2), 53. https://doi.org/10.4103/jss.JSS_9_19

Verma, V., Paul, S., Ghose, A., Eddleston, M., & Konradsen, F. (2017). Treatment of self-poisoning at a tertiary-level hospital in Bangladesh: Cost to patients and government. *Tropical Medicine & International Health: TM & IH, 22*(12), 1551–1560. https://doi.org/10.1111/tmi.12991

World Health Organization. (2021). *Suicide worldwide in 2019: Global health estimates*. WHO. Available online: https://www.who.int/publications/i/item/9789240026643. Accessed on September 15, 2021

World Health Organization. (2025). *Suicide worldwide in 2021: Global health estimates*. World Health Organization. https://www.who.int/publications/i/item/9789240110069. Accessed on October 18, 2025

World Health Organization. (2019). *Suicide in the world*. Global Health Estimates. https://apps.who.int/iris/bitstream/handle/10665/326948/WHO-MSD-MER-19.3-eng.pdf. Accessed on July 15, 2022

World Health Organization. (2014). Preventing suicide: a global imperative. https://apps.who.int/iris/handle/10665/131056. Accessed on July 15, 2022.

World Health Organization. (2022). Mental health atlas 2020 country profile: Bangladesh. https://www.who.int/publications/m/item/mental-health-atlas-bgd-2020-country-profile. Accessed on July 15, 2022.

World Health Organization. (2020) Bangladesh WHO special initiative for mental health situational assessment. WHO. (https://cdn.who.int/media/docs/default-source/mental-health/special-initiative/who-special-initiative-country-report%2D%2D-bangladesh%2D%2D-2020_f746e0ca-8099-4d00-b126-fa338a06ca6e.pdf?sfvrsn=c2122a0e_7. Accessed on July 15, 2022.

Zalsman, G., Hawton, K., Wasserman, D., van Heeringen, K., Arensman, E., Sarchiapone, M., Carli, V., Höschl, C., Barzilay, R., Balazs, J., Purebl, G., Kahn, J. P., Sáiz, P. A., Lipsicas, C. B., Bobes, J., Cozman, D., Hegerl, U., & Zohar, J. (2016). Suicide prevention strategies revisited: 10-year systematic review. *The Lancet Psychiatry, 3*(7), 646–659. https://doi.org/10.1016/S2215-0366(16)30030-X

Chapter 4
Cultural Perspectives of Suicide in Bangladesh

Anisur Rahman Khan

1 Introduction

Émile Durkheim's classic research *Le Suicide* (1897/2002) laid the foundation of empirical sociology by producing a methodical, extensive, coherent, and testable theory of suicide (Joiner, 2007), establishing him as the founder of the scientific study of suicide (Jaworski, 2016). Durkheim (1897/2002) viewed suicide as a much more complex social fact, embedded within a varied range of sociocultural (external) contexts and perspectives. For Durkheim, suicide is a manifestation of sociocultural norms, values, role expectations, interactions, needs, and circumstances specific to a given sociocultural milieu (Staples, 2012). In this sense, academic interest in examining the influence of cultural/social (structural) factors on suicide clearly derives from the Durkheimian tradition in sociology of suicide (Goldston et al., 2008).

Considering the implications of cultural factors in the context of growing rural suicide rates, Gessert (2003: 698) strongly asserted, "ultimately, suicide reflects a determination that death is preferable to life. Such a determination cannot be understood without a thorough understanding of the culture in which it occurs." To reiterate, suicide is culturally patterned everywhere, and each society has developed its own cultural narratives around it (Canetto, 2015). Cultural factors such as norms, values, and role expectations shape the suicidal acts in diverse ways, including the classifications/forms, methods, motivations/causes, and demographic distributions based on gender, age, social class, ethnicity, or other socio-economic variables. The

A. R. Khan (✉)
Department of Sociology, East West University, Dhaka, Bangladesh

Institute for Social and Health Science (ISHS), University of South Africa, Cape Town, South Africa
e-mail: arkhan@ewubd.edu

S. M. Y. Arafat (ed.), *Suicidal Behavior in Bangladesh*, Mental Health Systems and Policy in Low- and Middle-Income Countries,
https://doi.org/10.1007/978-981-95-8321-8_4

perceptions, understandings/meanings, and reactions to suicide may differ across cultures. Cultural contexts may also shape the risk and protective factors as well as the frameworks of prevention and intervention (Goldston et al., 2008; Lester, 2013; Stack, 2021; Staples, 2012).

Notwithstanding the difficulties associated with understanding the cultural meanings of suicide due to its diverse contestation across culture and society, scholarly efforts consistently highlight the obvious ramifications of culture on suicide (Cloucci, 2013; Maharajh & Abdool, 2005). Against this backdrop, this chapter examines the interface between culture and suicide (excluding suicide attempt or suicide intent) in the context of Bangladesh. Despite suicide being a grievous public health crisis in Bangladesh, its risk factors have not yet been studied meticulously (Arafat et al., 2022c). Considering the critical imprint of culture on suicide, any systematic assessment of this relationship may enhance the effectiveness of suicide reduction efforts (Maharajh & Abdool, 2005).

2 The Meaning of Culture

Culture as a concept has been used extensively to comprehend the ways of life of people. Core social science disciplines that deal with cultures, such as sociology and anthropology, have not only expressed the concept in varied ways but have also generated considerable controversies, disagreements, and paradoxes regarding its meaning and formation (Cheal, 2003; Cloussi, 2013). Culture is dynamic and also changeable. Its meaning-making, practices, and relationships are subject to continuous (re)reconstruction. Consequently, the culture of any society cannot be understood as a stable, measurable structure (Patel, 2017). For example, the extensive classical review by A.L. Kroeber and C. Kluckhohn, *Culture: A Critical Review of Concepts and History (1952)*, noted that there was very little agreement among scholars regarding the meaning of culture. Rather than highlighting the vast array of conceptual developments and incongruities of culture, I focus below on the key sociological and anthropological meanings of culture.

In *Primitive Culture*, E. B. Tylor (1871/1920:1), the renowned cultural anthropologist, offered the most formal, explicit, and widely prevailing definition of culture as, "that complex whole which includes knowledge, belief, art, law, morals, customs and any other capabilities and habits acquired by man as a member of society. The condition of culture among the various societies of mankind, in so far as it is capable of being investigated on general principles, is a subject apt for the study of laws of human thought and action". Briefly, for Tylor, culture comprises the names of things and events required for human beings (White, 1959).

In *Social Change*, sociologist W.B. Ogburn (1922) argued that culture makes a significant contribution to shaping societies and human behaviour. He categorically distinguished culture into two forms: material and nonmaterial. For Ogburn, material culture includes the tangible/physical/technological aspects of social life, whereas nonmaterial culture includes the intangible aspects, such as values, norms, customs, philosophies, and religions. Non-material culture often adapts more slowly than material culture, resulting in a period of maladjustment called *cultural lag*.

Kroeber and Kluckhohn (1952: 157), on the other hand, defined culture as follows: "culture is a product; is historical; includes ideas, patterns, and values; is selective; is learned; is based upon symbols; and is an abstraction from behaviour and the products of behaviour."

In *The Interpretation of Cultures*, Clifford Geertz (1973: 145) defined culture as follows: "culture is the fabric of meaning in terms of which human beings interpret their experience and guide their action; social structure is the form that action takes, the actually existing network of social relations. Culture and social structure are then but different abstractions from the same phenomena." Geertz (1973: 50) furthered noted, "our ideas, our values, our acts, even our emotions, are, like our nervous system itself, cultural products—products manufactured, indeed, out of tendencies, capacities, and dispositions with which we were born, but manufactured nonetheless." Considering the importance of culture on human behaviour, he (1973: 49) stated, "without men, no culture, certainly; but equally, and more significantly, without culture, no men.... We are, in sum, incomplete or unfinished animals who complete or finish ourselves through culture."

The elements that make up the behaviour of individuals and those that constitute culture are indistinguishable (White, 1959). As the eminent sociologist R.M. MacIver (1932: 322) once said, "culture is an expression of ourselves, of our nature." Such a statement implies that nothing in human nature or behaviour can be separated from or exist independently of culture. Thereby, suicide as an act cannot be separated from the cultural context. Culture influences the whole spectrum of suicide in diverse ways (Lester, 2008). Since all people clearly follow a culture, no matter whether recognisable consciously or unconsciously, it can have a direct impact on despairing behaviours, including suicide (Shiang, 1998). Without understanding the cultural context, it is not possible to appropriately comprehend suicide and suicidal people (Hjelmeland, 2011).

3 Cultural Elements In Suicide: An Overview

Since the concept of culture is so encompassing, caution is required when interpreting the cultural indexes associated with suicide. Herein, a brief overview is placed on the nexus between salient cultural variables and suicide, with examples drawn from different cultural contexts.

Culture shapes the demographic features of various groups for motivation towards suicide. Although the majority of suicide deaths (around 73%) occur in low- and middle-income countries, high-income countries record the highest age-standardised suicide rate (11.8 per 100,000). More than half (56%) of global suicides occurs before the age of 50, and it is one of the leading causes of death for young people aged 15–29 years (World Health Organisation [WHO], 2025). Rates of suicide for the elderly vary disproportionately across cultures or regions. In some regions, suicide rates increase considerably with age, while in others, they are higher among young adults (WHO, 2014; Stanley et al., 2016). However, suicide is a rare phenomenon among children (Amini et al., 2021).

Cultural contexts influence the categorisations of suicide as well. For example, Durkheim (1897/2002) articulated a four-fold categorisation of suicide based on two social/cultural forces: integration and regulation—the degree to which people are attached to and controlled by society and culture. Egoistic and altruistic suicides result from too little and too much social integration, respectively, while anomic and fatalistic suicides arise from too little and too much social regulation. Suicide may also be categorised as pact suicide, which occurs by mutual agreement between two individuals (Rastogi & Nagesh, 2008), and is often triggered by romantic, dramatic, or heroic events (Risal, 2017). Cluster suicide refers to suicide committed by individuals connected through time, space, or social relationships. Such suicides may also occur through means of contagion (Rezaeian, 2012). Mass suicide or simultaneous suicide is committed by the members of a particular social group who blatantly follow evocative social and cultural models, such as religious cults (e.g., the People's Temple or Heaven's Gate mass ritual suicides), as a means of attaining salvation (Misra et al., 2019).

Suicide is culturally disapproved when undertaken for selfish reasons but is viewed positively when committed for heroic or altruistic/self-sacrificial purposes (Misra et al., 2019). The acts of Muslim suicide bombers may generally be classified as suicide; however, for themselves or many other Muslims, such deaths are essentially linked to martyrdom, carried out in the name of holy war (*Jihad*) (Lester, 2013; Joiner, 2007). Martyrdom, based on a firm faith connected with holy war (*Jihad)* and the duty to defend one's homeland, is an essential duty in Islam. However, many Westerners consider it as martyrdom suicide or altruistic suicide (Abdel-Khalek, 2004). Similarly, *Sati*, an old Indian custom in which widows self-immolate on their deceased husbands' funeral pyres, is often defined as ritual or altruistic suicide, and sometimes as culpable homicide (Vijayakumar, 2004). Durkheim (1897/2002) specifically categorised *Sati* as an altruistic suicide, as this Hindu customary practice defines it as a woman's duty.

Gender plays a significant role in suicidality across different cultures. Durkheim (1897/2002) regarded suicide essentially as a 'male phenomenon', particularly because it occurs at substantially higher rates among males than females. Even today, suicide rates are higher among males than females across regions and socio-economic groups. The rates are 3.2 times higher in higher-income countries, 3.0 times higher in low-income countries, 2.3 times higher in lower-middle-income countries, and 1.7 times higher in upper-middle-income countries (WHO, 2025). Amongst others, social and cultural expectations on men to perform traditional masculine responsibilities are linked to a higher prevalence of male suicide. When men fail to conform to culturally ideal masculine standards (i.e., employment or ability to provide), they may resort to suicide as a means of escape (Platt, 2017; Khan &

Arendse, 2025). In contrast, women's lower suicide rates are due to their strong cultural attachment to various protective factors and reduced exposure to risk factors (Stack, 2021). Durkheimian proposition suggests that conjugal society has a harmful function for a woman, as it may aggravate their inclination to suicide (Durkheim, 1897/2005). Supporting this argument, an example can be drawn from a non-Western country such as India, where the demand for dowry is considered the leading cause of female suicides. When dowry expectations are not met, young brides are often abused or tortured by their husbands and in-laws, causing numerous female suicides, frequently by self-immolation (Chen et al., 2012).

Methods used for suicide vary across cultures and carry substantial cultural implications. Suicide is strongly connected with the availability of lethal means and their degree of social acceptability (Gross et al., 2007a, 2007b; Lester, 2008). For example, hanging and poisoning are the most widely used methods in South Asia (Arafat et al., 2021a, 2021b), whereas firearms are more prevalent in many Western countries (Lester, 2008). Ritual suicide, such as *hara-kiri* or *seppuku* (self-disembowelment), was considered an honourable method practiced by the *samurai* (military men) in Japan (van den Bergh et al., 2013). Certain well-known sites can also attain cultural symbolism as suicide hotspots (Gross et al., 2007a, 2007b). Examples include the Golden Gate Bridge in San Francisco (the world's leading suicide location), the Cliffs of Moher in the Republic of Ireland, Niagara Falls on the Canadian-US border, the London Underground Metro, and *Aokigahara,* the so-called Suicide Forest in Japan (Zhi et al., 2019). The use of suicide methods is also linked to the 'gender paradox of suicide', which expresses that men die by suicide more than women, although women attempt suicide more often (Canetto & Sakinofsky, 1998). This difference is largely attributed to women tending to choose less lethal means than men (Elnour & Harrison, 2008).

Religion, an integral element of culture, can play a significant role in reducing the risk of suicide. Certain faiths and religious practices have been found to categorically lower suicidal risks (Stack, 2021). For example, Islam, the world's second-largest religion with approximately 1.9 billion adherents, strongly prohibits suicide (Arafat et al., 2021a). The cultural scripts of the Quran explicitly mark suicide as an unforgivable sin, with the belief that those who commit suicide would serve in hell forever (Khan et al., 2022b). Consequently, suicide rates are generally lower in Muslim/Muslim-majority countries. The strong integration of faiths and adherence to Islamic practices provide important protective belts against suicide for the inhabitants of these countries (Arafat et al., 2021b; Arafat et al., 2022b).

An ecological study covering 46 Muslim-majority countries reported an average suicide rate of 5.45 per 100,000 in 2019, which is significantly lower than the global average, with a few exceptions, such as Burkina Faso, Chad, Guinea, Kazakhstan, and Somalia (Arafat et al., 2022b). Another extensive ecological study spanning 2000–2019 similarly noted that age-standardised suicide rates in most Muslim-majority countries remain consistently below the global average (Lew et al., 2022). Durkheim, in *Le Suicide* (1897/2002), noted that suicide rates are higher among Protestants than Catholics or Jews. He argued that Catholics and Jews have stronger cohesion and collectivism as a religious community that offers them better immunity to suicide. In contrast, Protestants are more exposed to egoistic suicide due to weaker integration within both the community and the Church. For Durkheim, without a strong collective belief, no religious society can be formed or unified. Understandably, the strong cultural and religious integration of Muslims, Catholics, and Jews provides them greater protection against suicidality.

The legal status of suicide also varies across cultures. Countries following Islamic or *Sharia* laws have specific legal provisions for suicide/attempted suicide. In most other countries, it is a criminal offense to provoke, encourage, or assist another person in taking his/her own life (Mishara & Weisstub, 2016). Notably, only a few developed countries, along with certain US states, have legalised euthanasia or assisted suicide on medical grounds (De Leo, 2022). Despite the emphasis on self-sufficiency, self-determination, and the right to a 'good death' as alternatives to prolonged excruciating suffering or incurable illness, many religions, including Islam, Judaism, and Catholicism, explicitly forbid both euthanasia and suicide (Pierre, 2015). From a Durkheimian (1897/2002) perspective, the degree of social integration strongly influences the debate over whether suicide should be criminalised or decriminalised.

Studies offer an inconclusive understanding of suicide rates in urban versus rural areas (Casant & Helbich, 2022). Given the predominance of rurality, higher rural suicide rates are found in several Asian cultures (Chen et al., 2012). A range of socio-cultural factors, such as poverty or relative deprivation, social isolation and disconnection, insufficient knowledge or stigma about mental illness, self-reliance in the face of illness, lack of help-seeking services, and easy access to lethal means (e.g., pesticides) are identified as critical factors to rural suicidality (Chen et al., 2012; Gessert, 2003; Casant & Helbich, 2022). Rural farmer suicide is deeply rooted in the cultural contexts, and farming as an occupation has been identified as a dangerous factor for suicide in many countries. In particular, India, Sri Lanka, the United States, Canada, England, and Australia have all recorded elevated suicide rates amongst farmers (Behere & Bhise, 2009). In India, severe socioeconomic hardships of small and marginal farmers, such as indebtedness and monetary concerns, crop failure, and other farming-related challenges, account for nearly 60% of suicide deaths (Rao et al., 2017). Drought, on the other hand, has been identified as a major precipitating factor for farmer suicides in Australia (Behere & Bhise, 2009).

There are etiological variations in suicide between high-income countries (HICs) and low- and middle-income countries (LMICs). A systematic meta-analysis noted that psychiatric disorders are strongly associated with high-income countries, accounting for 80% to 90% of suicide deaths. However, this association is less pronounced or less well understood in low-and middle-income countries. Conversely, socio-cultural factors such as poverty, unemployment, domestic violence, and easy access to lethal means (e.g., pesticides) are more prominent contributors in these countries (Knipe et al., 2019).

Unlike HICs, LMICs often have very limited mental health structures, making it challenging to identify individuals at risk of suicide. Therefore, it becomes more important to consider borderer social and cultural determinants when contextualising suicide in these countries (Bantjes et al., 2016). One specific example concerns female suicide trends in LMICs. Cai et al. (2021) noted that LMICs maintain relatively smaller male-female suicide ratios compared to high-income countries. The study concludes that the relatively higher female suicides in these countries are linked to deliberate social and structural discrimination directed toward women.

In terms of help-seeking behaviour, some cultural groups may be reluctant to use formal services due to stigma and anxieties or negative attitudes towards health services (Goldston et al., 2008). These stigmas and attitudes are deeply rooted in cultural contexts and can help explain the differences in help-seeking across cultures and regions (Reynders et al., 2015). For example, men are generally reactive towards seeking help during periods of suicidality. Rigid masculine ideals such as impassiveness, stoicism, and self-reliance deter men from seeking professional support or disclosing their feelings, which eventually increases their risks of suicide (Oliffe et al., 2020). Conversely, women, including the elderly, tend to demonstrate more positive help-seeking attitudes and higher intentions to seek help (Calear et al., 2014).

4 Cultural Elements in Suicide: Bangladesh Context

This ensuing analysis will highlight the cultural scripts of suicide in Bangladesh. The paucity of field-based empirical studies hinders the extraction of context-driven cultural practices related to suicide in the country. With few exceptions, no substantial interpretation can be derived from the available studies, as most studies are predominantly conceptual or based on secondary sources (Khan et al., 2020b, 2020c, 2020d).

Islam is the predominant religious faith in Bangladesh, with Muslims comprising 90.4% population (Bangladesh Bureau of Statistics, 2015). According to WHO's (2025) global suicide mortality estimates, the rate (2.9/100,000) of suicide for both sexes in Bangladesh is lower than that of neighbouring South Asian countries such as Bhutan (5.1/100,000), India (12.6/100,000), Sri Lanka (9.8/100,000), and Nepal (11.1/100,000), where Islam is not the major religious faith. As Islam plays a pivotal role in shaping and prescribing the personal and community lives of the followers in Bangladesh, the *Quran*'s warning against self-killing is likely to make a strong imprint on suicidal thoughts and actions. In this Muslim-majority society, suicide is culturally stigmatised. Therefore, families may hide information regarding suicide, leading to under-reporting and under-estimation of cases (Mashreky et al., 2013). Within this context of religious stigmatisation, Khan et al. (2022b) observed that suicide by Muslim men is often regarded as an unmanly or cowardly act before God. On a positive note, Islam also plays a pivotal role in shaping and dictating the personal and community lives of the followers in Bangladesh, a cultural framework that can help protect individuals from suicide.

Suicide, including attempted suicide, is a criminal offense in Bangladesh. Section 306 of the Penal Code 1860 states that, "if any person commits suicide, whoever abets the commission of such suicide, shall be punished with imprisonment of either description for a term which may extend to ten years and shall also be liable to fine". Similarly, Section 309 states that, "if a person who survives an attempt to suicide will also be liable for his intended action and has to face legal consequences. Attempt to commit suicide is punishable with imprisonment for a term which may extend to one year or with fine or both". These legal provisions reflect the deep-rooted cultural reservation against suicide, which are closely associated with the ideology of the country's major religious faith. While Bangladeshi scholars continue to debate on matters of decriminalization or criminalisation of suicide (see Soron, 2019; Arafat & Khan, 2019), any policy intervention should be pursued by prudently considering the socio-economic, cultural, ethical, moral, and religious contexts of Bangladesh (Khan et al., 2020a).

Demographic analyses consistently indicate that the younger groups, particularly those under the age of 30, are more vulnerable to suicide in Bangladesh (Arafat, 2019a; Arafat et al., 2018; Arafat et al., 2021b; Shah et al., 2017; Khan et al., 2021b). Given the escalating trend of students' suicide, as documented by a growing number of studies, it is essential to contextualise the cultural aspects of this phenomenon. Critical socio-cultural factors associated with suicide among tertiary-level students include academic persecution and stress, perfectionism, family problems, relationship break-up, lack of social support, and financial crisis (Urme et al., 2022; Arafat & Al Mamun, 2019; Mamun et al., 2020a, 2020b). In Bangladesh, the culture of exam-centric education puts a significant burden on students, as examination outcomes are closely linked to their future prospects (higher education and career pathways), the social status of the parents, the reputation of teachers and academic institutions, and even the overall public image of the government. Consequently, students are expected not only to meet their own aspirations but also to shoulder the expectations of their parents, teachers, and schools (Al Amin & Greenwood, 2018). The pressure is further compounded by the highly competitive university admission tests (Khan et al., 2021). Failure to secure admission into reputed educational institutions or the subject of choice often underestimates the social standing of students and families. Parental investment in children's education and accompanying high expectations intensify mental stress and workload for students, frequently depriving them of opportunities for social, recreational, and sports activities (Mahmud, 2021). Such circumstances create a highly stressful environment that can increase the risk of suicide.

Hanging and pesticide ingestion are the two common methods of suicide in Bangladesh (Arafat, 2016). While some researchers reported poisoning as being widely used in rural areas (Arafat et al., 2021b; Mashreky et al., 2013), other studies have identified hanging as the most common method (Khan et al., 2020b; Shah et al., 2017). One study documented the variations in ligature materials used for hanging; finding *dupatta/orna* (38.55%), jute rope (30.12%), and *sari* (16.86%) were the most common, followed by nylon rope, towel, *kamiz*, and electric wire

(Ahmad & Hossain, 2010). Another study also noted *dupatta/orna* (38.55%) as the most common ligature material, followed by nylon rope (28.21%) and *sari* (10.26%) (Begum et al., 2017). Ali et al. (2014) further highlighted gender dimensions, noting that men use both soft and hard materials for hanging, whereas women primarily use soft materials.

Clothing, as a form of material culture, shapes human values and behaviours. In Bangladesh, women and girls typically wear *saree* and *salwar kamiz* (Mahamud, 2016), with the latter being more popular. *Dopatta (orna)*, which accompanies *salwar kamiz*, often becomes a readily available ligature material for female suicides (Ahmad & Hossain, 2010). In contrast, the widespread use of pesticides for suicide is linked to their easy availability in rural areas. As an agrarian country, Bangladesh makes extensive use of pesticides and relevant substances (Khan et al., 2020a). Although Bangladesh has banned highly hazardous pesticides (HHPs) from agricultural use (Chowdhury et al., 2018), their enforcement is yet to be meticulously monitored (Khan et al., 2020b). Consequently, the free availability of pesticides contributes to higher suicide rates in Bangladesh. Notably, a wider survey reported that rural suicide rates are 17-fold higher than those in urban Bangladesh (Mashreky et al., 2013).

Since the country does not maintain a national suicide surveillance system, the exact male–female ratio cannot be reliably determined (Arafat, 2019b). Yet, the country has historically been noted as one of the few where suicide rates among females were higher than those among males. Several in-country studies consistently reported a greater frequency of female suicides (see Mashreky et al., 2013; Arafat, 2019b; Khan et al., 2020a). But WHO's (2021) estimates, for the first time, recorded a much higher male suicide rate (6.0/100,000) compared to the female rate (1.7/100,000). This suggests a remarkable reduction in the female suicide rate, which has significantly contributed to the overall decline in the national rate. WHO's (2025) most recent estimates also confirm the continuation of this decline. Nonetheless, certain groups remain consistently vulnerable to suicide, particularly married women from lower socio-economic strata (Arafat et al., 2021b), adolescents (10–19 years), and young adults (20–30 years) (Shahnaz et al., 2017; Arafat, 2019a). For females, critical socio-cultural risk factors include rigid patriarchal norms, early or forced marriage, dowry demands, marital conflict or disharmony, sexual abuse, poverty, infidelity, lack of economic opportunities, failure to meet spousal expectations, divorce, or expulsion from the family, and domestic violence (Bagley et al., 2017; Shahnaz et al., 2017; Mashreky et al., 2013; Arafat et al., 2021b). Specifically, Arafat et al. (2021b) found that sexual harassment can be a critical risk factor for female suicides before marriage, while marital disharmony or relationship predominates after marriage.

Within the purview of Bangladeshi family culture, women are expected not to expose their private problems to others. A strong sense of stigma and shame often compels them to silently endure suffering, which increases their vulnerability to suicide (Mamun et al., 2020a, 2020b). Most of these perspectives highlight the family as a central site of risk. Supporting this, Arafat et al. (2022c) confirmed that complicated family events serve as critical risk factors for both female and male suicides in Bangladesh.

The following discussions will extend the analysis to the cultural embodiments of male suicide in Bangladesh. Given the recent escalating trend of male suicide relative to female suicide, it is imperative to devote greater scholarly attention to the phenomenon of male suicidality in the country. In the context of Bangladesh, the ideal version of hegemonic masculinity or real manhood in the context of Bangladesh includes, among other attributes, the ability to earn an income, provide and protect the family, exercise dominance, display fearlessness and power, maintain control over family members and household matters, demonstrate physical and sexual competence, and embody honesty and strength of character (Khan et al., 2022a). In line with the attributes of manhood, an in-depth empirical study by Khan et al. (2022b) found that many cases of rural male suicide were disturbingly linked to challenges and pressures associated with hegemonic or traditional masculine ideals. The difficulties men faced prior to suicide include economic hardship and poverty, indebtedness, sexual impotency, failure to control or meet expectations of their spouses, loss of self-esteem and family respect, and long-term illness. Further, Khan et al. (2021a) highlighted that disturbing marital or intimate relationships, such as tensions surrounding provider and breadwinner responsibilities, complications arising from polygamous practices, difficulties in exercising control over wives, and perceived betrayal of loyalties through extramarital relations were critical factors prompting male suicides. Complementing these findings, a content analysis by Khan et al. (2021b), drawing on Durkheim's fourfold social typology of suicide, revealed that most male suicide cases fell within the egoistic category, followed by anomic, fatalistic, and altruistic suicides.

4.1 Case: Male Suicide and the Cultural Context

In 2020, the author conducted a study to explore the complex interplay between social or cultural aspects and suicidal acts in selected rural settings of the *Jhenaidah* district. *Jhenaidah* is considered one of the suicide-prone areas of the country, with an estimated standardised rate of 20.6/100,000 (Khan et al., 2020b). The study included 15 cases of male suicide, identified through purposive and snowball sampling, involving individuals aged 18 and above. Post hoc retrospective in-depth qualitative interviews were conducted with 45 individuals close to the deceased (e.g., family members, friends, and relatives). For one case of suicide, three persons close to the deceased were interviewed. As a qualitative study, specific to a location, caution is warranted in generalising the findings to the broader context of Bangladesh. Data were analysed following the steps of thematic analysis outlined by Braun and Clarke (2006). The incidents of suicide occurred between 2017 and 2020. Ethical approval for this research was granted by the Centre for Research and Training (CRT), East West University, Dhaka, Bangladesh.

4.2 Culture of Taboo

Several participants experienced disturbing relationship troubles that were deemed socially and culturally unacceptable in Bangladesh. These culturally non-endorsed relationships emerged as critical suicidal risk factors for the men involved. One example is presented below.

Niranjan, aged 19, a Hindu young man, was caught between two powerful cultural realities: religion and family. He approached his parents with the intention of marrying his fiancé, who was Muslim. His family rejected the relationship due to the prevailing inter-religious taboos. At the same time, the girl faced pressure from her own family to end the relationship on the same grounds. She eventually told Niranjan that she could only marry him if he converted to Islam. Unable to reconcile these two strong cultural impediments, Niranjan ultimately took his own life. His friend Hossain provided a crucial context:

> *Niranjan told the family that he wanted to marry the girl. But his family didn't agree and put him under a lot of pressure for not doing that. His family members also told him that if he did it, all his family members would commit suicide. Then he might have thought that as he was causing problems in the family, so he had better kill himself. That is how that incident took place.*

Babu, aged around 25, committed suicide by hanging with the same rope as his sister-in-law, Rinki. Babu had been in a romantic relationship with her. This case of a pact suicide drew huge public attention due to its connection to a social taboo—a romantic episode between a brother-in-law and sister-in-law (*shalika-dulabhai*). Babu had married Rinki's elder sister, Ruma, in 2014. The couple lived happily until their baby was born in 2016. Afterwards, Babu lost interest in Ruma and gradually became romantically involved with his unmarried sister-in-law, Rinki. At one stage, both of them eloped from home, but community leaders managed to bring them back home after a few days. A local arbitration was arranged to address this issue. Babu was physically punished and fined. After the event, Babu felt humiliated and found an opportunity to hang himself to death along with his sister-in-law. Babu's mother, Salma, said:

> *They arranged a big arbitration on the issue. My son was beaten severely and insulted in a disgraceful manner. As if my son did all the wrongdoings. That girl did not do anything. The arbitration charged us a penalty of Taka 10,000.*

4.3 Culture of Poverty

Some men went through lifelong struggles due to their poor financial conditions. Unable to perform their socially prescribed role of the family provider in an expected manner, they faced extreme pressure to maintain their families on a limited income. Eventually, they succumbed to this perceived failure and committed suicide.

Alam, a 70-year-old agricultural sharecropper, also died by suicide. Throughout his life, he lacked a stable income and battled intense poverty. As he approached old age, his physical health gradually deteriorated. He lost the ability to work on the field. Finding no other options, Alam borrowed money to maintain the family. Unfortunately, this loan became a bone of contention as he could not repay it on time. The Covid-19 lockdown further deteriorated his financial situation, leaving him with no means of recovery. Ultimately, he took his own life to escape his burdens. His nephew, Zalal, mentioned:

> *He borrowed a good amount of money from the association. Once the association finally pressured him for paying back the money within Tuesday of a week. The day he heard this, he committed suicide because he did not have any money at all.*

Abinash, aged 50, also died by suicide due to his long-standing financial worries. Despite being a graduate, he could not find a suitable means of livelihood that met his expectations. Consequently, he had to take up tutoring students in local areas. Despite this, he could not provide financial security and comforts for his family. Money was also desperately needed for the treatment of his throat tumour, his wife's medical care, and his children's educational expenses. He borrowed money and became deeply frustrated. Overwhelmed by his troubles, he ultimately decided to take his own life. His neighbour Hironmoy commented:

> *He escaped from society. Men should fight, not end their lives. He was a coward. All have sufferings in their own lives. We must be more courageous and fight. Suicide can never be a solution.*

4.4 Culture of Materialism

Few men committed suicide for failing to acquire material gains, as such success was symbolically important to demonstrate their manhood. For example, Faruk, aged approximately 19, died by hanging. He had constant demands for money and often forced his father to provide it. He had been demanding a motorbike for over a year and was obsessed with the idea of riding one with his friends. Meanwhile, his father purchased a piece of land for the family, which Faruk disapproved of as he wanted a motorbike. Afterwards, his father attempted to borrow money for the motorbike but failed. Finally, Faruk killed himself as he could not purchase one. In fact, owning a motorbike was a prestige issue for him among friends and peers. Faruk's father, Jalal, commented:

> *I think boys these days are more disorganised. They want to show people that they have motorcycles. Every young man in our neighbourhood has a motorcycle. This is a social problem.*

Amir, an 18-year-old unmarried and family-oriented young man, died by hanging. He always considered taking good care of the family a solemn duty. From a very young age, he did different kinds of work to provide for his family. Although the financial condition of the family was not bad, he was strongly committed to improving it. When his father sold the family's only piece of land to pay for his sister's wedding, Amir was deeply disturbed by the loss. Despite having no financial means to buy the land back again, he was keen to recover it. He often urged his father to take out a loan to repurchase it. One day during supper, he had a heated argument with his father about the land and property. Afterwards, he went out of home and died by suicide, hanging himself from a nearby tree. His aunt, Srea, said:

> *You don't need 100 reasons to commit suicide, isn't one enough? Yes, he committed suicide due to the land issue. At least he understood that land is the most precious asset for a man. He thought it is worthless to live without having any asset as a man.*

4.5 Culture of Social Dignity

Each culture has a strong sense of social dignity. Losing dignity, or finding oneself on the verge of its collapse, can have a deleterious effect on an individual. Hasan, aged 65, died by suicide after being caught sexually abusing his elder brother's minor granddaughter. The incident caused him an irreparable loss of dignity. Most villagers were profoundly shocked, as Hasan was known as a gentle and pious man with no prior history of misconduct with anyone in the village. The episode caused extreme embarrassment throughout the community, and the shame fell heavily upon Hasan. Soon after being caught, Hasan somehow managed to leave the spot secretly. The following morning, he was found dead, having hanged himself to death from a mango tree far from the village.

His brother, Rafiq, said:

> *He felt ashamed that he is an old man caused such an incident. Then everything became known everywhere. Then a realisation worked in his mind that he would never show his face to anyone again. With this in mind, he committed suicide. He might have thought that he made a great mistake. Then he thought of taking his own life.*

4.6 Culture of Male Control

Being a patriarchal society, husbands in Bangladesh often expect to hold authority within their marriages. However, some cases starkly contradicted this norm. For example, Palash, aged 19, quickly developed a contentious relationship with his wife after they were married. The ongoing turmoil left him feeling depressed and annoyed. Gradually, he felt he was losing control over his wife. The perceived failure to assert authority ultimately led to suicidal ideation. His friend, Gias, depicted the events leading to Palash's suicide as follows;

> *That day he quarreled with his wife because her phone had remained busy for a long time. He repeatedly asked her who she was talking to for so long, but she was too stubborn to*

answer that. After ending the conversation over the phone, he sat beside me in a depressed mood and asked me to take some marijuana together. I could realise that he was acting like a madman. I should have informed others about his mental condition that day. If I had done that, then he could have been saved from committing suicide. I still regret that I did not do it that day.

5 Cultural Considerations in Suicide Prevention and Research in Bangladesh

Sadly, Bangladesh grossly lacks a national suicide prevention strategy. There is no central suicide surveillance and monitoring system. Existing interventions are sporadic and operate only at certain levels, often remaining unknown to the general population. The culture of help-seeking behaviour is extremely underdeveloped, a situation exacerbated by low mental health literacy and poor public knowledge concerning suicidality. Consequently, the country has failed to cultivate a culture of suicide literacy (Arafat, 2019a; Arafat et al., 2022c; Arafat et al., 2022a).

The strong prevalence of social stigma, coupled with insufficient public education on the risks and protective factors associated with suicide, has obscured the urgency of formulating a national intervention strategy (Arafat et al., 2021b). Equally dismal is the lack of scholarly efforts to appropriately study the risk factors of suicide in Bangladesh, particularly given that suicidal acts in Bangladesh are exacerbated not only by individual and biological factors, but also by social and cultural factors (Arafat et al., 2022c). Any intervention not informed by scholarly efforts will fail to make expected imprints.

Furthermore, scholars in Bangladesh often examine suicide through individualised or medicalised lenses (psychological/psychiatric). Structural (social/cultural) perspectives of suicide are seemingly marginalised as a research focus (Khan et al., 2020b). Given the importance of the cultural dimensions, future research and interventions must prioritise these structural issues to better link knowledge and practice. Scholars have emphasised the importance of studying the cultural aspects of suicide, arguing that a meaningful understanding of this context will enable professionals to frame more culturally differentiated and effective services (Cloucci, 2013; Goldston et al., 2008).

6 Conclusion

Bangladesh suffers from a dearth of exclusive research on the cultural perspectives of suicide. This chapter travels in diverse ways to situate the connection between culture and suicide in the context of Bangladesh. While the primary focus remains on Bangladesh, it also incorporates pertinent cross-cultural evidence to capture the relationship between suicide and culture. The chapter synthesises relevant information from existing scholarship, integrating relevant findings from a recently conducted study on male suicide.

Culture is a fundamental sociological and anthropological concept that profoundly influences every aspect of human behaviour, including suicide. Evidence suggests that suicidal acts in Bangladesh are closely intertwined with various cultural elements, such as religious faith, the legal context, demographic profiles, chosen methods, and gender dimensions, as well as interventions and research. A key limitation to note is that this analysis cannot exclusively contextualise the interface between suicide and culture in Bangladesh, due to a dearth of relevant and specific literature. Both macro-level and micro/community-level studies are needed to address the gap.

Although Bangladesh is a Muslim-majority country, it is also home to a diverse population with distinct socio-cultural identities. Therefore, when developing an effective national suicide intervention strategy, it is imperative that Bangladesh prioritises and accommodates the cultural scripts of suicide relevant to its various cultural groups. As a social fact, culture holds different meanings to different groups, and consequently, it is likely to influence suicidal behaviour in group-specific ways. Furthermore, it is essential to develop small-scale, culturally sensitive, and appropriate interventions tailored to specific regions and groups. This approach would ensure that vulnerable individuals have access to help-seeking platforms available within their own communities. From an intervention perspective, such targeted efforts are crucial for addressing the prevalent culture of shame and the widespread low literacy surrounding suicidality.

References

Abdel-Khalek, A. M. (2004). Neither altruistic suicide, nor terrorism but martyrdom: A Muslim perspective. *Archives of Suicide Research, 8*(1), 99–113. https://doi.org/10.1080/13811110490243840

Ahmad, M., & Hossain, M. Z. (2010). Hanging as a method of suicide retrospective analysis of postmortem cases. *Journal of Armed Forces Medical College, 6*(2), 37–39. https://doi.org/10.3329/jafmc.v6i2.7273

Al Amin, M., & Greenwood, J. (2018). The examination system in Bangladesh and its impact: On curriculum, students, teachers and society. *Language Testing in Asia, 8*(4). https://doi.org/10.1186/s40468-018-0060-9

Ali, E., Maksud, M., Zubyra, S., Hossain, M. S., Debnath, P. R., Alam, A., & Chakrabarty, P. (2014). Suicide by hanging: A study of 334 cases. *Bangladesh Medical Journal, 43*(2), 90–93. https://doi.org/10.3329/bmj.v43i2.21390

Amini, S., Bagheri, P., Moradinazar, M., Basiri, M., Alimehr, M., & Ramazani, Y. (2021). Epidemiological status of suicide in the Middle East and North Africa countries (MENA) from 1990 to 2017. *Clinical Epidemiology and Global Health, 9*, 299–303. https://doi.org/10.1016/j.cegh.2020.10.002

Arafat, S. M. Y. (2016). Suicide in Bangladesh: A mini review. *Journal of Behavioral Health, 6*(1), 64–69. https://doi.org/10.5455/JBH.20160904090206

Arafat, S. M. Y. (2019a). Current challenges of suicide and future directions of management in Bangladesh: Asystematic review. *Global Psychiatry, 2*(1), 09–20. https://doi.org/10.2478/gp-2019-0001

Arafat, S. M. Y. (2019b). Females are dying more than males by suicide in Bangladesh. *Asian Journal of Psychiatry, 40*, 124–125. https://doi.org/10.1016/j.ajp.2018.10.014

Arafat, S. M. Y., & Al Mamun, M. A. (2019). Repeated suicides in the university of Dhaka (November 2018): Strategies to identify risky individuals. *Asian Journal of Psychiatry, 39*, 84–85. https://doi.org/10.1016/j.ajp.2018.12.014

Arafat, S. M. Y., Ali, S. A., Menon, V., Hussain, F., Ansari, D. S., Baminiwatta, A., Saleem, T., Singh, R., Varadharajan, N., Biyyala, D., Kar, S. K., & Khan, M. M. (2021a). Suicide methods in South Asia over two decades (2001-2020). *The International Journal of Social Psychiatry, 67*(7), 920–934. https://doi.org/10.1177/00207640211015700

Arafat, S. M. Y., Mohit, M. A., Mullick, M., Kabir, R., & Khan, M. M. (2021b). Risk factors for suicide in Bangladesh: Case-control psychological autopsy study. *BJPsych Open, 7*(1), e18. https://doi.org/10.1192/bjo.2020.152

Arafat, S. M. Y., Hussain, F., Hossain, M. F., Islam, M. A., & Menon, V. (2022a). Literacy and stigma of suicide in Bangladesh: Scales validation and status assessment among university students. *Brain and Behavior, 12*(1), e2432. https://doi.org/10.1002/brb3.2432

Arafat, S., Marthoenis, M., Khan, M. M., & Rezaeian, M. (2022b). Association between suicide rate and human development index, income, and the political system in 46 Muslim-majority countries: An ecological study. *European Journal of Investigation in Health, Psychology and Education, 12*(7), 754–764. https://doi.org/10.3390/ejihpe12070055

Arafat, S. M. Y., Saleem, T., Edwards, T. M., Ali, S. A., & Khan, M. M. (2022c). Suicide prevention in Bangladesh: The role of family. *Brain and Behavior, 12*(5), e2562. https://doi.org/10.1002/brb3.2562

Arafat, S. M. Y., & Khan, S. T. (2019). Suicide prevention in Bangladesh: Only decriminalisation would not be beneficial in an expected fashion. *Asian Journal of Psychiatry, 36*, 22–23. https://doi.org/10.1016/j.ajp.2019.03.027

Arafat, S. M. Y., Mali, B., & Akter, H. (2018). Demography and risk factors of suicidal behaviour in Bangladesh: A retrospective online news content analysis. *Asian Journal of Psychiatry, 36*, 96–99. https://doi.org/10.1016/j.ajp.2018.07.008

Bagley, C. A., Shahnaz, A., & Simkhada, P. (2017). High rates of suicide and violence in the lives of girls and young women in Bangladesh: Issues for feminist intervention. *Social Sciences, 6*(140), 1–17. https://doi.org/10.3390/socsci6040140

Bangladesh Bureau of Statistics. (2015). *Population monograph of Bangladesh.* http://203.112.218.65:8008/WebTestApplication/userfiles/Image/PopMonographs/Volume9_Age-Sex.pdf.

Bantjes, J., Iemmi, V., Coast, E., Channer, K., Leone, T., McDaid, D., Palfreyman, A., Stephens, B., & Lund, C. (2016). Poverty and suicide research in low- and middle-income countries: Systematic mapping of literature published in English and a proposed research agenda. *Global Mental Health (Cambridge, England), 3*, e32. https://doi.org/10.1017/gmh.2016.27

Begum, A., Khan, N. T., Shafiuzzaman, A., Shahid, F., Anam, A. A., Ahmed, K. S., Begum, R. A., & Fahmi, S. (2017). Suicidal death due to hanging. *Delta Medical College Journal, 5*(2), 89–93. https://doi.org/10.3329/dmcj.v5i2.33347

Behere, P. B., & Bhise, M. C. (2009). Farmers' suicide: Across culture. *Indian Journal of Psychiatry, 51*(4), 242–243. https://doi.org/10.4103/0019-5545.58286

Braun, V., & Clarke, V. (2006). Using thematic analysis in psychology. *Qualitative Research in Psychology, 3*(2), 77–101. https://psycnet.apa.org. https://doi.org/10.1191/1478088706qp063oa

Cai, Z., Canetto, S. S., Chang, Q., & Yip, P. S. F. (2021). Women's suicide in low-, middle-, and high-income countries: Do laws discriminating against women matter? *Social Science & Medicine, 282*, 114035. https://doi.org/10.1016/j.socscimed.2021.114035

Calear, A. L., Batterham, P. J., & Christensen, H. (2014). Predictors of help-seeking for suicidal ideation in the community: Risks and opportunities for public suicide prevention campaigns. *Psychiatry Research, 219*(3), 525–530. https://doi.org/10.1016/j.psychres.2014.06.027

Canetto, S. S. (2015). Suicidal behaviors among Muslim women. Patterns, pathways, meanings, and prevention. *Crisis, 36*(6), 447–458. https://doi.org/10.1027/0227-5910/a000347

Canetto, S. S., & Sakinofsky, I. (1998). The gender paradox in suicide. *Suicide & Life-threatening Behaviour, 28*(1), 1–23. https://doi.org/10.1111/j.1943-278X.1998.tb00622.x
Casant, J., & Helbich, M. (2022). Inequalities of suicide mortality across urban and rural areas: A literature review. *International Journal of Environmental Research and Public Health, 19*(5), 2669. https://doi.org/10.3390/ijerph19052669
Chowdhury, F. R., Dewan, G., Verma, V. R., Knipe, D. W., Isha, I. T., Faiz, M. A., & Eddleston, M. (2018). Bans of WHO class I pesticides in Bangladesh-suicide prevention without hampering agricultural output. *International Journal of Epidemiology, 47*(1), 175–184. https://doi.org/10.1093/ije/dyx157
Cheal, D. (2003). General introduction. In D Cheal (edt.) *Culture: Critical concepts in sociology* (pp. 1-19). Routledge.
Chen, Y.-Y., Wu, K. C.-C., Yousuf, S., & Yip, P. S. F. (2012). Suicide in Asia: Opportunities and challenges. *Epidemiologic Reviews, 34*(1), 129–144. https://doi.org/10.1093/epirev/mxr025
Cloucci, E. (2013). Culture, cultural meaning(s), and suicide. In E. Colucci, D. Lester, H., Hjelmeland & B. C. Ben Park (Eds.). Suicide and culture understanding the context (pp.25–46). Hogrefe.
Gross, C., Piper, T. M., Bucciarelli, A., et al. (2007a). Suicide tourism in Manhattan, New York City, 1990–2004. *Journal of Urban Health, 84*, 755. https://doi.org/10.1007/s11524-007-9224-0
Gross, C., Piper, T. M., Bucciarelli, A., Tardiff, K., Vlahov, D., & Galea, S. (2007b). Suicide tourism in Manhattan, New York City, 1990–2004. *Journal of Urban Health, 84*, 755. https://doi.org/10.1007/s11524-007-9224-0
De Leo, D. (2022). Late-life suicide in an aging world. *Nature Aging, 2*, 7–12. https://doi.org/10.1038/s43587-021-00160-1
Durkheim, É. (1897/2002). *Suicide: A study in sociology*. Taylor & Francis Group.
Elnour, A. A., & Harrison, J. (2008). Lethality of suicide methods. *Injury Prevention, 14*(1), 39–45. https://doi.org/10.1136/ip.2007.016246
Geertz, C. (1973). *The interpretation of cultures*. Basic Books.
Gessert, C. E. (2003). Rurality and suicide. *American Journal of Public Health, 93*(5), 698–698. https://doi.org/10.2105/AJPH.93.5.698
Goldston, D., Molock, S., Whitbeck, L., Murakami, J., Zayas, L., & Hall, G. (2008). Cultural considerations in adolescent suicide prevention and psychosocial treatment. *American Psychologist, 63*(1), 14–31. https://doi.org/10.1037/0003-066X.63.1.14
Hjelmeland, H. (2011). Cultural context is crucial in suicide research and prevention. *Crisis, 32*(2), 61–64. https://doi.org/10.1027/0227-5910/a000097
Jaworski, K. (2016). *The gender of suicide: Knowledge production, theory and suicidology*. Ashgate.
Joiner, T. (2007). *Why people die by suicide*. Harvard University Press.
Khan, A. R., & Arendse, N. (2025). Understanding male suicide in rural Bangladesh: A narrative case analysis through hegemonic masculinity and the interpersonal theory of suicide. *OMEGA Journal of Death and Dying, 0*(0). https://doi.org/10.1177/00302228251362651
Khan, A. R., Arendse, N., & Ratele, K. (2020a). Suicide prevention in Bangladesh: The current state and the way forward. *Asian Social Work and Policy Review, 15*(1), 15–23. https://doi.org/10.1111/aswp.12214
Khan, A. R., Ratele, K., Arendse, N., Islam, M. Z., & Dery, I. (2020b). Suicide and attempted suicide in Jhenaidah district. Bangladesh, 2010–2018. *Crisis, 41*(4), 304–312. https://doi.org/10.1027/0227-5910/a000631
Khan, R. A., Ratele, K., & Dery, I. (2020c). (Re)animating sociology of suicide in Bangladesh. *Italian Sociological Review, 10*(1), 55–75. https://doi.org/10.13136/isr.v10i1.317
Khan, A. R., Ratele, K., & Helman, R. (2020d). Suicidal behaviour in South Africa and Bangladesh: A review of empirical work. *African Safety Promotion: A Journal of Injury and Violence Prevention, 18*(1), 1–35.
Khan, A. R., Arendse, N., & Ratele, K. (2021a). Intimate relationships and suicidal behaviour of men in Bangladesh. *Mortality, 28*(1), 106–125. https://doi.org/10.1080/13576275.2021.1879755

Khan, A. R., Shimul, S. A. K., & Uddin, H. (2021b). Demographic risk factors and motives of male suicide in Bangladesh: A retrospective content analysis. *Acta Counseling and Humanities, 1*(2), 66–80. https://doi.org/10.46637/ach.v1i2.7

Khan, A. R., Dery, I., & Helman, D. (2022a). Masculinity and men's suicide attempts in Bangladesh. *Journal of Loss and Trauma, 27*(4), 367–385. https://doi.org/10.1080/15325024.2021.1987037

Khan, A. R., Ratele, K., Helman, R., Dlamini, S., & Makama, R. (2022b). Masculinity and suicide in Bangladesh. *Omega, 86*(1), 218–240. https://doi.org/10.1177/0030222820966239

Knipe, D., Williams, A. J., Hannam-Swain, S., Upton, S., Brown, K., Bandara, P., Chang, S. S., & Kapur, N. (2019). Psychiatric morbidity and suicidal behaviour in low- and middle-income countries: A systematic review and meta-analysis. *PLoS Medicine, 16*(10), e1002905. https://doi.org/10.1371/journal.pmed.1002905

Kroeber, A. L., & Kluckhohn, C. (1952). *Culture: A critical review of concepts and definitions*. Pantianos Classic.

Lester, D. (2008). Suicide and culture. *World Cultural Psychiatry Research Review, 3*(2), 51–56.

Lester, D. (2013). The cultural meaning of suicide: What does it mean? In E. Colucci, D. Lester, H. Hjelmeland, & B. C. B. Park (Eds.), *Suicide and culture understanding the context* (pp. 47–58). Hogrefe.

Lew, B., Lester, D., Kõlves, K., et al. (2022). An analysis of age-standardized suicide rates in Muslim-majority countries in 2000-2019. *BMC Public Health, 22*, 882. https://doi.org/10.1186/s12889-022-13101-3

MacIver, R. M. (1932). Civilization versus culture. *University of Toronto Quarterly, 1*(3), 316–332.

Maharajh, H. D., & Abdool, P. S. (2005). Cultural aspects of suicide. *The Scientific World Journal, 5*, 736–746. https://doi.org/10.1100/tsw.2005.88

Mahmud, R. (2021). Learning in the shadows: Parents' investments, family burden, and students' workload in Dhaka, Bangladesh. *Asia Pacific Education Review, 22*(1), 41–52. https://doi.org/10.1007/s12564-020-09655-9

Mahamud, S. (2016). Traditional costume heritage of Bangladesh and how it is connected to our culture. *ASRJETS, 26*(4), 391–405.

Mamun, M. A., Misti, J. M., & Griffiths, M. D. (2020a). Suicide of Bangladeshi medical students: Risk factor trends based on Bangladeshi press reports. *Asian Journal of Psychiatry, 48*, 101905. https://doi.org/10.1016/j.ajp.2019.101905

Mamun, M. A., Siddique, A. B., Sikder, M. T., & Griffiths, M. D. (2020b). Student suicide risk and gender: A retrospective study from Bangladeshi press reports. *International Journal of Mental Health and Addiction, 20*, 1438–1445. https://doi.org/10.1007/s11469-020-00267-3

Mashreky, S. R., Rahman, F., & Rahman, A. (2013). Suicide kills more than 10,000 people every year in Bangladesh. *Archives of Suicide Research, 17*(4), 387–396. https://doi.org/10.1080/13811118.2013.801809

Mishara, B. L., & Weisstub, D. N. (2016). The legal status of suicide: A global review. *International Journal of Law and Psychiatry, 44*, 54–74. https://doi.org/10.1016/j.ijlp.2015.08.032

Misra, N., Jha, H., & Tiwari, K. (2019). Psychosocial autopsy of mass suicides: Changing patterns in contemporary times. In K. F. Shad & K. H. Dogan (Eds.), *Neurological and mental disorders*. IntechOpen. https://doi.org/10.5772/intechopen.89439

Oliffe, J. L., Broom, A., Rossnagel, E., Kelly, M. T., Affleck, W., & Rice, S. M. (2020). Help-seeking prior to male suicide: Bereaved men perspectives. *Social Science & Medicine (1982), 261*, 113173. https://doi.org/10.1016/j.socscimed.2020.113173

Ogburn, W. F. (1922). *Social change with respect to culture and original nature*. Huebsch.

Patel, T. (2017). Multiparadigmaticstudies of culture: Needs, challenges and recommendations for management scholars. *European Management Review, 14*(1), 83–100. https://doi.org/10.1111/emre.12089

Platt, S. (2017). Suicide in men: What is the problem? *Trends in Urology & Men's Health, 8*(4), 9–12. https://doi.org/10.1002/tre.587

Pierre, J. M. (2015). Culturally sanctioned suicide: Euthanasia, seppuku, and terrorist martyrdom. *World Journal of Psychiatry, 5*(1), 4–14. https://doi.org/10.5498/wjp.v5.i1.4

Reynders, A., Kerkhof, A. J., Molenberghs, G., & Van Audenhove, C. (2015). Help-seeking, stigma and attitudes of people with and without a suicidal past. A comparison between a low and a high suicide rate country. *Journal of Affective Disorders, 178*, 5–11. https://doi.org/10.1016/j.jad.2015.02.01

Rao, S. T. S., Gowda, M. R., Ramachandran, K., & Andrade, C. (2017). Prevention of farmer suicides: Greater need for state role than for a mental health professional's role. *Indian Journal of Psychiatry, 59*(1), 3–5. https://doi.org/10.4103/psychiatry.IndianJPsychiatry_89_17

Rastogi, P., & Nagesh, K. R. (2008). Suicide pact by hanging. *Medicine, Science and the Law, 48*(3), 266–268. https://doi.org/10.1258/rsmmsl.48.3.266

Rezaeian, M. (2012). Suicide clusters: Introducing a novel type of categorisation. *Violence and Victims, 27*(1), 125–132. https://doi.org/10.1891/0886-6708.27.1.125

Risal, A. (2017). Attempted suicide pact by married couple: A case study. *Journal of Psychiatrists' Association of Nepal, 5*(1), 49–52. https://doi.org/10.3126/jpan.v5i1.18332

Shah, M. M. A., Ahmed, S., & Arafat, S. M. Y. (2017). Demography and risk factors of suicide in Bangladesh: A six-month paper content analysis. *Psychiatry Journal*, 1–5. https://doi.org/10.1155/2017/3047025

Shahnaz, A., Bagley, C., Simkhada, P., & Kadri, S. (2017). Suicidal behaviour in Bangladesh: A scoping literature review and a proposed public health prevention model. *Open Journal of Social Sciences, 5*, 254–282. https://doi.org/10.4236/jss.2017.57016

Shiang, J. (1998). Does culture make a difference? Racial/ethnic patterns of completed suicide in San Francisco, CA 1987-1996 and clinical applications. *Suicide & Life-threatening Behaviour, 28*(4), 338–354. https://doi.org/10.1111/j.1943-278X.1998.tb00970.x

Soron, T. R. (2019). Decriminalising suicide in Bangladesh. *Asian Journal of Psychiatry, 39*, 91–92. https://doi.org/10.1016/j.ajp.2018.12.012

Stack, S. (2021). Contributing factors to suicide: Political, social, cultural and economic. *Preventive Medicine, 152*(Pt 1), 106498. https://doi.org/10.1016/j.ypmed.2021.10649

Stanley, I. H., Hom, M. A., Rogers, M. L., Hagan, C. R., & Joiner, T. E., Jr. (2016). Understanding suicide among older adults: A review of psychological and sociological theories of suicide. *Aging & Mental Health, 20*(2), 113–122. https://doi.org/10.1080/13607863.2015.1012045

Staples, J. (2012). Introduction: Suicide in South Asia: Ethnographicperspectives. *Contributions to Indian Sociology, 46*(1–2), 1–28. https://doi.org/10.1177/006996671104600202

The Penal Code. (1860). *Penal Code1860.* Chapter XVI. http://bdlaws.minlaw.gov.bd/act-11/section-3140.htmlA.

Tylor, E. (1871/1920). *Primitive culture*. J.P. Putnam's Sons.

Urme, S. A., Islam, M. S., Begum, H., & Awal Chowdhury, N. (2022). Risk factors of suicide among public university students of Bangladesh: A qualitative exploration. *Heliyon, 8*(6), e09659. https://doi.org/10.1016/j.heliyon.2022.e09659

White, L. A. (1959). The concept of culture. *American Anthropologist, 61*(2), 227–251. https://doi.org/10.1525/aa.1959.61.2.02a00040

WHO. (2014). *Preventing suicide: A global imperative.* http://apps.who.int/iris/bitstream/10665/131056/8/9789241564878_eng.pdf?ua=1&ua=1.

WHO. (2021). *Suicide worldwide in 2019: Global health estimates.* https://www.who.int/publications/i/item/9789240026643.

World Health Organization. (2025). Suicide worldwide in 2021: Global health estimates. https://iris.who.int/bitstream/handle/10665/381495/9789240110069-eng.pdf?sequence=1.

van den Bergh, W. M., van Westerloo, D. J., & de Jong, V. M. (2013). Self-disembowelment. *Critical Care (London, England), 17*(1), 403. https://doi.org/10.1186/cc11878

Vijayakumar, L. (2004). Altruistic suicide in India. *Archives of Suicide Research, 8*(1), 73–80. https://doi.org/10.1080/13811110490243804

Zhi, G., Flaherty, G. T., & Hallahan, B. (2019). Final journeys: Exploring the realities of suicide tourism. *Journal of Travel Medicine, 26*(3), taz016. https://doi.org/10.1093/jtm/taz016

Chapter 5
Suicidal Behavior in Bangladesh: A Socioecological Analysis

S. M. Yasir Arafat and Tamkeen Saleem

1 Introduction

1.1 Suicidal Behavior in Global Perspective

Suicide is a global public health crisis, causing the demise of 727,000 people in a year (World Health Organization, 2025). It is one of the leading causes of death in all age groups and the third important cause of death in the 15–29-year-old age group (World Health Organization, 2025). About two-thirds of the suicide deaths occur in low- and middle-income countries (LMICs). Against a suicide, there are about 20 additional attempts, which indicate the burden of suicidal behavior (Turecki & Brent, 2016; World Health Organization, 2014). Despite all possible efforts over the past about half of the century, the trend is not in control (World Health Organization, 2014).

Suicide affects family members, close friends, community members, and the country. One study noted that about 135 persons are exposed to a suicide and about six persons are bereaved by a suicide death, which may result in suicidal behavior among the grieved persons, posttraumatic stress disorder, depression, and prolonged grief (Cerel et al., 2016; Turecki & Brent, 2016).

Suicidal behavior is an outcome of complex interaction among various factors ranging from biological (genetic factors), environmental factors, psychological

S. M. Y. Arafat (✉)
Department of Psychiatry, Bangladesh Specialized Hospital, Dhaka, Bangladesh

Department of Public and Community Health, Faculty of Medicine and Health Sciences, Frontier University Garowe, Garowe, Somalia

T. Saleem
Department of Clinical Psychology, Shifa Tameer-r-Millat University, Islamabad, Pakistan

S. M. Y. Arafat (ed.), *Suicidal Behavior in Bangladesh*, Mental Health Systems and Policy in Low- and Middle-Income Countries,
https://doi.org/10.1007/978-981-95-8321-8_5

(personal factors), social factors, and cultural factors participating as various roles like predisposing, precipitating and immediate factors (Zalsman et al., 2016; Turecki & Brent, 2016; Favril et al., 2022). Due to the complex interactions, identification of a risk factor on the basis of cause–effect association is nearly impossible for suicides attempt till date (World Health Organization, 2014; Zalsman et al., 2016). Socioecological factors play roles as developmental factors over the years (Arafat & Kar, 2025; Turecki & Brent, 2016).

1.2 Suicidal Behavior in Bangladesh

In Bangladesh, suicidal and self-harm behavior is a public health crisis, which is yet to receive academic and service attention (Arafat, 2019). It does not have a national suicide surveillance system and national data on suicidal and self-harm behavior. Any nation-wide study assessing epidemiology, burden, and risk factors for suicidal behavior among the general population has not been done yet (Arafat, 2024). In the current legal status in Bangladesh, according to *the Penal Code*, 1860 (Section 309), suicide attempt is a criminal offense (Laws of Bangladesh, nd; Arafat, 2017). There is a high social stigma and low suicide literacy, enduring disfavored religious and cultural constructs make suicide a hidden issue (Arafat & Ali, 2026). Due to the legal status, there are concerns of police harassment while investigating the suicide deaths. All these situations contribute to underreporting and misclassification of suicides.

Social and economic factors such as poverty, unemployment, domestic violence, marital disharmony, familial discord, and masculinity associated with mental health issues play a greater role than clinical factors (Arafat et al., 2021a, 2021b; Gibson & Hossain, 2017; Khan, 2026). Several studies revealed personal issues, family factors, peer relationships, and school-level risk factors for suicidal behavior in Bangladesh (Arafat et al., 2021a, 2022a, 2024, 2025a; Feroz et al., 2012; Reza et al., 2014; Tasfi & Mostofa, 2024; Sharmin Salam et al., 2017). Along with that, there are some additional challenges for suicide prevention in the country, such as criminal legal status, inadequate clinical services, extremely limited fund, improper media reporting, and lack of quality data (Hoque and Arafat, 2026; Arafat & Khan, 2024).

Suicide research in the recent decade has received academic attention in Bangladesh (Uddin & Arafat, 2026). Studies covering the broader socioecological variables (Arafat & Kar, 2025) are yet to be conducted in the country. This chapter delves into the interactions of multiple systems proposed in the Ecological Systems Theory and tries to fit the risk factors for suicidal behavior, as well as proposes system-wise preventive measures based on available evidence, expertise, strengths, and weaknesses. It is important to understand suicidal behavior in Bangladesh in the light of interactions between the levels of the wider socioecological systems and variables to formulate a national suicide prevention strategy, as well as to allocate available limited resources for maximum preventive outcome.

1.3 Ecological Systems Theory

The Ecological Systems Theory was proposed by Urie Bronfenbrenner (1977, 1979). It explains the interactions of an individual with the enduring surrounding interconnected systems, such as individual characteristics, family and school, and a wider environment, such as neighbors, climate, and time. It divides the environment into several systems that surround an individual, mentioned as microsystem, mesosystem, exosystem, macrosystem, and chronosystem (Fig. 5.1, for systems). The center of the systems puts an individual reflected by the personal characteristics and makes the ontogenic system (Ayyash-Abdo, 2002). The microsystem immediately surrounds the ontogenic system, which is composed of interaction with/of family members, school environment, religious institutions, close friends, and available health services (Henderson, 2020). The mesosystem surrounds the microsystem, and it is considered a "system of microsystems" due to its influence on the microsystem. The outcome is determined by enduring interactions among various dimensions of relationships among the microsystems. The exosystem encircles the mesosystem, which is comprised of social systems, social support, wider variables such as stigma, mass media, political system, and economy of the country. The macrosystem encircles the exosystem, which is composed of enduring cultural norms, ethics, beliefs, and standards regulating human behavior. And the chronosystem encircles the macrosystem, which indicates social changes over the decades, such as climate change, rising temperature, and melting of polar ice.

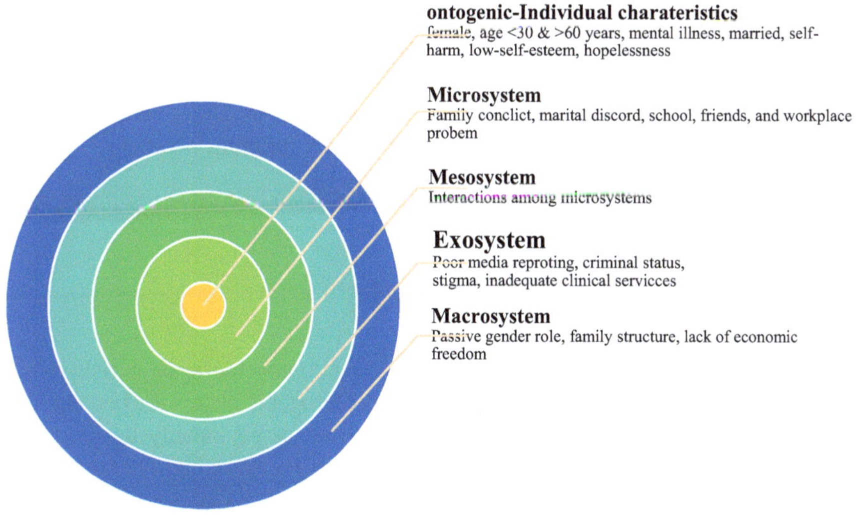

Fig. 5.1 Risk factors for suicidal behavior in Bangladesh in different ecological systems. (Adapted from Arafat & Saleem, 2025)

1.4 Socioecological Model

The Social-ecological Model (SEM) of suicidal behavior depicts the wider and complex interactions among sociocultural and environmental variables and their influence on an individual's suicidal behavior (Centers for Disease Control and Prevention, 2024; Cramer & Kapusta, 2017; Zulkiply & Rosliza, 2022). It dictates the multifaceted nature of suicidal behavior and acknowledges that the human mind is influenced by various wider variables of the environment. Current ecological studies establish various associations among the wider socioecological variables and suicidal behavior, reinforcing the model. As a result, while considering the prevention of suicidal behavior, it is important to acknowledge the roles and ensure adequate efforts to address their impacts. The various interactions of an individual with the different systems, that is, microsystem, mesosystem, exosystem, and macrosystem, should be considered (Henderson, 2020). The SEM and its interconnected layers provide a holistic framework to understand suicidal behavior as well as to prevent it.

2 Risk Factors for Suicidal Behavior in Bangladesh in Different Ecological Systems

The Socioecological Model (SEM) is a framework used to understand the multifaceted and interactive effects of personal and environmental factors that influence behaviors like suicidal behavior. It can be used as a baseline for the development of public health interventions; SEM is particularly useful for analyzing how risk and protective factors function at various levels of the ecological environment of an individual. Risk factors for suicidal behavior in Bangladesh are inadequately studied. However, it is well established in suicidology, especially while explaining the SEM, that there are complex interactions among risk factors across various ecological systems. Here, risk factors are categorized into different ecological systems speculatively revealed by different studies (Fig. 5.1).

2.1 Risk Factors in Ontogenic System

Available studies revealed several individual-level/ontogenic system risk factors associated with suicidal behavior in Bangladesh. Ontogenic factors are personal and have an impact on behavior, mental health aspects, or personality development. Females are dying more than males; suicides and self-harm are highly noted among persons under the age of 30 years (Arafat, 2019; Arafat et al., 2021a, 2024, 2025a). One community-based research noted the highest rate among older adults (60+ age group) (Mashreky et al., 2013). The other sociodemographic factors indicate that mental illness (depression, personality disorder, and substance abuse), married persons, unemployment, negative life events, and past self-harm behavior are important risk factors that fit the ontogenic system (Arafat et al., 2021a, 2024, 2025a; Arafat, 2026; Feroz et al., 2012; Reza et al., 2014). A study conducted in rural areas found that unskilled laborers were 16 times more prone to suicide attempts than students attending schools (Sharmin Salam et al., 2017). There may be overlaps while considering risk factors. Unskilled laborers may have issues with the workplace, which is a part of the microsystem. Additionally, one factor may lead to other factors within the same or different systems. For example, mental illness may result in unemployment and vice versa. Also, mental illness can cause workplace problems and vice versa. A psychological autopsy found that there exists a higher risk of suicidal behavior among individuals with psychiatric disorders (15.3 times), experiences of adverse life events (17.8 times), or individuals with previous suicide attempts (65.3 times), and those with a history of sexual abuse (92.3 times) in Dhaka, Bangladesh (Arafat et al., 2021a). Some individual factors, such as low self-esteem, increase the chances of experiencing suicidal ideation and suicidal attempts. Feelings of low self-worth or hopelessness can also lead to psychological distress or depression, which play a critical role in the development of suicidal ideation and behavior (Tasfi & Mostofa, 2024).

2.2 *Risk Factors in Microsystem*

It includes family dynamics, educational institutions like the school environment, religious institutions, close friends, and health services (Henderson, 2020). This system is important in Bangladesh as family discord and marital disharmony are the prominent risk factors for suicide and self-harm. Problems with close persons, marital issues, domestic or intimate partner violence, enduring gender roles and expectations, and enduring practice in the extended family structures are attributed to suicidality in South Asian culture, which is not an exception in Bangladesh (Khan, 2002). A case-control psychological autopsy study observed that about 86% of suicides would not have happened if the negative life events had been prevented (Arafat et al., 2021b). The notable risk factors are mentioned as marital discord, family disputes, unfaithful conjugal relationships, extramarital love affairs, premarital affair disputes, and intimate partner violence (Shah et al., 2017; Arafat, 2019; Arafat et al., 2021a, 2024, 2025a; Sara et al., 2024). Sibling rivalry, failure in joint family business, and relationship problems among the siblings were found as risk factors within the family system (Arafat et al., 2022a). The psychological autopsy study found that 40% of the life events were related to interpersonal relationship problems linked with marital and sexual issues, including marital discord, extramarital love affairs, forceful marriage by parents, disputes related to premarital love relationships, and family disharmony (Arafat et al., 2021a). Similarly, a history of family mental illness and having a family suicide attempt history is strongly related to suicide completion (Rasheduzzaman et al., 2022).

Academic stress and problems, exam failure, and bullying or ragging in university and schools are attributed to suicide attempts. Some of the factors are closely related and may lead to others. For example, being bullied in the university results in mental illness and poor academic performance that may lead to suicidality (Urme et al., 2022). Parent–child interaction (parenting), like infrequent parental supervision, isolation in the family, was associated with a higher likelihood of suicidality in schools among students (Marthoenis & Yasir Arafat, 2022; Arafat et al., 2022b).

2.3 *Risk Factors in Mesosystem*

It is the interrelationships among two or more microsystems in which an individual lives, such as the relationship between family and school or school and religious institutions. One microsystem can influence the others, which is reflected in the mesosystem. For example, home environment affects performance in school and workplace and vice versa (Eamon, 2001). One study found that unemployment, poverty, poor interpersonal relationships, and drug abuse were associated with low self-esteem and suicidal thoughts (Tasfi & Mostofa, 2024). There are extreme examples noted in Bangladesh where suicide happens due to the unfulfillment of an immediate demand by young kids, such as being scolded or bitten by teachers, or not buying an expected dress (Shah et al., 2017; Arafat, 2019).

2.4 *Risk Factors in Exosystem*

This system dictates associations among social systems, social support, wider variables such as stigma, mass media, political system, legal structure, and the economy of the country. There are various challenges in these areas. Bangladesh is a lower-middle-income country with a population of about 170 million, where more than 90% are Muslim. Here, suicide attempt is a criminal offense (Laws of Bangladesh, nd). It hinders the help-seeking behavior, raises stigma, and underreporting of suicide (Arafat & Ali, 2026). Suicide is a sin in Islam. Therefore, the religious prohibition and punitive legal status make suicide a taboo and perpetuate a high stigma that challenges prevention. High stigma hinders people from help-seeking as well as discussing it openly, which may lead to hopelessness and result in the development of suicidal behavior (Arafat et al., 2022a; Shahnaz et al., 2017; Urme et al., 2022).

Due to the income category and a small budgetary allocation, currently, there are no dedicated clinical services for suicidal behavior (Arafat, 2024).

Mass media presents suicidality without caring about its impact on further suicidal behavior. The quality of media reporting of suicide was found to be poor when they are compared to the World Health Organization (WHO) reporting guidelines (Arafat & Anik, 2026; Arafat et al., 2019, 2020, 2025b, 2025c).

2.5 Risk Factors in Macrosystem

It covers extremely wide variables such as enduring social norms and cultures of living in a region or culture. It includes gender roles, economic freedom, and the trend of family dynamics. In Bangladeshi families, parents take care of the expenses of their child(ren) even after marriage, maintain a joint family environment, and dominate family decisions of their children, which may create conflicts (Ghuman, 2000; Arafat et al., 2022a). Perhaps, therefore, previous studies identified multiple risk factors related to familial disharmony (Arafat, 2019; Arafat et al., 2021a, 2024, 2025a).

Historically, females have passive gender roles and low economic freedom in Bangladesh, which may contribute to the female suicides (Arafat, 2017). Additionally, there are expected gender roles of daughter-in-law and mother-in-law, which create conflicts in families living together and lead to suicidal behavior among daughters-in-law.

2.6 Risk Factors in Chronosystem

Bangladesh is a disaster-prone region where recent environmental and climate changes have been noted. It has been reflected by increasing temperature and humidity, deforestation due to urbanization, which in turns causes displacement and additional disasters. Climate change and exposure to disasters affect mental well-being and suicidal behavior (Wahid et al., 2024).

3 Potential Suicide Preventive Measures in Bangladesh in Different Ecological Systems

Prevention strategies should be based on the risk factors. In this section, we propose potential preventive measures according to the ecological systems based on a previous review conducted by Arafat and Saleem (2025) (Fig. 5.2).

3.1 Prevention Strategies in Ontogenic System

3.1.1 Psychiatric Services

Psychiatric illness is a vital risk factor for suicidal behavior. Previous studies revealed that 61% of suicides had at least one mental illness, and 71% of persons exhibiting self-harm behavior had mental illness (Arafat et al., 2021a, 2024).

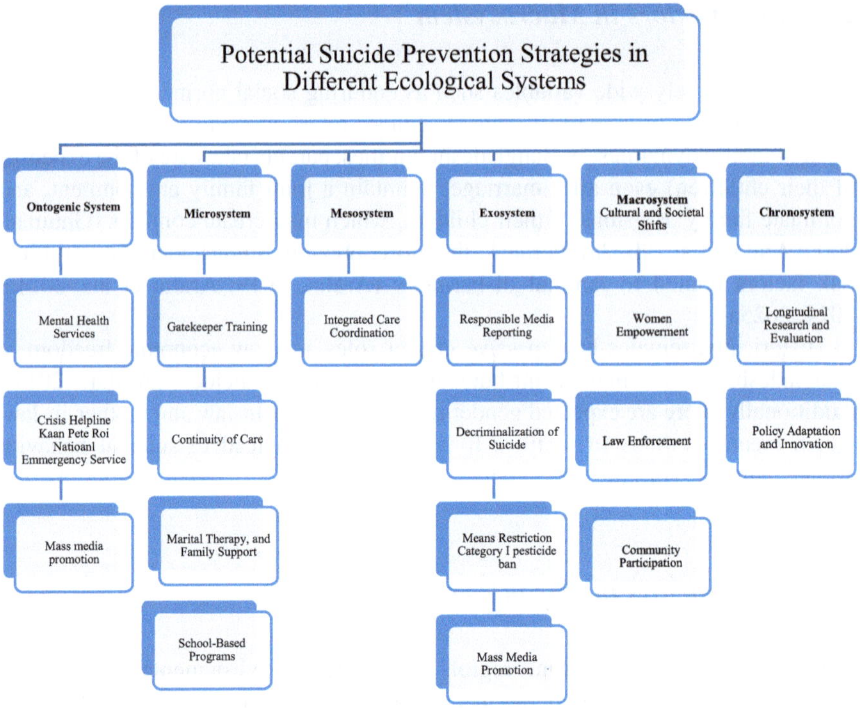

Fig. 5.2 Potential prevention strategies for suicidal behavior in different ecological systems in Bangladesh. (Adapted from Arafat & Saleem, 2025)

Treatment of mental illness is a vital suicide prevention strategy (Zalsman et al., 2016). Hence, adequate clinical services are needed in Bangladesh to prevent suicidal behavior. Unfortunately, there are no specialized services for suicidal behavior in the country. Two specialized clinics were started that ceased recently (Arafat, 2024). Additionally, measures should be taken to extend the services to the community level.

3.1.2 Crisis Helplines

Crisis lines are a potential suicide preventive measure (World Health Organization, 2014; Zalsman et al., 2016). Relationship problems with family members and spouse are an important domain of risk factors for suicide attempt in Bangladesh (Arafat, 2019; Arafat et al., 2021a, 2024). Therefore, crisis lines for immediate emotional distress relief have shown promises (Arafat et al., 2025d). "Kaan Pete Roi" is the first suicide prevention crisis line established more than 10 years ago (Arafat et al., 2025d). It is available for 12 hours (3 pm to 3 am) and has shown efficacy in reducing suicide attempts. Among the 60,000 calls, it successfully neutralized 1–3% of callers with thoughts of active suicide attempt. The National Emergency Services

(NES, 999) was started on 12 December 2017 and has shown promises in stopping suicide attempts (Arafat et al., 2025d). A national dedicated public toll-free crisis line for suicide prevention is warranted.

3.1.3 Mass Media Promotion

Mass media promotion plays a significant role in suicide prevention in improving suicide literacy among individuals and reducing stigma, which enables individuals to seek help when necessary (Zalsman et al., 2016; World Health Organization, 2023; Arafat et al., 2022c).

3.2 Prevention Strategies in Microsystem

3.2.1 Gatekeeper Training

It has shown efficacy in suicide prevention where gatekeepers (family members, teachers, peers, physicians, and religious leaders) are trained so that they can easily identify a risky individual for suicidal behavior and refer to preventive services (Kingi-Uluave et al., 2025; Zalsman et al., 2016; World Health Organization, 2014). It needs to be started in Bangladesh, where persons in the microsystem can identify the risky individuals.

3.2.2 Continuity of Care

Psychiatric disorders are an important risk factor for suicide attempts. The early days after discharge from the hospital are a potentially vulnerable time for a suicide attempt. Therefore, continuity of care is necessary for individuals with mental illness. In that case, family members play a vital role (Arafat et al., 2022a; Edwards et al., 2021).

3.2.3 Marital Therapy and Family Support

Relationship problems with spouse and family members, including extramarital love relationships, premarital affair-related conflicts, are prominent immediate negative life events attributed to suicidal behavior in Bangladesh. As a result, marital therapy and counseling for resolving family-centric issues could be a potential prevention strategy (Edwards et al., 2021; Ayyash-Abdo, 2002).

3.2.4 School-Based Interventions

Schools are a vital place where students pass a significant portion of their lives when they interact with peers and teachers. It guides thoughts, motivation, and lifelong behaviors (Arafat et al., 2021c). Initiation of school-based suicide prevention programs that teach students and teachers about mental well-being, coping skills, and peer support in distress. Peers and teachers can be a significant source of identification of the at-risk individuals and support for mental health difficulties.

3.3 Prevention Strategies in Mesosystem

Collaboration and integration of different suicide prevention strategies affecting the microsystems would be an important measure. Enduring collaboration among various stakeholders in the microsystem is warranted. Additionally, prioritization of limited resources would be important to decide. Enduring collaboration, cooperation, and integration need to be ensured.

3.4 Prevention Strategies in Exosystem

3.4.1 Sensible Media Reporting

As mentioned previously, the quality of media reporting is poor when compared to the WHO media reporting guidelines. Immense efforts are needed in this area as the attempted measures seem inadequate. The detailed effort and status of media reporting of suicide is mentioned in the chapter of this book (Arafat & Anik, 2026).

3.4.2 Decriminalization of Suicide Attempt

Criminalized legal status would hinder the help-seeking behavior and foster the chances of misclassification and underreporting of suicide. Therefore, decriminalization of suicide attempts would be a major initiative in suicide prevention in Bangladesh (Hoque and Arafat, 2026; Arafat, 2025a).

3.4.3 Means Restriction

In compliance with international efforts, Bangladesh restricted category I pesticides in agriculture in 2000 (Chowdhury et al., 2018). It reduced suicides by pesticide poisoning. However, benzodiazepines are an important substance for overdose that needs to be restricted. One report revealed that online dispensing of benzodiazepines could be stopped to prevent overdose attempts (Arafat, 2025b).

3.4.4 Mass Media Promotion

Regular promotions in mass media aiming at improving suicide literacy, reducing stigma among the general population, available services for suicide emergency cases should be continued. There is strong evidence that suicides increase after media stories about suicides by celebrities, particularly those that highlight the suicide method. Following evidence from the Papageno effect (Niederkrotenthaler et al., 2022), media can decrease suicide risk by portraying the stories of individuals who overcame suicidal behavior through positive coping, help-seeking, and support from friends and family. Such narratives can help in counteracting a sense of despair, instill hope, and provide individuals with constructive alternatives to suicide related behavior.

3.5 Prevention Strategies in Macrosystem

As a long-term plan, Bangladesh needs to plan for intervention measures to modify the social fabric where the passive gender roles for females and their lack of economic freedom would be changed. Additional efforts are warranted to change the enduring culture of expected roles in the in-laws' family.

3.5.1 Gender Empowerment

Attempts may be made to expand access of girls to higher education, confidence and capacity building, and entrepreneurship programs for establishing economic independence and decision-making abilities.

3.5.2 Law Enforcement

Strengthen enforcement of laws protecting women's rights in marriage, inheritance, and the workplace. Along with this, cultural transformation initiatives are required where public awareness campaigns are needed to challenge and modify orthodox gender norms and enhance equitable relationships within families, including immediate family and with in-laws.

3.5.3 Community Participation

There may be the establishment of community-based dialogue programs where religious leaders, local influencers, and digital media may be involved to normalize the concept of shared household responsibilities and mutual respect in families.

Modification in the enduring culture of prescribed roles between daughters-in-law and in-laws will require systematic and well-coordinated educational, social, and legal reforms. This may require sustaining it over decades, fueled and supported by grassroots activism and national policy development.

3.6 Prevention Strategies in Chronosystem

Bangladesh needs to consider the chorological variables of the environment, disaster, mental health, and suicidal behavior. Cautious observations and national policy-level adjustments are warranted. Adequate fund allocations in suicide prevention and augmented research would be warranted.

4 Conclusion

Suicide is more of a social event in Bangladesh; however, it should be kept in mind that suicide is extremely complex. Understanding the socioecological perspectives is essential for formulating an effective national suicide prevention program that is culture-sensitive and locally tailored. This chapter conceptualizes suicidal behavior in Bangladesh through the lens of socioecological models that may foster the development of the national suicide prevention strategy, considering the limited resources and maximum outcome. By implementing interventions at each of these levels, Bangladesh can create a comprehensive approach to suicide prevention and intervention that addresses individual needs while also considering the influences of families, schools, and communities on mental health and well-being. By using this approach, a supportive environment can be created that promotes mental health, reduces suicide risk, and enhances the overall well-being of its population. However, empirical studies are warranted to test the speculations.

References

Arafat, S. M. Y., & Anik, A. I. (2026). Media and suicidal behavior in Bangladesh. In S. M. Y. Arafat (Ed.), *Suicidal behavior in Bangladesh*. Springer. https://doi.org/10.1007/978-981-95-8321-8_11

Arafat, S. M. Y., & Ali, S. A. Z. (2026). Literacy and stigma of suicidal behavior in Bangladesh. In S. M. Y. Arafat (Ed.), *Suicidal behavior in Bangladesh*. Springer. https://doi.org/10.1007/978-981-95-8321-8_10

Arafat, S. M. Y. (2026). Mental health and suicidal behavior in Bangladesh. In S. M. Y. Arafat (Ed.), *Suicidal behavior in Bangladesh*. Springer. https://doi.org/10.1007/978-981-95-8321-8_3

Arafat, S. M. Y., & Saleem, T. (2025). Suicide in Bangladesh: An ecological systems analysis. *Brain and Behavior, 15*(1), e70233. https://doi.org/10.1002/brb3.70233

Arafat, S. Y., & Kar, S. K.. (2025). *Ecological and social determinants of suicidal behavior*. https://doi.org/10.1007/978-981-96-4028-7

Arafat, S. M. Y., Mali, B., & Mazumder, A. H. (2025a). Nonsuicidal self-injury in Bangladesh: A narrative review. *Health Science Reports, 8*(5), e70790. https://doi.org/10.1002/hsr2.70790

Arafat, S. M. Y., Jalil, S. B., Alam, M. S., Sultana, N., Ahmed, M. I. U., Abedin, M. M., & Armstrong, G. (2025b). Suicide in Bangla movie and Drama: A content analysis. *Omega, 91*(2), 1058–1071. https://doi.org/10.1177/00302228221148286

Arafat, S. M. Y., Sultana, Y., & Akter, H. (2025c). Quality of news reporting of celebrity suicide in Bangladesh against World Health Organization guidelines. *Global Psychiatry Archives, 8*(1), 1–7. https://doi.org/10.52095/gpa.2025.7579.1100

Arafat, S. M. Y., Mourin, C., & Jahan, R. (2025d). Crisis help line and suicide prevention in Bangladesh: Challenges and ways ahead. *Asian Journal of Psychiatry, 109*, 104565. https://doi.org/10.1016/j.ajp.2025.104565

Arafat, S. M. Y. (2025a). Suicide prevention in Bangladesh: Critical analysis of mental health law, policy and strategy. *BJPsych International, 22*(4), 138–141. https://doi.org/10.1192/bji.2025.10042

Arafat, S. M. Y. (2025b). Online dispensing of benzodiazepines can be an emerging threat for suicide prevention in Bangladesh: A case and potential preventive measures. *Asian Journal of Psychiatry, 106*, 104446. https://doi.org/10.1016/j.ajp.2025.104446

Arafat, S. M. Y., Shormi, F. R., & Kibria, M. G. (2024). Psychiatric disorder and life-event in self harm: A cross-sectional study among clinical population in Bangladesh. *Heliyon, 10*(19), e38627. https://doi.org/10.1016/j.heliyon.2024.e38627

Arafat, S. M. Y. (2024). Suicidal behavior and suicide prevention in Bangladesh. In S. M. Y. Arafat (Ed.), *Mental health in Bangladesh*. Springer. https://doi.org/10.1007/978-981-97-0610-5_11

Arafat, S. M. Y., & Khan, A. R. (2024). Suicidal behavior in Bangladesh. In S. M. Y. Arafat, M. Rezaeian, & M. M. Khan (Eds.), *Suicidal behavior in Muslim majority countries*. Springer. https://doi.org/10.1007/978-981-97-2519-9_4

Arafat, S. M. Y., Saleem, T., Edwards, T. M., Ali, S. A., & Khan, M. M. (2022a). Suicide prevention in Bangladesh: The role of family. *Brain and Behavior, 12*(5), e2562. https://doi.org/10.1002/brb3.2562

Arafat, S. Y., Menon, V., Dinesh, M., & Kabir, R. (2022b). Parenting style and suicidal behavior: A focused review. *Mental Illness, 2022*(1), 2138650. https://doi.org/10.1155/2022/2138650

Arafat, S., Hussain, F., Hossain, M. F., Islam, M. A., & Menon, V. (2022c). Literacy and stigma of suicide in Bangladesh: Scales validation and status assessment among university students. *Brain and Behavior, 12*(1), e2432. https://doi.org/10.1002/brb3.2432

Arafat, S. M. Y., Mohit, M. A., Mullick, M., Kabir, R., & Khan, M. M. (2021a). Risk factors for suicide in Bangladesh: Case-control psychological autopsy study. *BJPsych Open, 7*(1), e18. https://doi.org/10.1192/bjo.2020.152

Arafat, S., Khan, M., Knipe, D., & Khan, M. M. (2021b). Population attributable fractions of clinical and social risk factors for suicide in Bangladesh: Finding from a case-control psychological autopsy study. *Brain and Behavior, 11*(12), e2409. https://doi.org/10.1002/brb3.2409

Arafat, S. M. Y., Majumder, M. A. A., Kabir, R., Papadopoulos, K., & Uddin, M. S. (2021c). Health literacy in school. In *Research anthology on mental health stigma, education, and treatment* (pp. 920–942). Medical Information Science Reference/IGI Global. https://doi.org/10.4018/978-1-7998-8544-3.ch053

Arafat, S. M. Y., Khan, M. M., Niederkrotenthaler, T., Ueda, M., & Armstrong, G. (2020). Assessing the quality of media reporting of suicide deaths in Bangladesh against world health organization guidelines. *Crisis, 41*(1), 47–53. https://doi.org/10.1027/0227-5910/a000603

Arafat, S. M. Y., Mali, B., & Akter, H. (2019). Quality of online news reporting of suicidal behavior in Bangladesh against World Health Organization guidelines. *Asian Journal of Psychiatry, 40*, 126–129. https://doi.org/10.1016/j.ajp.2018.10.010

Arafat, S. M. Y. (2019). Current challenges of suicide and future directions of management in Bangladesh: A systematic review. *Global Psychiatry, 2*(1), 09–20. https://doi.org/10.2478/gp-2019-0001

Arafat, S. M. Y. (2017). Suicide in Bangladesh: A mini review. *Journal of Behavioral Health, 6*(1), 66–69. https://doi.org/10.5455/jbh.20160904090206

Ayyash-Abdo, H. (2002). Adolescent suicide: An ecological approach. *Psychology in the Schools, 39*(4), 459–475. https://doi.org/10.1002/pits.10042

Bronfenbrenner, U. (1977). Toward an experimental ecology of human development. *American Psychologist, 32*, 513–531.

Bronfenbrenner, U. (1979). *The ecology of human development*. Harvard University Press.

Cramer, R. J., & Kapusta, N. D. (2017). A social-ecological framework of theory, assessment, and prevention of suicide. *Frontiers in Psychology, 8*, 1756. https://doi.org/10.3389/fpsyg.2017.01756

Centers for Disease Control and Prevention, 2024. Centers for Disease Control and Prevention (2017). *The social-ecological model: a framework for prevention*. Accessed Apr 29, 2024, from https://www.cdc.gov/violenceprevention/about/social-ecologicalmodel.html

Cerel, J., Maple, M., van de Venne, J., Moore, M., Flaherty, C., & Brown, M. (2016). Exposure to suicide in the community: Prevalence and correlates in one U.S. State. *Public Health Reports, 131*(1), 100–107. https://doi.org/10.1177/003335491613100116

Chowdhury, F. R., Dewan, G., Verma, V. R., Knipe, D. W., Isha, I. T., Faiz, M. A., Gunnell, D. J., & Eddleston, M. (2018). Bans of WHO class I pesticides in Bangladesh-suicide prevention without hampering agricultural output. *International Journal of Epidemiology, 47*(1), 175–184. https://doi.org/10.1093/ije/dyx157

Eamon, M. K. (2001). The effects of poverty on childrens socioemotional development: An ecological systems analysis. *Social Work, 46*(3), 256–266. https://doi.org/10.1093/sw/46.3.256

Edwards, T. M., Patterson, J. E., & Griffith, J. L. (2021). Suicide prevention: The role of families and carers. *Asia-Pacific Psychiatry, 13*(3), e12453. https://doi.org/10.1111/appy.12453

Favril, L., Yu, R., Uyar, A., Sharpe, M., & Fazel, S. (2022). Risk factors for suicide in adults: Systematic review and meta-analysis of psychological autopsy studies. *Evidence-Based Mental Health, 25*(4), 148–155. https://doi.org/10.1136/ebmental-2022-300549

Feroz, A., Islam, S., Reza, S., Rahman, A., Sen, J., Mowla, M., & Rahman, M. (2012). A community survey on the prevalence of suicidal attempts and deaths in a selected rural area of Bangladesh. *Journal of Medicine, 13*(1), 3–9. https://doi.org/10.3329/jom.v13i1.10042

Gibson, R., & Hossain, D. (2017). Understanding the psychosocial context of suicide through the 'voice of the bereaved' in Bangladesh: A qualitative study. *International Journal of Social Psychiatry, 63*(7), 646–655. https://doi.org/10.1177/0020764017734341

Ghuman, P. A. S. (2000). Acculturation of south Asian adolescents in Australia. *British Journal of Educational Psychology, 70*(3), 305–316. https://doi.org/10.1348/000709900158128

Henderson, D. (2020). *A social-ecological approach to adolescent suicide in rural New Mexico*. The University of New Mexico.

Hoque, M. B., & Arafat, S. M. Y. (2026). Suicidal behavior in Bangladesh: The preventive measures. In S. Y. Arafat (Ed.), *Suicidal behavior in Bangladesh*. Springer.

Khan, M. M. (2002). Suicide on the Indian subcontinent. *Crisis: The Journal of Crisis Intervention and Suicide Prevention, 23*(3), 104–107. https://doi.org/10.1027/0227-5910.23.3.104

Khan, A. R. (2026). Cultural perspectives of suicide in Bangladesh. In S. M. Y. Arafat (Ed.), *Suicidal behavior in Bangladesh*. Springer.

Kingi-Uluave, D., Taufa, N., Tuesday, R., Cargo, T., Stasiak, K., Merry, S., & Hetrick, S. (2025). A review of systematic reviews: Gatekeeper training for suicide prevention with a focus on effectiveness and findings. *Archives of Suicide Research, 29*(2), 329–346. https://doi.org/10.1080/13811118.2024.2358411

Laws of Bangladesh. (n.d.). *The penal code, 1860*. Accessed June 06, 2025, from http://bdlaws.minlaw.gov.bd/act-11/section-3140.html

Marthoenis, M., & Yasir Arafat, S. M. (2022). Rate and associated factors of suicidal behavior among adolescents in Bangladesh and Indonesia: Global school-based student health survey data analysis. *Scientifica, 2022*, 8625345. https://doi.org/10.1155/2022/8625345

Mashreky, S. R., Rahman, F., & Rahman, A. (2013). Suicide kills more than 10,000 people every year in Bangladesh. *Archives of Suicide Research, 17*(4), 387–396. https://doi.org/10.1080/13811118.2013.801809

Niederkrotenthaler, T., Till, B., Kirchner, S., Sinyor, M., Braun, M., Pirkis, J., Tran, U. S., Voracek, M., Arendt, F., Ftanou, M., Kovacs, R., King, K., Schlichthorst, M., Stack, S., & Spittal, M. J. (2022). Effects of media stories of hope and recovery on suicidal ideation and help-seeking attitudes and intentions: Systematic review and meta-analysis. *The Lancet. Public health, 7*(2), e156–e168. https://doi.org/10.1016/S2468-2667(21)00274-7

Rasheduzzaman, M., Al-Mamun, F., Hosen, I., Akter, T., Hossain, M., Griffiths, M. D., & Mamun, M. A. (2022). Suicidal behaviors among Bangladeshi university students: Prevalence and risk factors. *PLoS One, 17*(1), e0262006. https://doi.org/10.1371/journal.pone.0262006

Reza, A. S., Feroz, A. H. M., Islam, S. N., Karim, M., Rabbani, M., Shah Alam, M., Rahman, M., Rahman, M., Ahmed, H. U., Bhowmik, A., Khan, M., Sarkar, M., Alam, M., & Jalal Uddin, M. M. (2014). Risk factors of suicide and Para suicide in rural Bangladesh. *Journal of Medicine, 14*(2), 123–129. https://doi.org/10.3329/jom.v14i2.19653

Sara, S. S., Rahman, M. A., Rahman, R., & Talukder, A. (2024). Prediction of suicidal ideation with associated risk factors among university students in the southern part of Bangladesh: Machine learning approach. *Journal of Affective Disorders, 349*, 502–508. https://doi.org/10.1016/j.jad.2024.01.092

Shah, M. M. A., Ahmed, S., & Arafat, S. M. Y. (2017). Demography and risk factors of suicide in Bangladesh: A six-month paper content analysis. *Psychiatry Journal, 2017*, 3047025. https://doi.org/10.1155/2017/3047025

Sharmin Salam, S., Alonge, O., Islam, M. I., Hoque, D. M. E., Wadhwaniya, S., Ul Baset, M. K., et al. (2017). The burden of suicide in rural Bangladesh: Magnitude and risk factors. *International Journal of Environmental Research and Public Health, 14*(9), 1032. https://doi.org/10.3390/ijerph14091032

Shahnaz, A., Bagley, C., Simkhada, P., & Kadri, S. (2017). Suicidal behaviour in Bangladesh: A scoping literature review and a proposed public health prevention model. *Open Journal of Social Sciences, 5*(07), 254. https://doi.org/10.4236/jss.2017.57016

Tasfi, J. T., & Mostofa, S. M. (2024). Understanding complex causes of suicidal behaviour among graduates in Bangladesh. *BMC Public Health, 24*(1), 560. https://doi.org/10.1186/s12889-024-17989-x

Turecki, G., & Brent, D. A. (2016). Suicide and suicidal behaviour. *Lancet (London, England), 387*(10024), 1227–1239. https://doi.org/10.1016/S0140-6736(15)00234-2

Uddin, M. S., & Arafat, S. M. Y. (2026). Suicide research in Bangladesh. In S. M. Y. Arafat (Ed.), *Suicidal behavior in Bangladesh*. Springer.

Urme, S. A., Islam, M. S., Begum, H., & Awal Chowdhury, N. M. R. (2022). Risk factors of suicide among public university students of Bangladesh: A qualitative exploration. *Heliyon, 8*(6), e09659. https://doi.org/10.1016/j.heliyon.2022.e09659

Wahid, S. S., Islam, M. N., & Raza, W. A. (2024). Climate change and mental health in Bangladesh: Vulnerability, inequality, and the crucial need for intervention on the frontlines of the climate crisis. In S. M. Y. Arafat (Ed.), *Mental health in Bangladesh*. Springer. https://doi.org/10.1007/978-981-97-0610-5_15

World health organization. (2025). *Suicide*. Accessed June 05, 2025, from https://www.who.int/news-room/fact-sheets/detail/suicide

World Health Organization. (2023). *Preventing suicide: A resource for media professionals, update 2023*. Accessed Nov 14, 2024, from https://www.who.int/publications/i/item/9789240076846

World Health Organization. (2014). *Preventing suicide: A global imperative*. Geneva. Accessed Apr 29, 2024, from https://www.who.int/publications/i/item/9789241564779

Zalsman, G., Hawton, K., Wasserman, D., van Heeringen, K., Arensman, E., Sarchiapone, M., Carli, V., Höschl, C., Barzilay, R., Balazs, J., Purebl, G., Kahn, J. P., Sáiz, P. A., Lipsicas, C. B., Bobes, J., Cozman, D., Hegerl, U., & Zohar, J. (2016). Suicide prevention strategies revisited: 10-year systematic review. *The Lancet Psychiatry, 3*(7), 646–659. https://doi.org/10.1016/S2215-0366(16)30030-X

Zulkiply, S. H., & Rosliza, A. M. (2022). Application of socio-ecological model in developing preventive strategies against suicidal ideation and suicidal attempt among youth in low and middle-income countries: A scoping review. *The Medical Journal of Malaysia, 77*(6), 755–763.

Chapter 6
Family Dynamics and Suicidal Behavior in Bangladesh

S. M. Yasir Arafat and Tamkeen Saleem

1 Introduction

Suicidal behavior is a global public health problem. A recent estimate (2025) of suicide revealed that 727,000 people die by suicide every year worldwide, and many more attempt to do so (World Health Organization, 2025). It has been estimated that approximately three-fourths of suicide deaths (73%) occur in lower and middle-income countries (LMICs) due to the greater size of their populations and lack of preventive measures for suicidal behavior (World Health Organization, 2025). Currently, suicide is the fourth leading injury-related cause of death in Bangladesh (Khan et al., 2021). Despite the burden of suicidal behaviors in Bangladesh, there are no longitudinal, nationwide, interventional, and epidemiological studies on suicide, especially on suicide prevention (Arafat et al., 2021a). The majority of the previous studies explore the individual risk factors of suicide, such as depression, substance use, prior suicide attempt, financial crisis, and so on (Arafat et al., 2021b; Urme et al., 2022). However, studies also identified negative life events related to family dynamics that affect suicidal behavior in Bangladesh (Arafat et al., 2021b, 2024, 2025a; Feroz et al., 2012; Khan et al., 2020; Marthoenis & Arafat, 2022). Therefore, there is a need to assess the contribution of family dynamics in suicidal behavior and consider prevention measures to reduce suicidal behavior based on family dynamics (Arafat, et al. 2022a; Edwards et al., 2021; Frey & Cerel, 2015).

S. M. Y. Arafat (✉)
Department of Psychiatry, Bangladesh Specialized Hospital, Dhaka, Bangladesh

Department of Public and Community Health, Faculty of Medicine and Health Sciences, Frontier University Garowe, Garowe, Somalia

T. Saleem
Department of Clinical Psychology, Shifa Tameer-r-Millat University, Islamabad, Pakistan

S. M. Y. Arafat (ed.), *Suicidal Behavior in Bangladesh*, Mental Health Systems and Policy in Low- and Middle-Income Countries,
https://doi.org/10.1007/978-981-95-8321-8_6

Worldwide, suicide is the third leading cause of death among people aged 15–29 years (World Health Organization, 2025). In Bangladesh, the majority of suicides happen among persons under the age of 30 years (Arafat, 2019). Dysfunction, conflicts, socioeconomic conditions, violence, and stress in family are frequently associated with suicide risk behaviors for adolescents (Khan et al., 2020; Randell et al., 2006). A number of studies revealed that more than half of the suicides occurred due to emotional reasons within the family (Reza et al., 2014; Shahnaz et al., 2017). Marital disharmony, family stress, extra- and premarital issues, relationship strife, and poverty were found as the most common risk factors within the family environment (Arafat et al., 2021a, 2022a). Although there is a paucity of research on suicide prevention in Bangladesh, supportive and healthy family environment, raising awareness, gatekeeper involvement, identification of protective factors, continuity of care, and increasing access to marital therapy were speculated as prevention methods by engaging family members (Arafat et al., 2022a; Edwards et al., 2021). Parental homework check would also be a prevention strategy of suicide among the school-going adolescents in Bangladesh (Khan et al., 2020). As there is no national surveillance system or suicide database, criminal legal status, and social stigma, suicide has been underreported (Arafat, 2019; Arafat et al., 2021a). This chapter aims to explore the association between suicidal behavior and family dynamics in Bangladesh and speculate a way forward for suicide prevention and future studies in the country.

2 Family Structure in Bangladesh

2.1 Family Dynamics

Family is a culturally constructed unit that is a building block of social structure for all societies. It is defined as a group of people who have interacted and communicated with each other by marriage, blood, or adoption, constructing a single unit and also sharing a common culture or common beliefs (Arafat et al., 2022a; Uddin, 2009). Minuchin (1974, 1982) discussed the structural model of family systems in three primary subsystems" namely, spousal, sibling, and parent–child subsystems. The spousal subsystem is noted as the most important as it links three generations, namely, the marriage, child(ren), and each of their family of origin. Changes in sibling and parent–child subsystems are interconnected. Any expected and effective change in children is often enabled through a modification in the spousal subsystem, and a change in the spousal subsystem usually affects other subsystems.

Being a Muslim-majority country, it is imperative to view the family dynamics from an Islamic standpoint, where the family is not only a social unit but also a divinely ordained institution that serves as the foundation of moral, spiritual, and social order. In light of Minuchin's structural model of the family, the spousal subsystem resonates strongly with the Holy Qur'an, that the marital bond is the core upon which the family system is built. The Holy Qur'an narrates marriage as a source of *sakinah* (tranquility), *mawaddah* (affection), and *rahmah* (mercy), which are essential for maintaining harmony across all family relationships. Quran quotes: "And among His signs is that He created for you from yourselves mates that you may find tranquility in them; and He placed between you affection and mercy…" (Qur'an 30:21).

Islamic teachings highlight the importance of a stable marital relationship as being central to the well-being of children and overall family bonds. A healthy spousal bond aids in mutual respect, cooperation, and compassion, which naturally extends to the sibling relations and parent–child connections (Al-Azhar University, 2005). Supporting the argument, it has been noted that parenting styles and child rearing practices affect suicidality among child(ren) (Arafat et al., 2022b).

2.2 *Family in Bangladeshi Culture*

In Bangladeshi society, the family is much more than just a domestic arrangement; it is like a living social organism that holds the collective ethics, memory, values, and survival strategies of generations. It has its roots in a blend of South Asian traditions as well as Islamic principles; the family operates both as a private sanctuary and a public marker of identity. A typical Bangladeshi family emphasizes interdependence, profound respect for elders, and strong kinship bonds (Arafat et al., 2022a). In Bangladesh, most of the families are governed by patriarchal lineage, and males have the decision-making authority, where women are dominated by their husbands and their in-law's family members. But through modernization and urbanization, there has been a change as women are involved in employment and playing a more active role in the decision-making of families and societies (Arafat et al., 2022a; Bhandari & Titzmann, 2017; Samad, 2015; Zahangir, 2011).

The family structure and size are also changing in Bangladesh, from extended family to nuclear family, because of the participation of women in economic activity, which was not so common before (Samad, 2015). A study focused on the changing family patterns in Bangladesh demonstrates that the fertility rate is declining due to the role of family planning methods in both rural and urban areas. Furthermore, age at marriage is rising by reducing child marriage, increasing awareness about reproductive health, implementing marriage-related laws, enhancing the education rate, and reducing existing social taboos on early marriage (Samad, 2015). With the changing rate of divorce in Bangladesh, a new family pattern, single parenthood, has been trending (Afroz, 2019). The household size has decreased from 5.7 in 1981 to 4.2 in 2019 (Arafat, et al., 2022a). About 35% of women in Bangladesh have experienced domestic violence at home, where their marital age, number of children, decision-making role in family, lack of support from family members, and household food insecurity are associated with this violence (Arafat et al., 2022a).

Bangladeshi families have a higher level of solidarity, interconnectedness, and amalgamation between the household members. Parents must look after their children before their marriage and sometimes even after marriage when the children are in an economic crisis in their in-law's household. The children, especially the male children, also take the responsibility of their parents after getting jobs. Bangladeshi parents decide what their children will do in the future, and the children follow their instructions without raising any complaints (Arafat et al., 2022a).

3 Risk Factors for Suicidal Behavior in Bangladesh Related to Family

We discussed the risk factors for suicide in Bangladesh in Chap. 1 of this book (Arafat & Kabir, 2026). Here, risk factors related to family have been emphasized. The French sociologist *Emile Durkheim* explains that suicide is a social fact that occurs due to less social integration with family, friends, and so on, and also a lack of social norms and regulations on behavior would force one to take their life by suicide (Mueller et al., 2021). The previously noted common risk factors of suicide are previous suicide attempt, physical and sexual violence, psychiatric disorders (such as depression, anxiety and stress, personality disorders, substance abuse), hopelessness, loneliness, familial psychiatric history, familial suicide predisposition (such as not reared by biological parents, marital discord and family disharmony), relationship problems (such as loss of loved one or loss of family relationship), financial hardship, and unemployment (Arafat et al., 2021b, 2024, 2025a; Shahnaz et al., 2017; Feroz et al., 2012; Reza et al., 2014). Many of the risk factors of suicide are related to familial issues (Arafat et al., 2022a; Arafat, 2019). One study identified that approximately 93% of the participants took their own lives due to familial and marital disputes, which was sorted by assessing newspaper contents (Shah et al., 2017). A community-based survey in selected rural areas of Bangladesh showed 63% of suicide cases occurred due to family issues, among them 57% had a family conflict (Feroz et al., 2012). A case-control study found 65.5% of suicides occurred due to family events including romantic relationship problem, death of a near kin, academic persecution, financial hardship, marital disharmony, family quarrels and not reared by biological parents (Reza et al., 2014). An extreme case of family involvement was noted in 2007, where nine members of a family took their own lives together due to their delusion regarding religion (Selim, 2010). A narrative review demonstrated that conflict between husband and wife, family discords, widowhood, broken family, and relationship breakups were the leading causes of suicide in Bangladesh (Arafat, 2017). Another study showed that exam failure, suicidal death of close kin, marital dispute, and not being raised by biological parents were frequently reported as the risk factors for suicidal behavior (Shahnaz et al., 2017). A recent case-control psychological autopsy study found several life events related to family events such as extramarital affair, family conflict, marital discord, and broken engagement (Arafat et al., 2021b). About 40% of the life events were closely related to marital and sexual affairs, including conjugal strife, premarital

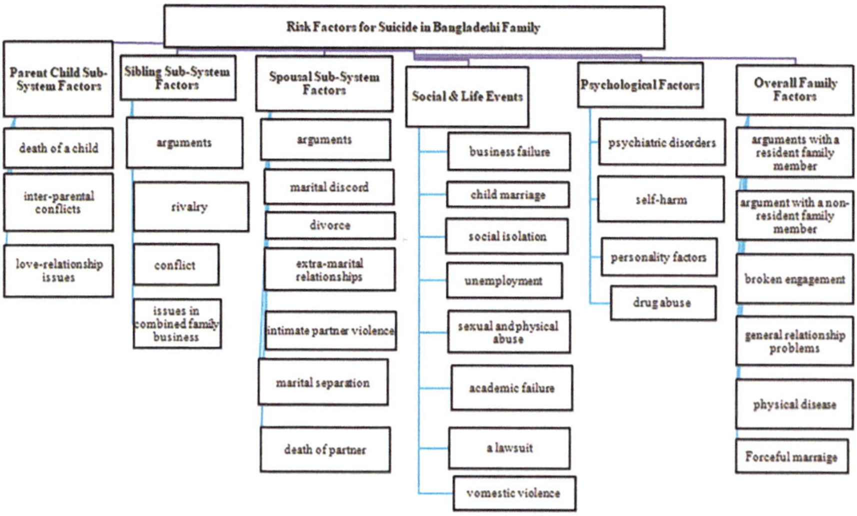

Fig. 6.1 Risk factors for suicide in Bangladeshi families. (Adapted from Arafat et al., 2022a)

romantic relationship, illicit love relationship, forcible wedlock, and contention with kins that contribute to suicidal ideation (Arafat et al., 2021b, 2022a). In addition, a few risk factors of suicide relevant to the parent–children subsystem are also perceived, such as early marriage, academic failure, death of children, romantic relationships, negative parenting, domestic abuse by the parents, and experiencing psychosocial, physical, and sexual abuse by teachers or peers in schools (Arafat et al., 2022a). Another risk factor is sibling subsystems, which may be affected by intrafamilial abuse, such as sibling conflicts, financial issues, family business failures, etc. (Arafat et al., 2022a). In rare cases, filicide-extended suicides have been noted in lower socioeconomic conditions attributed to poverty and marital discord (Arafat et al., 2025b). The risk factors have been presented in different subsystems of a family in Fig. 6.1.

4 Potential Family-Centric Suicide Prevention Strategies

Every suicide has an impact on a family's well-being in various ways (Shahnaz et al., 2017). In other ways, engaging and involving the family members is vital to developing an effective suicide prevention program. Family members and caregivers may play an important role in reducing suicidal tendency by creating a supportive family environment, good communications between family members, and strong relationships between them (Arafat et al., 2022a; Edwards et al., 2021). If the deceased person had a friendly environment in his/her family, that individual could

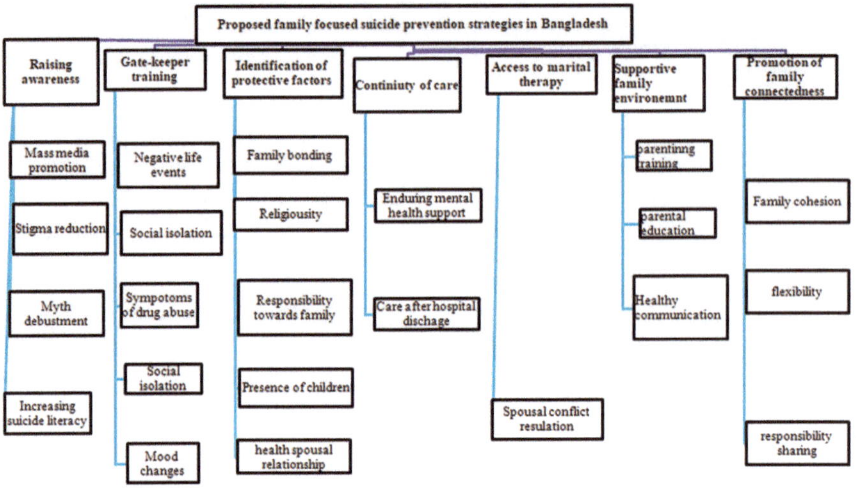

Fig. 6.2 Potential role of family in suicide prevention in Bangladesh. (Adapted from Arafat et al., 2022a)

share about his/her discomfort, which can keep him/her far away from suicide (Edwards et al., 2021; Shahnaz et al., 2017).

A recent qualitative study that focuses on public university students of Bangladesh reported some suicide prevention strategies that are also related to the family. For example, parenting skills training and workshops can be arranged at the community level, ensuring follow-up care for the suicide attempt survivors by the support of family, raising awareness among all the general people through advertising, and staging a drama are urgently needed for diminishing suicidal death (Urme et al., 2022). Stigma and taboo attached to mental health disorder patients and suicide survivors negatively play a role both for posttrauma counseling and suicide prevention (Arafat et al., 2022b; Shahnaz et al., 2017; Urme et al., 2022). The family-oriented prevention strategies would be raising awareness, gatekeeper training, identification of protective factors, access to psychiatric services, treatment facilities for suicidal behavior, continuity of care, access to marital therapy, supportive family environment, and promotion of family interactions (Edwards et al., 2021; Zalsman et al., 2016; Arafat & Kabir, 2017; Arafat et al., 2022a, Fig. 6.2).

4.1 Improving Suicide Literacy

There is a need to organize awareness-raising programs regarding suicide and suicide prevention for educating the general population, including parents and family members, through mass media (Zalsman et al., 2016). Efforts could be aimed at increasing suicide literacy, decreasing suicide stigma, identifying risky individuals, and making available nearby health services. The parents will be more interested in seeking mental health treatment for their children when the existing myths are allayed by society (Arafat et al. 2022a; Edwards et al. 2021). Bangladeshi families prefer to hide suicidal thoughts or death due to ignoring the social stigma and legal harassment, so arranging awareness-raising programs at the community level would be beneficial (Arafat et al., 2022a, 2022c; Urme et al., 2022).

4.2 Gatekeeper Interventions

Family members can play a role as a gatekeeper, as they have a connection with their kin who have a suicidal tendency. It is a potential preventive strategy by which the vulnerable populations can be identified (Zalsman et al., 2016). Additionally, family interventions help to identify the warning signs of suicide among adolescents (Zalsman et al., 2016). So, a formal training for the gatekeepers must be arranged to execute a problem-solving discussion on how to reduce suicidal ideation, attempt, and death.

4.3 Healthy Communication in Family

Everyone must have good communication and engagement with family members, by which parent-child conflict and sibling disputes can be reduced in the family environment (Arafat et al., 2022a; Edwards et al., 2021). Effective and supportive communication between family members can help them combat depression, anxiety, hopelessness, and suicidal behavior (Arafat et al., 2022a).

4.4 Family Cohesion and Monitoring

With modernization, the nuclear family systems are increasing, and parents have less time to spend with children. Warmth, routine check-ins, and active parental monitoring correlate with lower adolescent suicidality; family dysfunction is repeatedly linked to higher risk. Although much Bangladeshi work is risk-oriented, synthesis across local studies and regional data supports strengthening family function as a protective pathway (Arafat et al., 2024).

4.5 Religiosity (Promoting the Protective Factor)

Being a Muslim country in Bangladesh, religiosity/spirituality is associated with lower suicide risk and better treatment adherence; Bangladeshi reviews recommend engaging religious resources as part of family coping and stigma reduction. Families may enhance discussions regarding religious concepts that reframe life's challenges as tests, emphasizing reward for endurance and help-seeking. Share Hadith and Qur'anic verses highlighting patience (ṣabr), hope in Allah's mercy, and the prohibition of suicide as gentle reminders of faith-based resilience. They may make steps to regularly offer family prayers (Salat) at home or at the masjid and Qur'an recitation together to create shared spiritual moments. This will add to the quality time spent together and strengthen the bonds.

4.6 Life Event Focused Couple Counseling

Marital conflict and familial discord are potential life events for suicide exposures (Arafat et al. 2021c). In addition, the spousal subsystem affects the parent–child or sibling subsystem, so organizing a program for the couple's needs can play a prominent role in keeping a healthy relationship between family members. From this program, they can be benefitted knowing how to manage marital discords (Arafat et al., 2022a).

4.7 Continuity of Care

Hospitalization or follow-up care is urgently needed for the suicide survivors who have had prior suicide attempts. In this respect, information from the patients themselves and also from close kin members is important to assess the risk factors of suicide (Edwards et al. 2021). Additionally, the time after discharge from the hospital has been identified as a vulnerable period. Therefore, family members should be careful about suicidal behavior during this period and should ensure regular follow-ups.

4.8 Postvention

Suicide survivors are more stigmatized and ostracized by the community people rather than survivors of other types of death. This is also true for the deceased person's parents, who lose their child to suicide. After being negatively judged by society, the survivors sometimes keep themselves isolated from any social networks, a process called self-stigmatization; although this situation has changed over time (Cerel et al., 2008). The family members need care after any suicide attempt (fatal or non-fatal) in the family. Care for the vulnerable family members to keep them away from mental health crisis helps to reduce further risk of suicidal behavior, as recommended by the WHO (Arafat, 2021; WHO, 2018). But family members always try to keep their close kin's mental health sickness a secret because they think that the community can stigmatize them for this (Arafat, 2021). Sometimes suicide is contagious, one person can be influenced by another person's death, especially if the deceased person was his/her closed one (Urme et al., 2022). In this regard, postvention is urgently required, which can be worked as an effective prevention method.

5 Conclusions

This chapter examines the relationship between the risk factors of suicide that are relevant to the family, which can be helpful for developing and implementing effective suicide prevention strategies in Bangladesh. The common reasons behind self-destruction related to family, such as marital discord, familial disharmony, extramarital affair, premarital love relationship, conflicts with family members, or weak interrelation with them, should be taken into account for developing suicide prevention programs where family members have roles and responsibilities. This chapter discusses the potential areas of involvement of family members while considering suicide prevention.

References

Afroz, S. (2019). The rise of divorce in Bangladesh: A review in the change of marriage dynamics. *Social Sciences, 8*(5), 261. https://doi.org/10.11648/j.ss.20190805.17

Al-Azhar University. (2005). *Family in Islam*. Al-Azhar Publications. Accessed Aug 18, 2025, fromhttps://resourcecentre.savethechildren.net/pdf/children_in_islam_english.pdf

Arafat, S. M. Y., & Kabir, R. (2026). Data is silent, epidemiology is blur: Suicidal behavior in Bangladesh-what is known and what needs to improve. In S. M. Y. Arafat (Ed.), *Suicidal behavior in Bangladesh*. Springer. https://doi.org/10.1007/978-981-95-8321-8_1

Arafat, S. M. Y., Mali, B., & Mazumder, A. H. (2025a). Nonsuicidal self-injury in Bangladesh: A narrative review. *Health Science Reports, 8*(5), e70790. https://doi.org/10.1002/hsr2.70790

Arafat, S. M. Y., Hossain, S., & Mali, B. (2025b). Filicide-extended suicide in Bangladesh: A socio-demographic analysis from media reports. *South East Asian Journal of Suicide Prevention, 2*(1) Retrieved from https://seajsp.qvjournal.com/index.php/about/article/view/9

Arafat, S. M. Y., Shormi, F. R., & Kibria, M. G. (2024). Psychiatric disorder and life-event in self harm: A cross-sectional study among clinical population in Bangladesh. *Heliyon, 10*(19), e38627. https://doi.org/10.1016/j.heliyon.2024.e38627

Arafat, S. M. Y., Hussain, F., Jakaria, K. M., Itu, Z. T., & Islam, M. A. (2021a). Empirical studies on suicide in Bangladesh in a decade (2011-2020). *Global Psychiatry Archives, 4*(1), 109–122. https://doi.org/10.52095/gp.2021.10692

Arafat, S. M. Y., Mohit, M. A., Mullick, M. S. I., Kabir, R., & Khan, M. M. (2021b). Risk factors for suicide in Bangladesh: Case–control psychological autopsy study. *BJPsych Open, 7*(1), 1–5. https://doi.org/10.1192/bjo.2020.152

Arafat, S. M. Y., Khan, M. A. S., Knipe, D., & Khan, M. M. (2021c). Population attributable fractions of clinical and social risk factors for suicide in Bangladesh: Finding from a case–control psychological autopsy study. *Brain and Behavior, 11*(12), e2409. https://doi.org/10.1002/brb3.2409

Arafat, S. M. Y. (2021). Practical challenges of addressing suicidal behaviors for a clinician in Bangladesh. *International Journal of Mental Health and Addiction, 19*(6), 2175–2177. https://doi.org/10.1007/s11469-020-00310-3

Arafat, S. M. Y., Saleem, T., Edwards, T. M., Ali, S. A. e. Z., & Khan, M. M. (2022a). Suicide prevention in Bangladesh: The role of family. *Brain and Behavior, 12*(5), 1–7. https://doi.org/10.1002/brb3.2562

Arafat, S. Y., Menon, V., Dinesh, M., & Kabir, R. (2022b). Parenting style and suicidal behavior: A focused review. *Mental Illness, 2022*(1), 2138650. https://doi.org/10.1155/2022/2138650

Arafat, S. M. Y., Hussain, F., Hossain, M. F., Islam, M. A., & Menon, V. (2022c). Literacy and stigma of suicide in Bangladesh: Scales validation and status assessment among university students. *Brain and Behavior, 12*(1), e2432. https://doi.org/10.1002/brb3.2432

Arafat, S. M. Y., & Kabir, R. (2017). Suicide prevention strategies: Which one to consider? *South East Asia Journal of Public Health, 7*, 1–5. https://doi.org/10.3329/seajph.v7i1.34671

Arafat, S. (2017). Suicide in Bangladesh: A mini review. *Journal of Behavioral Health, 6*(1), 66. https://doi.org/10.5455/jbh.20160904090206

Arafat, S. M. Y. (2019). Current challenges of suicide and future directions of management in Bangladesh: A systematic review. *Global Psychiatry, 2*(1), 9–20. https://doi.org/10.2478/gp-2019-0001

Bhandari, P., & Titzmann, F.-M. (2017). Introduction. Family realities in South Asia: Adaptations and resilience. *South Asia Multidisciplinary Academic Journal, 16*, 0–13. https://doi.org/10.4000/samaj.4365

Cerel, J., Jordan, J. R., & Duberstein, P. R. (2008). The impact of suicide on the family. *Crisis, 29*(1), 38–44. https://doi.org/10.1027/0227-5910.29.1.38

Edwards, T. M., Patterson, J. E., & Griffith, J. L. (2021). Suicide prevention: The role of families and carers. *Asia-Pacific Psychiatry, 13*(3), e12453. https://doi.org/10.1111/appy.12453

Feroz, A. H. M., Islam, S. M. N., Reza, S., Rahman, A. K. M. M., Sen, J., Mowla, M., & Rahman, M. R. (2012). A community survey on the prevalence of suicidal attempts and deaths in a selected rural area of Bangladesh. *Journal of Medicine, 13*, 3–9. https://doi.org/10.3329/jom.v13i1.10042

Frey, L. M., & Cerel, J. (2015). Risk for suicide and the role of family: A narrative review. *Journal of Family Issues, 36*(6), 716–736. https://doi.org/10.1177/0192513X13515885

Khan, A. R., Arendse, N., & Ratele, K. (2021). Suicide prevention in Bangladesh: The current state and the way forward. *Asian Social Work and Policy Review, 15*(1), 15–23. https://doi.org/10.1111/aswp.12214

Khan, M. M. A., Rahman, M. M., Islam, M. R., Karim, M., Hasan, M., & Jesmin, S. S. (2020). Suicidal behavior among school-going adolescents in Bangladesh: Findings of the global school-based student health survey. *Social Psychiatry and Psychiatric Epidemiology, 55*(11), 1491–1502. https://doi.org/10.1007/s00127-020-01867-z

Marthoenis, M., & Arafat, S. M. Y. (2022). Rate and associated factors of suicidal behavior among adolescents in Bangladesh and Indonesia: Global school-based student health survey data analysis. *Scientifica, 2022*, 8625345. https://doi.org/10.1155/2022/8625345

Minuchin, S. (1974). *Families and family therapy*. Harvard University Press.

Minuchin, S. (1982). Reflection on boundaries. *American Journal of Orthopsychiatry, 52*, 655–663.

Mueller, A. S., Abrutyn, S., Pescosolido, B., & Diefendorf, S. (2021). The social roots of suicide: Theorizing how the external social world matters to suicide and suicide prevention. *Frontiers in Psychology, 12*, 621569. https://doi.org/10.3389/fpsyg.2021.621569

Randell, B. P., Wang, W. L., Herting, J. R., & Eggert, L. L. (2006). Family factors predicting categories of suicide risk. *Journal of Child and Family Studies, 15*(3), 255–270. https://doi.org/10.1007/s10826-006-9020-6

Reza, A. M. S., Feroz, A. H. M., Islam, S. M. N., Karim, M. N., Rabbani, M. G., Shah Alam, M., et al. (2014). Risk factors of suicide and Para suicide in rural Bangladesh. *Journal of Medicine, 14*, 123–129. https://doi.org/10.3329/jom.v14i2.19653

Shahnaz, A., Bagley, C., Simkhada, P., & Kadri, S. (2017). Suicidal behaviour in Bangladesh: A scoping literature review and a proposed public health prevention model. *Open Journal of Social Sciences, 05*(07), 254–282. https://doi.org/10.4236/jss.2017.57016

Samad, M. A. (2015). Marriage in changing family pattern of Bangladesh: The present trends. *International Journal of Social Work and Human Services Practice, 3*, 155–161. https://www.hrpub.org/download/20151130/IJRH4-19290354.pdf

Selim, N. (2010). An extraordinary truth? The Ādam "suicide" notes from Bangladesh. *Mental Health, Religion and Culture, 13*(3), 223–244. https://doi.org/10.1080/13674670903061230

Shah, M. M. A., Ahmed, S., & Arafat, S. M. Y. (2017). Demography and risk factors of suicide in Bangladesh: A six-month paper content analysis. *Psychiatry Journal, 2017*, 3047025. https://doi.org/10.1155/2017/3047025

Uddin, M. E. (2009). Family structure between Muslim and Santal communities in rural Bangladesh. *International Journal of Humanities and Social Sciences, 3*, 1433–1442.

Urme, S. A., Islam, M. S., Begum, H., & Awal Chowdhury, N. M. R. (2022). Risk factors of suicide among public university students of Bangladesh: A qualitative exploration. *Heliyon, 8*, E09659. https://doi.org/10.1016/j.heliyon.2022.e09659

World Health Organization. (2025). *Suicide*; WHO. Accessed May 23, 2025, from https://www.who.int/news-room/fact-sheets/detail/suicide

World Health Organization (WHO). (2018). National suicide prevention strategies: Progress, examples and indicators. https://apps.who.int/iris/bitstream/handle/10665/279765/9789241515016-eng.pdf

Zahangir, M. S. (2011). *Early and very early family formation in Bangladesh*. Retrieved from http://www.diva-portal.org/smash/record.jsf?pid=diva2:432607&dswid=-7466

Zalsman, G., Hawton, K., Wasserman, D., van Heeringen, K., Arensman, E., Sarchiapone, M., et al. (2016). Suicide prevention strategies revisited: 10-year systematic review. *The Lancet Psychiatry, 3*(7), 646–659. https://doi.org/10.1016/S2215-0366(16)30030-X

Chapter 7
Crisis, Trauma, Coping, and Suicide in Bangladesh

Muhammad Kamruzzaman Mozumder

1 Suicide Crisis Syndrome

Understanding and predicting suicidal behavior has received significant attention among mental health professionals and researchers. The urge to identify warning signs for longer- and shorter-term prediction of suicide has led to the development of checklists and scales for assessing and predicting suicide risks. Closely aligned with the goal of prediction, Galynker et al. (2024) proposed the suicide crisis syndrome. The five dimensions of the proposed syndrome include entrapment, affective disturbance, loss of cognitive control, hyperarousal, and social withdrawal (see Melzer et al., 2024). To understand the suicide crisis Stanley et al. (2023) described a suicide risk curve where they proposed four stages, that is, start of crisis, escalating, danger of acting suicidal feeling, and subsiding.

In recent times, the socio-ecological model that proposes an interplay of individual, sociocultural, and environmental factors in understanding suicidal behavior is gaining popularity. Using an ecological system analysis, Arafat and Saleem (2025) discussed a range of individual, micro-, meso-, exo-, and macrosystem factors contributing to suicide in Bangladesh. They reported being female, aged below 30 years or above 60 years, being married, and having a mental disorder as the individual factors, while family conflict, marital discord, and problems at workplace or school were the microsystem factors of suicide in Bangladesh (Arafat & Saleem, 2025). They further discussed improper media reporting, stigma, and inadequate clinical services as exosystem factors, along with passive gender role, family structure, and economic factors as the macrosystem contributors of suicidal behavior in Bangladesh (Arafat & Saleem, 2025).

M. K. Mozumder (✉)
Department of Clinical Psychology, University of Dhaka, Dhaka, Bangladesh
e-mail: mozumder@du.ac.bd

S. M. Y. Arafat (ed.), *Suicidal Behavior in Bangladesh*, Mental Health Systems and Policy in Low- and Middle-Income Countries,
https://doi.org/10.1007/978-981-95-8321-8_7

For a very long time, individual factors, especially depression, have been regarded as the key markers of suicidal behavior. However, it is being increasingly recognized as an ineffective strategy for suicide prevention to solely focus on the management of depression. Recent works suggest directly intervening in suicidal behavior as well as improving coping skills and self-management skills to be more effective in curbing suicidality compared to treating underlying depression (see Stanley et al., 2023). Subsequently, a range of factors, namely, crisis, trauma, and coping, are now gaining attention in understanding suicide and its prevention.

2 Crisis and Suicide

Individuals with a history of suicidal behavior can be generally classified into two broad categories: individuals with relatively persistent thoughts of suicide and individuals with impulsive or spur-of-the-moment thoughts of suicide. Irrespective of such classification, crisis plays an important role in generating suicidal thoughts and attempting suicide. This connection between crisis and suicide is well reflected in the naming, approach, and methods used in suicide prevention services.

Crisis can be defined as "acute emotional upset in an individual's usual steady state, accompanied by a perceived breakdown of his or her usual coping abilities" (Ell, 1996). Crises can originate from the reaction to external events or from internal conflicts between psychological systems. A crisis is closely associated with a certain state of mind, such as shock, fear, anxiety, uncertainty, hopelessness, helplessness, and denial (Centers for Disease Control and Prevention, 2019). These same features are also common among suicidal individuals. Increased suicidality with different types of crises has been well-reported and researched. Economic crisis and unemployment are among the strongest contributors to suicidality (see Gunnell et al., 2009). Crisis in the form of relationship problems and financial problems has been reported to be associated with suicide in Bangladesh (Arafat, 2019; Arafat et al., 2021a, 2021b; Feroz et al., 2012; Reza et al., 2013). Other forms of crisis, such as academic failure, failure in business, being a victim of sexual harassment, forced marriage, relationship crisis, domestic violence, dowry, the death of a spouse, and divorce, have also been linked with suicidality in Bangladesh (Arafat, 2019; Arafat et al., 2021b; Faruk et al., 2025).

In recent times, the link between the pandemic-induced crisis and suicide in Bangladesh has been studied by researchers from multiple disciplines. The crisis related to the recent COVID-19 pandemic has been reported to contribute to suicide among individuals across different districts of Bangladesh. Khan et al. (2022) analyzed several such suicidal cases using Durkheim's sociological perspective, where they found these COVID-related suicides and suicide attempts in Bangladesh to fall under the egoistic, anomic, and fatalistic categories. The cases reported by them indicated the presence of crisis in several aspects of life, including adverse interpersonal comments, failure to cope with restrictions, state of uncertainty, financial hardship, and failure to fulfil basic needs (hunger). Similar findings on suicide from a social and economic crisis during the COVID-19 pandemic have been reported by other researchers from Bangladesh (Bhuiyan et al., 2021; Mamun, 2021).

Exposure to and experience of crisis usually cause significant distress. When, due to limited coping resources, the person feels overwhelmed by the crisis, it can result in trauma, which is another marker for suicidality for many individuals. A crisis is generally conceptualized as a transient state, while trauma is reported as a comparatively longer-lasting emotional state. The development of psychological trauma from exposure to crisis depends on several vulnerabilities in the individuals, which include the presence of chronic stressors in life, pre-existing mental illness, limited problem-solving skills, and poor coping. Due to the persistent nature of distress in trauma, a person with trauma may often be more likely to attempt suicide repeatedly.

3 Trauma and Suicide

Risk factors of suicide are generally understudied in Bangladesh. However, distressing life events, sexual abuse, psychiatric illness, and previous attempts have been found as major risk factors for suicide in this context (Arafat, 2019; Arafat et al., 2021b, 2022b; Faruk et al., 2025). Mozumder et al. (2023) reported a relation between mental health and suicidal behaviors among male homosexuals in Bangladesh. Having experienced stressful life events in the past year has also been found to be a significant risk factor for suicide ideation, planning, and attempts in Bangladesh (Rasheduzzaman et al., 2022). The connection between trauma and suicidal ideation or attempt has been well established through research in the international context (LeBouthillier et al., 2015; Whiteman et al., 2019). The link between post-traumatic stress disorder (PTSD) and suicidal behavior has been consistently reported in research literature (see Akbar et al., 2023). Vulnerability to suicide has also been demonstrated among patients with acute physical trauma, where nightmares and insomnia in the first 2 months of traumatic injury have been found to be linked with a high rate (42.9%) of suicidal ideation (Reffi et al., 2025).

Exposure to trauma has a long-standing impact. Having a history of childhood trauma has been linked with suicidal behavior in adulthood. O'Connor et al. (2018) reported the presence of a history of childhood trauma among 78.7% adults who attempt suicide and among 37.7% adults with suicidal ideation. From a meta-analysis of 68 studies, Angelakis et al. (2019) indicated a two to fivefold higher risk of suicide attempts among adults who have a history of childhood abuses (sexual, physical, emotional, others, or complex abuse) compared to those without such a history. Childhood maltreatment, a common source of trauma, has been found to be linked with suicidal ideation among adults in Bangladesh (Zakir & Haque, 2024).

Due to the lack of research evidence, the exact magnitude of trauma-induced suicide cannot be ascertained in Bangladesh. However, with evidence of the connection between suicidality and the experience of distressing life events in Bangladesh (Rasheduzzaman et al., 2022), it is not difficult to assume that trauma may have a greater impact on suicidality in this context. Experience from clinical practices and anecdotal evidence also suggests the presence of trauma in inducing suicidal ideation and attempt in the Bangladesh context (Mamun & Griffiths, 2020). The association between a traumatic event and suicidal ideation in Bangladeshi individuals has been reported by Rahman et al. (2022). Kabir et al. (2019) demonstrated the presence of suicidal thoughts among individuals with trauma from the infamous Rana Plaza building collapse in Bangladesh.

Despite the wide acceptability of the connectivity between trauma and suicide, most theories of suicide fall short of explaining this relationship. The interpersonal theory of suicide (IPTS; Van Orden et al., 2010) introduces three concepts associated with suicide attempts that can be used to explain the connection between trauma and suicide. The first of the three concepts, *thwarted belongingness*, indicates a limited sense of belongingness with others, which is often caused by the known traumatic risk factors of suicide, namely, social isolation, family conflict, shame, or childhood abuse. As per the theory, the sense of thwarted belongingness, along with *perceived burdensomeness* (the second concept in IPTS), creates passive suicidal ideation in the person. With a prolonged experience of thwarted belongingness and perceived burdensomeness, the person moves gradually toward active suicide ideation. The third concept, that is, *capability for suicide,* suggests that the person must have the capacity to actually attempt suicide. It requires the person to overcome the fear of attempting suicide. Those with trauma often have repeated physically and psychologically painful experiences and exposure to dreadful events. The experience of trauma may be perceived as more painful or terrifying than the pain and fear associated with attempting suicide, thus helping the person move from ideation (Smith et al., 2016). In a Bangladeshi study, Arafat et al. (2022a) found higher perceived burdensomeness among females and higher thwarted belongingness among those with past suicide attempts.

A common feature among suicidal cases is their lack of coping resources. All suicidal cases demonstrate a severe level of distress and/or helplessness associated with their life circumstances, be it an external distressing event, personal psychological problem, internal existential crisis, or a combination of all of these. A person with access to well-developed coping strategies can handle these stressors appropriately. However, those with poor coping resources often experience trauma and helplessness. Repeated and persistent exposure to such distress and trauma can result in hopelessness, which is well-recognized as a key indicator of suicidal thoughts and behavior. Therefore, coping can be seen as a common link between suicide and trauma.

4 Coping and Trauma

Psychological trauma can be defined as an emotional response to dreadful life events (American Psychological Association, 2022). However, the experience of trauma is not limited to emotional responses; it is also closely associated with cognitive, behavioral, and physiological responses of the individual experiencing the traumatic events. Although closely connected, all exposure to traumatic events may not result in trauma for a person. A country-wide survey in Bangladesh indicated that 96% of the children had experienced at least one traumatic event, while the average score on the measure for posttraumatic stress disorder (PTSD) was below the cutoff value (Deeba & Rapee, 2015).

Due to the unusual and dreadful nature of the life events involved in trauma, it is generally associated with intense stress and taxes on the person's coping resources, which explains the individual variations of trauma experience even from exposure to the same dreadful life events. There is considerable research evidence indicating close ties between trauma and coping skills (Jenzer et al., 2020). When exposed to distressing events, individuals with poor coping skills are more likely to have trauma reactions. On the other hand, exposure to traumatic events has been found to cause poorer coping among individuals.

Coping helps protect a person from adverse internal emotional, cognitive, or physiological states generated from either internal or external sources. Researchers tried to categorize qualitative differences among the varied coping strategies used by human beings (Carver, 1997; Folkman & Lazarus, 1988). These different types are often broadly clustered under functional or dysfunctional coping approaches. Irrespective of the functionality, all types of coping are aimed at protecting the person's well-being from distress, or at an extreme level, from trauma.

Among all the species in the animal kingdom, humans have been the most powerful in terms of having control over their surroundings. This sense of agency can be the Achilles' heel for humankind. While enjoying the experiences of agency, we have very little preparation for coping with moments when our agency is lost. Dreadful incidents thus brought forth such moments where we find a lack of agency and feel threatened. Threat perception triggers survival instincts and arouses the sympathetic nervous system. This process alters the allocation of energy in different regions of the brain, resulting in increased activity in the subcortical brain (survival brain) while decreased activity in the cerebral cortex (thinking center). With the survival brain being in control, it initiates a series of bodily reactions, including rapid breathing to increase oxygen intake, faster heart beating to help circulate the oxygen to the mitochondrion throughout the body and increasing muscle tension to move fast. While our biology frantically tries to avert the threat, our mind goes blank due to reduced activities in the frontal cortex, resulting in helplessness and strengthening of the threat perception. This process of intense stress serves as the basis for trauma.

When a person has sufficient coping resources, he or she is less likely to feel threatened compared to one with insufficient resources in dreadful life circumstances (see Fig. 7.1). People with well-developed coping resources are, therefore, more likely to make a proper decision and to stay in control of their internal state and hence less likely to develop trauma.

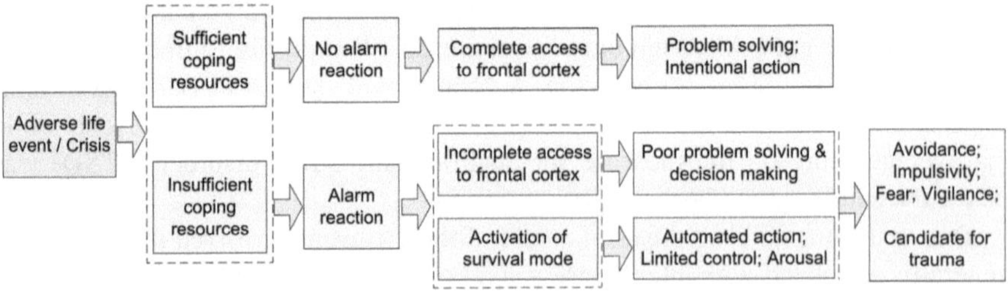

Fig. 7.1 Schematic diagram depicting the relation between adverse life experience, coping, and outcome

5 Triadic Relationship Between Trauma, Coping, and Suicide

Glennie (2010) nicely stated, "Coping skills are intentional responses to resolve stress that are distinct from involuntary reactions." Coping resources are known to have an important role in providing a reason for living, which is inversely related to suicidality (Yi et al., 2021). Several negative coping styles, such as suppression, denial, addiction, self-distraction, and behavioral disengagement, have been shown to be associated with suicidality (Josepho & Plutchik, 1994; Liang et al., 2020; Yi et al., 2021). Similar coping styles, such as disengagement and avoidant coping, have been found to be associated with trauma (Fortier et al., 2009; Sheerin et al., 2018). Coping resources often mediate the relationship between suicidality and traumatic experiences. Kılınç et al. (2022) demonstrated the mediating role of coping flexibility in the relationship between psychological maltreatment and death obsession during the COVID-19 pandemic. In another study, Whiteman et al. (2019) demonstrated the link between trauma, cognitive distortion, and suicidality. Apart from the direct effect of trauma on suicide ideation, they also found that trauma contributes to cognitive distortion, which in turn contributes to suicidal ideation (Whiteman et al., 2019).

Development of coping skills starts very early in childhood when an infant is required to develop skills to adapt to numerous challenges and the potential threat that he or she faces (Compas, 1987). Coping skills developed in childhood shape our ongoing coping and responses to our surroundings. Severely adverse experiences in childhood often leave the child with inadequate coping resources, the scar of trauma, and the possibility of experiencing future victimization and trauma (see Cloitre & Rosenberg, 2006). A history of childhood abuse has been found to result in coping difficulties such as emotional dysregulation, affective lability, and socially inappropriate expression of emotion (Shields & Cicchetti, 1998). Childhood sexual abuse has also been found to increase suicidality. Study findings suggest that one-third of the youth with experience of childhood sexual abuse attempt suicide, while approximately half experience suicidal ideation from the abuse (Plunkett et al., 2001). A case-control psychological autopsy study conducted in Bangladesh identified that sexual abuse was attributed to twelve suicides in females, and among these twelve females, more than 91% (n = 11) were adolescents (Arafat et al., 2021b). Studies also revealed that 40% of the suicide triggering life events were related to sexual and marital issues (Arafat & Khan, 2021). Childhood trauma has also been linked with suicide among prisoners (Navarro-Atienzar et al., 2019).

6 The Traumatic Impact of Suicide

There is a circular relationship between trauma and suicide. Similar to the impact of trauma in triggering suicide and suicidal thoughts, the impact of suicide is well-reported for its ability to trigger trauma reactions in others. Any form of death can be traumatic. However, exposure to death from suicide can be especially traumatic due to the often violent nature of the suicidal death (Spillane et al., 2018). The loss of family members or loved ones from suicide can also be traumatic. Exposure to suicide in the family can also initiate suicidal ideation among other members of the family (Pereira & Campos, 2022). A recent study on the university student population indicated that the history of suicide attempts in the family is a significant risk factor for both suicide ideation and suicide attempt in Bangladesh (Rasheduzzaman et al., 2022).

Research findings indicate the initiation of trauma reactions among mental health professionals who experience suicide in their clients (Castelli Dransart et al., 2014). The person attempting suicide can also experience trauma from the attempt (see Stanley et al., 2019). Suicidal behavior is considered a criminal offence in Bangladesh (Arafat, 2019). Therefore, surviving attempted suicide can cause additional stress to the person as well as the family members. Despite the gradual move toward individualism, the society and families in Bangladesh are still connected to the ideas of collectivism, where people are, to some extent, accountable to the larger system. This connection with the larger system (e.g., society, extended family) and stigmas ingrained in the system often put an added burden on the person and/or the family affected by suicide. It may be noted here that a high degree of stigma against suicidal individuals is observed in Bangladesh (Jahan et al., 2023).

7 Assessment of Trauma in Suicidality: Missing Links

The instruments used for assessing suicidal risk can be categorized into three groups. First, there are tools such as the Beck Hopelessness Scale (BHS; Beck & Steer, 1988), the Beck Depression Inventory-II (BDI-II; Beck et al., 1996), and the Patient Health Questionnaire (PHQ-9; Kroenke et al., 2001), which are used for assessing different psychological constructs and indirectly indicate suicide risk. The second category of tools includes instruments that assess suicidality directly by using items exclusively on suicide and death. These include the Suicidal Ideation

Questionnaire (SIQ; Reynolds, 1987) and Beck Scale for Suicide Ideation (BSS; Beck & Steer, 1993). Third, there are instruments that assess the risk of suicide through a combination of items assessing the risk factors and suicidality. These include the Tool for Assessment of Suicide Risk (TASR; Kutcher & Chehil, 2007) and the Suicide Risk Assessment Matrix (World Health Organization, 2009).

Assessment of depression and hopelessness is at the core of many instruments that assess suicide. However, the assessment of suicide seems to ignore the need for the inclusion of items on trauma. Only a few assessment tools, such as the Suicide Status Form (SSF; Jobes et al., 1997), came a little closer by including items about distress. Ignoring trauma in the assessment of suicide may have manyfold impacts. First, the sole assessment of suicide will provide only a partial conceptualization of the case, resulting in inadequate formulation and a subsequent narrow intervention plan. Second, ongoing trauma affects information processing and interaction of the person with the environment; if left unaccounted for, it has the potential to bring detrimental consequences to therapy. Third, addressing suicide without managing the trauma may generate only transient outcomes. As the vulnerability will still be there, the person may continue with repeated suicidal attempts, rendering unnecessary duplication of work. Finally, unmanaged trauma has a pervasive negative impact on the overall well-being of the person. Therefore, leaving the person with unmanaged trauma is morally and ethically unacceptable.

8 Trauma-Informed Suicide Prevention in Bangladesh

A thorough assessment of trauma, along with suicidality, is essential for the proper management of suicide cases. Additionally, working with suicidal cognition and behavior may increase the risk of re-traumatization if the service provider is unaware or ignorant about the ongoing or past trauma of the patient. Inscoe et al. (2022) provided a detailed qualitative analysis of trauma-informed youth suicide prevention intervention. They emphasized the importance of involving the caregiver in the intervention, providing psychoeducation, building therapeutic alliance (utilizing clinician authenticity, genuineness, and warmth), and the therapist being oriented about and being able to recognize trauma (Inscoe et al., 2022).

Ensuring trauma-informed suicide management in clinical practice poses some major challenges for Bangladesh. Becoming a trauma-informed therapist requires not only knowledge and awareness but more of mindset and preparation to become one. As suggested by the Substance Abuse and Mental Health Services Administration (2014), it requires active involvement of service providers in terms of realizing the widespread impact of trauma, recognizing signs of trauma, responding to trauma with the integration of knowledge and policies, and being focused on resisting retraumatization. Being a resource-constrained country, Bangladesh has an extremely high (92%) mental health treatment gap (World Health Organization, 2020). One of the prime reasons for this treatment gap is the limited availability of professionals. With extremely high patient loads in government hospitals, the average per-patient consultation time for a psychiatrist is generally less than 10 min. Although clinical psychologists generally maintain the standard of a 50-min consultation time, the waiting time to get an appointment is often too long. Therefore, limited access to qualified mental health professionals and getting sufficient time needed for intensive trauma-focused suicide management can be challenging in Bangladesh.

Suicide prevention helplines are doing a good job of providing support to individuals with crisis, trauma, and suicidal ideation in Bangladesh. Most notable among these is *Kan Pete Roi*, a volunteer-based nongovernment organization that provides telephone crisis support services. Trained volunteers provide a listening ear with basic psychological support to intervene in the immediate crisis that the callers present with. The government also has a generic 999 telephone-based service for all citizens, as well as a specific "women and children"-focused toll-free 109 telephone-based service, that addresses crisis and plays a significant role in preventing suicide in Bangladesh. Nonetheless, these telephone-based services with partially trained volunteers and staff are limited in dealing with and healing trauma.

Inclusion of a detailed orientation on trauma, as well as on suicide, needs to be incorporated into mental health professional training programs in Bangladesh. Training programs in clinical psychology, counseling psychology, and educational psychology have recently been seen to arrange sporadic orientation training on the assessment and management of suicide and trauma. However, the regularization of these trainings and organizing them as part of continuing professional development through professional associations would be of real value.

9 Coping Skills Enhancement in Curbing Suicidality

As mentioned earlier, research literature has demonstrated an inverse relation between suicidal ideation and use of positive coping skills, irrespective of these skills being therapist-taught or spontaneous self-guided strategies adopted by the individual (Gómez-Tabares et al., 2022; Mirkovic et al., 2015; Stanley et al., 2021). Enhancement of coping skills among the suicidal individuals has therefore been increasingly recognized as a key component in reducing suicidal behavior (see McManama O'Brien et al., 2021). Psychological therapies, especially the structured approaches (e.g., cognitive behavior therapy, dialectical behavior therapy), focus heavily on skill building of the suicidal individuals as a preventive strategy. Stanley et al. (2021) reported the effectiveness of distraction or positive activity-based coping (e.g., keeping busy, socializing, positive thinking, and doing something good for oneself) in lowering the intensity of suicidal thoughts. A recent meta-analysis by Darvishi et al. (2023) concluded that interventions using problem-solving skills effectively reduce suicide risk. Liang et al. (2020) suggested the use of adaptive coping skills, such as actively reducing stressors or the use of cognitive reframing, in preventing suicidal behavior among students. Through case-control psychological autopsy, Arafat et al. (2021b) reported the use of personal coping as a preventive component for suicide in Bangladesh.

10 Conclusion

Immediate adverse life events, trauma, and crises are closely associated with suicide and suicidal behavior in Bangladesh. Sadly, at the same time, informal social support is declining with urbanization and other transitions in society. Despite the lack of research evidence, it seems likely that the clinicians in Bangladesh will have to deal with an increasing number of cases with a dual presentation of suicide and trauma in the coming days. Dialogues around suicide and trauma are hugely important for ensuring trauma-informed suicide management. Participation of stakeholders from all spheres of society is warranted to ensure a holistic approach to reducing crisis-related suicides in the country. Although slow in growth, the increasing interest in research and availability of psychological therapies, as well as trauma-focused interventions, are welcoming signs for suicide prevention in Bangladesh.

References

Akbar, R., Arya, V., Conroy, E., Wilcox, H. C., & Page, A. (2023). Posttraumatic stress disorder and risk of suicidal behavior: A systematic review and meta-analysis. *Suicide and Life-threatening Behavior, 53*(1), 163–184. https://doi.org/10.1111/sltb.12931

American Psychological Association. (2022). *Trauma*. Retrieved October 01, 2022 from https://www.apa.org/topics/trauma

Angelakis, I., Gillespie, E. L., & Panagioti, M. (2019). Childhood maltreatment and adult suicidality: A comprehensive systematic review with meta-analysis. *Psychological Medicine, 49*(7), 1057–1078. https://doi.org/10.1017/S0033291718003823

Arafat, S. M. Y. (2019). Current challenges of suicide and future directions of management in Bangladesh: A systematic review. *Global Psychiatry, 2*(1), 09–20. https://doi.org/10.2478/gp-2019-0001

Arafat, S. M. Y., Hussain, F., Zaman, M. S., Tabassum, T., Islam, M. K., Shormi, F. R., Khan, A. R., Islam, M. R., Redwan, A. S. M., Giasuddin, N. A., Mubashir, A., & Khan, M. A. S. (2022a). Thwarted belongingness, perceived burdensomeness, and acquired capability for suicide among university students of Bangladesh: Scales validation and status assessment. *Frontiers in Psychiatry, 13*. https://doi.org/10.3389/fpsyt.2022.1025976

Arafat, S. M. Y., Khan, M. A. S., Knipe, D., & Khan, M. M. (2021a). Population attributable fractions of clinical and social risk factors for suicide in Bangladesh: Finding from a case–control psychological autopsy study. *Brain and Behavior, 11*(12), e2409. https://doi.org/10.1002/brb3.2409

Arafat, S. M. Y., & Khan, M. M. (2021). Sexual violence and suicide in Bangladesh. *Health Science Reports, 4*(2), e269. https://doi.org/10.1002/hsr2.269

Arafat, S. M. Y., Mohit, M. A., Mullick, M. S. I., Kabir, R., & Khan, M. M. (2021b). Risk factors for suicide in Bangladesh: Case–control psychological autopsy study. *BJPsych Open, 7*(1), e18. https://doi.org/10.1192/bjo.2020.152

Arafat, S. M. Y., & Saleem, T. (2025). Suicide in Bangladesh: An ecological systems analysis. *Brain and Behavior, 15*(1), e70233. https://doi.org/10.1002/brb3.70233

Arafat, S. M. Y., Saleem, T., Edwards, T. M., Ali, S. A.-e.-Z., & Khan, M. M. (2022b). Suicide prevention in Bangladesh: The role of family. *Brain and Behavior, 12*(5), e2562. https://doi.org/10.1002/brb3.2562

Beck, A. T., & Steer, R. A. (1988). *Beck hopelessness scale*. Psychological Corporation.

Beck, A. T., & Steer, R. A. (1993). *Beck scale for suicide ideation (BSS)*. Pearson.

Beck, A. T., Steer, R. A., & Brown, G. K. (1996). *Manual for the beck depression inventory-II*. Psychological Corporation.

Bhuiyan, A. K. M. I., Sakib, N., Pakpour, A. H., Griffiths, M. D., & Mamun, M. A. (2021). COVID-19-related suicides in Bangladesh due to lockdown and economic factors: Case study evidence from media reports. *International Journal of Mental Health and Addiction, 19*(6), 2110–2115. https://doi.org/10.1007/s11469-020-00307-y

Carver, C. S. (1997). You want to measure coping but your protocol' too long: Consider the brief cope. *International Journal of Behavioral Medicine, 4*(1), 92–100. https://doi.org/10.1207/s15327558ijbm0401_6

Castelli Dransart, D. A., Gutjahr, E., Gulfi, A., Kaufmann Didisheim, N., & Séguin, M. (2014). Patient suicide in institutions: Emotional responses and traumatic impact on Swiss mental health professionals. *Death Studies, 38*(5), 315–321. https://doi.org/10.1080/07481187.2013.766651

Centers for Disease Control and Prevention. (2019). *CERC: Psychology of a crisis*. US Department of Health Human Services.

Cloitre, M., & Rosenberg, A. (2006). Sexual revictimization: Risk factors and prevention. In V. C. Follette & J. I. Ruzek (Eds.), *Cognitive-behavioral therapies for trauma* (pp. 321–361). Guilford.

Compas, B. E. (1987). Coping with stress during childhood and adolescence. *Psychological Bulletin, 101*(3), 393–403. https://doi.org/10.1037/0033-2909.101.3.393

Darvishi, N., Farhadi, M., Azmi-Naei, B., & Poorolajal, J. (2023). The role of problem-solving skills in the prevention of suicidal behaviors: A systematic review and meta-analysis. *PLoS One, 18*(10), e0293620. https://doi.org/10.1371/journal.pone.0293620

Deeba, F., & Rapee, R. M. (2015). Prevalence of traumatic events and risk for psychological symptoms among community and at-risk children and adolescents from Bangladesh. *Child and Adolescent Mental Health, 20*(4), 218–224. https://doi.org/10.1111/camh.12093

Ell, K. (1996). Crisis theory and social work practice. In F. J. Turner (Ed.), *Social work treatment 4th Edition* (pp. 168–190). The Free Press.

Faruk, M. O., Awal, A., & Chowdhury, K. U. A. (2025). Factors contributing to the higher prevalence of suicide in Jhenaidah, Bangladesh: A qualitative exploration. *BMJ Open, 15*(6), e089985. https://doi.org/10.1136/bmjopen-2024-089985

Feroz, A., Islam, S. N., Reza, S., Rahman, A. M., Sen, J., Mowla, M., & Rahman, M. R. (2012). A community survey on the prevalence of suicidal attempts and deaths in a selected rural area of Bangladesh. *Journal of Medicine, 13*(1), 3–9. https://doi.org/10.3329/jom.v13i1.10042

Folkman, S., & Lazarus, R. S. (1988). *Ways of coping questionnaire: Research edition*. Consulting Psychologists Press.

Fortier, M. A., DiLillo, D., Messman-Moore, T. L., Peugh, J., DeNardi, K. A., & Gaffey, K. J. (2009). Severity of child sexual abuse and Revictimization: The mediating role of coping and trauma symptoms. *Psychology of Women Quarterly, 33*(3), 308–320. https://doi.org/10.1111/j.1471-6402.2009.01503.x

Galynker, I., Bloch-Elkouby, S., & Cohen, L. J. (2024). Suicide crisis syndrome: a specific diagnosis to aid suicide prevention. *World Psychiatry, 23*(3), 362–363. https://doi.org/10.1002/wps.21229

Glennie, E. J. (2010). Coping and resilience. In J. A. Rosen, E. J. Glennie, B. W. Dalton, J. M. Lennon, & R. N. Bozick (Eds.), *Noncognitive skills in the classroom: New perspectives on educational research* (pp. 169–194). RTI Press.

Gómez-Tabares, A. S., Marín, J. P. C., Vanegas, A. M., Martinez, D. A. L., & Gallego, E. M. M. (2022). The effect of coping strategies on the risk for suicidal ideation and behavior in adolescents. *Mediterranean Journal of Clinical Psychology, 10*(2). https://doi.org/10.13129/2282-1619/mjcp-3436

Gunnell, D., Platt, S., & Hawton, K. (2009). The economic crisis and suicide. *BMJ (Clinical research ed.), 338*, b1891. https://doi.org/10.1136/bmj.b1891

Inscoe, A. B., Donisch, K., Cheek, S., Stokes, C., Goldston, D. B., & Asarnow, J. R. (2022). Trauma-informed care for youth suicide prevention: A qualitative analysis of caregivers' perspectives. *Psychological Trauma: Theory, Research, Practice, and Policy, 14*, 653–660. https://doi.org/10.1037/tra0001054

Jahan, I., Sharif, A. B., & Hasan, A. B. M. N. (2023). Suicide stigma and suicide literacy among Bangladeshi young adults: A cross-sectional study [original research]. *Frontiers in Psychiatry, 14*. https://www.frontiersin.org/journals/psychiatry/articles/10.3389/fpsyt.2023.1160955

Jenzer, T., Meisel, S. N., Blayney, J. A., Colder, C. R., & Read, J. P. (2020). Reciprocal processes in trauma and coping: Bidirectional effects over a four-year period. *Psychological Trauma, 12*(2), 207–218. https://doi.org/10.1037/tra0000500

Jobes, D. A., Jacoby, A. M., Cimbolic, P., & Hustead, L. A. T. (1997). Assessment and treatment of suicidal clients in a university counseling center. *Journal of Counseling Psychology, 44*, 368–377. https://doi.org/10.1037/0022-0167.44.4.368

Josepho, S. A., & Plutchik, R. (1994). Stress, coping, and suicide risk in psychiatric inpatients. *Suicide and Life-threatening Behavior, 24*(1), 48–57. https://doi.org/10.1111/j.1943-278X.1994.tb00662.x

Kabir, H., Maple, M., Islam, M. S., & Usher, K. (2019). The current health and wellbeing of the survivors of the Rana plaza building collapse in Bangladesh: A qualitative study. *International Journal of Environmental Research and Public Health, 16*(13), 2342. https://www.mdpi.com/1660-4601/16/13/2342

Khan, A. R., Uddin, H., Shimul, A. K., & Billah, M. (2022). Coronavirus (COVID-19) crisis and suicide in Bangladesh: Some explanations through Durkheim's sociology of suicide. *Journal of Community Positive Practices, 3*, 3–17. https://doi.org/10.35782/JCPP.2022.3.01

Kılınç, M., Arslan, G., Çakar, F. S., & Yıldırım, M. (2022). Psychological maltreatment, coping flexibility, and death obsession during the COVID-19 pandemic: A multi-mediation analysis. *Current Psychology*. https://doi.org/10.1007/s12144-021-02576-9

Kroenke, K., Spitzer, R. L., & Williams, J. B. (2001). The PHQ-9: Validity of a brief depression severity measure. *Journal of General Internal Medicine, 16*(9), 606–613. https://doi.org/10.1046/j.1525-1497.2001.016009606.x

Kutcher, S., & Chehil, S. (2007). Putting it all together: The tool for assessment of suicide risk (TASR). In S. Kutcher & S. Chehil (Eds.), *Suicide risk management: A manual for health professionals*. Wiley-Blackwell.

LeBouthillier, D. M., McMillan, K. A., Thibodeau, M. A., & Asmundson, G. J. G. (2015). Types and number of traumas associated with suicidal ideation and suicide attempts in PTSD: Findings from a U.S. nationally representative sample. *Journal of Traumatic Stress, 28*(3), 183–190. https://doi.org/10.1002/jts.22010

Liang, J., Kõlves, K., Lew, B., de Leo, D., Yuan, L., Abu Talib, M., & Jia, C.-x. (2020). Coping strategies and suicidality: A cross-sectional study from China [original research]. *Frontiers in Psychiatry, 11*. https://doi.org/10.3389/fpsyt.2020.00129

Mamun, M. A. (2021). Suicide and suicidal behaviors in the context of COVID-19 pandemic in Bangladesh: A systematic review. *Psychology Research and Behavior Management, 14*, 695–704. https://doi.org/10.2147/prbm.s315760

Mamun, M. A., & Griffiths, M. D. (2020). PTSD-related suicide six years after the Rana plaza collapse in Bangladesh. *Psychiatry Research, 287*, 112645. https://doi.org/10.1016/j.psychres.2019.112645

McManama O'Brien, K. H., Almeida, J., View, L., Schofield, M., Hall, W., Aguinaldo, L., Ryan, C. A., & Maneta, E. (2021). A safety and coping planning intervention for suicidal adolescents in acute psychiatric care. *Cognitive and Behavioral Practice, 28*(1), 22–39. https://doi.org/10.1016/j.cbpra.2019.08.003

Melzer, L., Forkmann, T., & Teismann, T. (2024). Suicide crisis syndrome: A systematic review. *Suicide and Life-threatening Behavior, 54*(3), 556–574. https://doi.org/10.1111/sltb.13065

Mirkovic, B., Labelle, R., Guilé, J. M., Belloncle, V., Bodeau, N., Knafo, A., Condat, A., Bapt-Cazalets, N., Marguet, C., Breton, J. J., Cohen, D., & Gérardin, P. (2015). Coping skills among adolescent suicide attempters: Results of a multisite study. *Canadian Journal of Psychiatry, 60*(2 Suppl 1), S37–S45.

Mozumder, M. K., Jasmine, U. H., Haque, M. A., & Haque, S. (2023). Mental health and suicide risk among homosexual males in Bangladesh. *PLoS One, 18*(8), e0289597. https://doi.org/10.1371/journal.pone.0289597

Navarro-Atienzar, F., Zabala-Baños, C., & Ricarte-Trives, J. J. (2019). Childhood trauma as a risk factor for suicidal behaviour in prisons. *Rev Esp Sanid Penit, 21*(1), 42–51.

O'Connor, D. B., Green, J. A., Ferguson, E., O'Carroll, R. E., & O'Connor, R. C. (2018). Effects of childhood trauma on cortisol levels in suicide attempters and ideators. *Psychoneuroendocrinology, 88*, 9–16. https://doi.org/10.1016/j.psyneuen.2017.11.004

Pereira, A. M., & Campos, R. C. (2022). Exposure to suicide in the family and suicidal ideation in Portugal during the Covid-19 pandemic: The mediating role of unbearable psychache. *The British Journal of Clinical Psychology, 61*(3), 598–612. https://doi.org/10.1111/bjc.12325

Plunkett, A., O'Toole, B., Swanston, H., Oates, R. K., Shrimpton, S., & Parkinson, P. (2001). Suicide risk following child sexual abuse. *Ambulatory Pediatrics, 1*(5), 262–266. https://doi.org/10.1367/1539-4409(2001)001<0262:srfcsa>2.0.co;2

Rahman, M. E., Saiful Islam, M., Mamun, M. A., Moonajilin, M. S., & Yi, S. (2022). Prevalence and factors associated with suicidal ideation among university students in Bangladesh. *Archives of Suicide Research, 26*(2), 975–984. https://doi.org/10.1080/13811118.2020.1833800

Rasheduzzaman, M., al-Mamun, F., Hosen, I., Akter, T., Hossain, M., Griffiths, M. D., & Mamun, M. A. (2022). Suicidal behaviors among Bangladeshi university students: Prevalence and risk factors. *PLoS One, 17*(1), e0262006. https://doi.org/10.1371/journal.pone.0262006

Reffi, A. N., Kalmbach, D. A., Cheng, P., Moore, D. A., Jennings, M. B., Mahr, G. C., Seymour, G. M., Jankowiak, L., & Drake, C. L. (2025). Nightmares and insomnia within the acute aftermath of trauma prospectively predict suicidal ideation. *Journal of Clinical Sleep Medicine, 21*(9). https://doi.org/10.5664/jcsm.11744

Reynolds, W. M. (1987). *Suicidal ideation questionnaire (SIQ)*. Psychological Assessment Resources.

Reza, A. M. S., Feroz, A. H. M., Islam, S. M. N., Karim, M. N., Rabbani, M. G., Alam, M. S., Rahman, M. M., Rahman, M. R., Ahmed, H. U., Bhowmik, A. D., Khan, M. Z. R., Sarkar, M., Alam, M. T., & Uddin, M. M. J. (2013). Risk factors of suicide and Para suicide in rural Bangladesh. *Journal of Medicine, 14*(2). https://doi.org/10.3329/jom.v14i2.19653

Sheerin, C. M., Chowdhury, N., Lind, M. J., Kurtz, E. D., Rappaport, L. M., Berenz, E. C., Brown, R. C., Pickett, T., McDonald, S. D., Danielson, C. K., & Amstadter, A. B. (2018). Relation between coping and posttrauma cognitions on PTSD in a combat-trauma population. *Military Psychology, 30*(2), 98–107. https://doi.org/10.1080/08995605.2017.1420980

Shields, A., & Cicchetti, D. (1998). Reactive aggression among maltreated children: The contributions of attention and emotion dysregulation. *Journal of Clinical Child Psychology, 27*(4), 381–395. https://doi.org/10.1207/s15374424jccp2704_2

Smith, P. N., Kuhlman, S., Wolford-Clevenger, C., Faulk, R., D'Amato, D., & Granato, S. (2016). Interpersonal trauma, posttraumatic stress disorder symptoms, and the interpersonal theory of suicide in women seeking shelter from intimate partner violence. *Journal of Aggression, Maltreatment & Trauma, 25*(8), 812–830. https://doi.org/10.1080/10926771.2016.1214937

Spillane, A., Matvienko-Sikar, K., Larkin, C., Corcoran, P., & Arensman, E. (2018). What are the physical and psychological health effects of suicide bereavement on family members? An observational and interview mixed-methods study in Ireland. *BMJ Open, 8*(1), e019472. https://doi.org/10.1136/bmjopen-2017-019472

Stanley, B., Brodsky, B., & Monahan, M. (2023). Brief and ultra-brief suicide-specific interventions. *Focus, 21*(2), 129–136. https://doi.org/10.1176/appi.focus.20220083

Stanley, B., Martínez-Alés, G., Gratch, I., Rizk, M., Galfalvy, H., Choo, T.-H., & Mann, J. J. (2021). Coping strategies that reduce suicidal ideation: An ecological momentary assessment study. *Journal of Psychiatric Research, 133*, 32–37. https://doi.org/10.1016/j.jpsychires.2020.12.012

Stanley, I. H., Boffa, J. W., & Joiner, T. E. (2019). PTSD from a suicide attempt: Phenomenological and diagnostic considerations. *Psychiatry, 82*(1), 57–71. https://doi.org/10.1080/00332747.2018.1485373

Substance Abuse and Mental Health Services Administration. (2014). *SAMHSA'S concept of trauma and guidance for a traumainformed approach*. U.S. Department of Health and Human Services. Retrieved from https://store.samhsa.gov/sites/default/files/d7/priv/sma14-4884.pdf

Van Orden, K. A., Witte, T. K., Cukrowicz, K. C., Braithwaite, S. R., Selby, E. A., & Joiner, T. E., Jr. (2010). The interpersonal theory of suicide. *Psychological Review, 117*(2), 575–600. https://doi.org/10.1037/a0018697

Whiteman, S. E., Kramer, L. B., Petri, J. M., & Weathers, F. W. (2019). Trauma type and suicidal ideation: The mediating effect of cognitive distortions. *Traumatology, 25*(4), 262–268. https://doi.org/10.1037/trm0000192

World Health Organization. (2009). *HIV counselling handbook for the Asia-Pacific*. (9746851128). WHO Regional Office for South-East Asia Retrieved from https://apps.who.int/iris/handle/10665/205268

World Health Organization. (2020). *Bangladesh: WHO special initiative for mental health, situational assessment*. W. H. Organization https://www.who.int/docs/default-source/mental-health/special-initiative/who-special-initiative-country-report%2D%2D-bangladesh%2D%2D-2020.pdf?sfvrsn=c2122a0e_2

Yi, S., Chang, E. C., Chang, O. D., Seward, N. J., McAvoy, L. B., Krause, E. R., Schaffer, M. R., Novak, C. J., Ip, K., & Hirsch, J. K. (2021). Coping and suicide in college students. *Crisis, 42*(1), 5–12. https://doi.org/10.1027/0227-5910/a000662

Zakir, T., & Haque, M. (2024). The relationship between childhood maltreatment and suicidal ideation among adults. *Dhaka University Journal of Biological Sciences, 33*(1), 47–55. https://doi.org/10.3329/dujbs.v33i1.72479

Chapter 8
Suicide After an Immediate Negative Life Event: Protest, Defeat, Bargain, or Impulse?

S. M. Yasir Arafat, Rizwana Amin, and David Lester

1 Introduction

Those who die by suicide often have long-standing psychological or psychiatric problems, but suicide can also be triggered by a traumatic event in the person's life. Receiving a diagnosis of a serious, possibly terminal, illness can trigger suicidal behavior, as can a romantic break-up and other negative life events.

Suicidal behavior can be impulsive. For example, Simon et al. (2001) found that 24% of attempted suicides made their suicide attempt within 5 min of having suicidal ideation, and Deisenhammer et al. (2009) found that 48% of participants attempted 10 min or less after thinking about suicide. Cheah et al. (2008) reported the case of a young man who had embezzled some money and lost it gambling. He was crossing a bridge and, one-third of the way across, began to worry about his crime. At the top of the bridge (49 meters high), he decided to die by suicide and jumped. The planning process, therefore, took only a few seconds. As soon as he jumped, he regretted his decision, got into the pin-drop position (legs straight and toes pointed), and survived the jump (only three jumpers out of 32 had survived this jump in the past.)

S. M. Y. Arafat (✉)
Department of Psychiatry, Bangladesh Specialized Hospital, Dhaka, Bangladesh

Department of Public and Community Health, Faculty of Medicine and Health Sciences, Frontier University Garowe, Garowe, Somalia

R. Amin
Department of Psychology, Effat University Jeddah, Jeddah, Saudi Arabia

D. Lester
Stockton University, Galloway, NJ, USA

S. M. Y. Arafat (ed.), *Suicidal Behavior in Bangladesh*, Mental Health Systems and Policy in Low- and Middle-Income Countries,
https://doi.org/10.1007/978-981-95-8321-8_8

Suicide can be staged dramatically as a protest. Protesting tyranny has a long history, but modern protests began with that of Thich Quang Duc, a Buddhist monk who set fire to himself in South Vietnam on June 11, 1963, at the age of 66, to protest the persecution of Buddhists by the president, Ngo Dinh Diem. Another notable protest self-immolation was that of Norman Morrison, 31 years old, on November 2, 1965, outside the Pentagon office of Robert McNamara (Secretary of Defense) to protest the Vietnam War. Morrison took his 1-year-old daughter, Emily, with him, and gave her to a bystander (or set her down) before he set fire to himself. Jan Palach, a 20-year-old Czech student, set fire to himself in Prague on January 16, 1969, to protest the Soviet invasion of Czechoslovakia.

These self-immolations stirred the world but had no immediate impact. In contrast, the self-immolation of Mohamed Bouazizi on December 17, 2010, in Ben Arous, a town in Tunisia, to protest his harassment by the local government as he tried to support himself as a vendor on the streets, had a tremendous impact. Protests began within hours, and the president of Tunisia, Ben Ali, fled on January 14, 2011, the first victory of the *Arab Spring*, which led people in many Arab nations to rise up and attempt to overthrow their governments, some successfully.

This chapter presents five cases of this type of suicidal behavior that occurred in Bangladesh (Table 8.1).

Case 1

Gazi Anisur Rahman, aged 50, was a businessman (a contractor) who set himself on fire in front of the National Press Club in Dhaka and died as a result. Rahman was owed money from a large company that had refused to pay him.

Table 8.1 Description of cases

Event	Age of the person	Gender	Occupation	Life event	Summary
Case 1 (2022)	50 years	Male	Businessman	Failure to recover a loan	The person burnt himself in front of the National Press Club (NPC) in response to failed attempts at loan recovery.
Case 2 (2022)	35 years	Female	Housewife	Eviction from home	The lady set herself and her three children on fire in front of the NPC, protesting their eviction from their home.
Case 3 (2025)	23 years	Male	Garment worker	Failure in job permanence	The person took poison in response to failure to get a permanent job after 1 year of service.
Case 4 (2025)	25 years	Female		Disagree to marry by the lover	The lady attempted a hunger strike and said that she would attempt suicide if her boyfriend would not marry her.
Case 5 (2024)	15 years	Female	Student	Marriage	The adolescent girl took medication to avoid her marriage.

Case 2
Zunaid Khan, husband of Shirin, bought four khatas of land from Hannan Soud (a local leader of the Awami League) in Bhargaon area in 2015. Later, he built a two-story building on the land and started living there. A notice was sent to his family eight months later from Basic Bank's Karwan Bazar unit, urging them to leave the house as a bank loan taken remained unpaid.

Shirin (aged 35) disputed this with Hannan and, later, lodged a complaint with the Taltala police outpost. Shirin attempted to die by suicide by pouring kerosene over herself in front of the National Press Club, and on Saturday, she again attempted to die by suicide along with her three children. She survived, and Hannan was later jailed for cheating Shirin.

Case 3
Idris Ali (23), a worker in Gazipur, died by suicide by drinking toxic chemicals after posting on Facebook alleging irregularities against the factory authorities, police said. The incident occurred during the night shift at a ready-made garment factory, and the authorities declared a holiday at the factory after the suicide. Ali's employment had not been made permanent even after a year, and his superiors abused him verbally when he asked them about this. Ali posted about his intent to die by suicide and the reasons for his suicide on Facebook. After Ali's suicide, his co-workers accused their superiors of mental and physical torture.

Case 4
A 25-year-old unmarried female attempted a hunger strike and threatened suicide if her boyfriend would not marry her. She was in love with him, but her boyfriend had declined to marry her.

Case 5
A 15-year-old girl (a class 10 student of a local secondary school) in Brahmanpara, Comilla, attempted suicide by taking medicine to escape marriage. The teenager attempted suicide out of anger toward her family members for trying to force her into marriage with a young man who had recently returned from abroad. The girl consumed a large amount of montelukast, calcium, and metronidazole tablets in the house on a Wednesday evening. Her family took her to the local hospital, where she was treated.

2 Discussion

Suicide as a response to unexpected negative life circumstances is a complicated issue influenced by several social, psychological, and cultural factors (Rajkumar, 2025) and can be motivated by different factors. Acute stressors can lead to suicide impulsively and for a variety of psychological reasons (protest, bargaining, defeat, entrapment) (Macintyre et al., 2021; Dee et al., 2023). The urge to die by suicide often arises as a desperate response to feelings of helplessness in individuals who feel powerless, silenced, or constrained by social norms, cultural pressures, or systemic issues (Tapoi et al., 2024). The psychological processes involved include intense anger, moral outrage, and frustration, often paired with a sense of futility about changing their situation through traditional means.

2.1 *Protest Suicide*

In a social setting, suicide as a form of protest can signal perceived injustice and disagreement, holding both individual and collective importance (Ansloos & White, 2025; Rezvi et al., 2025). The desire for dramatic expression might be heightened by cultural factors such as honor-based codes or the stigmatization of victimhood. This act is often carefully planned and meant to send a strong message. Therefore, suicide is more than simple self-destruction. It acts as a form of communication aimed at drawing attention to injustice as well as personal suffering.

In Bangladesh, protest suicides reflect a unique sociocultural resonance. Social hierarchies, entrenched patriarchal norms, and limited avenues for redress can amplify individuals' feelings of powerlessness. Research indicates that suicidal behavior in Bangladesh may be a response to social oppression, familial pressures, and systemic injustice (Arafat et al., 2024). Economic hardship, political marginalization, and widespread social stigma, particularly stigma associated with gender and class, enhance the attractiveness of radical, symbolic protest. For women in arranged marriages, experiencing domestic violence, or facing restricted social mobility, may resort to protest suicides as a means of expressing their resistance (Arafat et al., 2021). Similarly, adolescents facing educational or occupational disparities may perceive suicide as the sole means to express their grievances (Tasfi & Mostofa, 2024). It is essential to consider communal and media factors in the analysis of suicide as a form of protest in Bangladesh. The performative dimensions of protest suicide can enhance social awareness, foster community solidarity, and stimulate policy discussions through the dissemination of specific instances (Arafat et al., 2025). Consequently, it is essential to implement culturally responsive prevention strategies, such as psychosocial support, grievance mechanisms, and mental health education for the broader community.

2.2 *Bargaining*

Suicide as a bargain is another psychological phenomenon where people use threats of self-destruction to influence others. Unlike protest, which focuses on voicing grievances or injustices, bargaining suicides are relational and instrumental, relying on the perceived power of self-destruction to elicit a response from someone other than the individual enacting self-harm (Syme, 2021). Research often describes bargaining suicides as situations in which people have conflicts or feel they cannot communicate their needs and, therefore, resort to suicide to manipulate others (Sikveland et al., 2022). Strong attachment needs, fear of abandonment, and the belief that self-destructive behavior will make the other individuals comply are the causes. These can be manipulative, with the performer using suicide threats to negotiate or blackmail (Marsh et al., 2022). The most prevalent tactics are hang-on strikes, verbal intimidation, or blatant plots to harm oneself, albeit the notion that the bargaining target would intervene or give in minimizes their significance.

Culture influences bargaining suicides in Bangladesh. Family-honor and gender-role norms may heighten the psychological stakes in interpersonal conflict (Kirmayer, 2022). The case study discussed earlier highlights the cultural expectations of love and marriage. In Bangladesh, where personal relationships may be perceived as social relativity and where familial authority can exert influence in personal matters, excessive behaviors, such as self-harm, might be regarded as the sole avenue for asserting power or agency in deeply intimate situations (Arafat et al., 2021). Women may face constraints in direct negotiations due to patriarchal views and the risk of social repercussions. Engaging in self-harm appears to be a method for influencing outcomes in relationships that are heavily governed by social norms. The action is centered on the individual, is socially constructed, and is influenced by cultural factors, involving personal attachment, perceived agency insufficiency, and sociocultural frameworks.

2.3 *Psychological Defeat/Being Trapped*

The despair and lack of purpose seen in suicides stemming from situations of defeat and entrapment reflect the profound experience of being entangled in an inescapable cycle of suffering (Pollak et al., 2021). Confronted with this type of situation, individuals experience a foreboding sense that all options for relief are unavailable and that there is no viable alternative to escape embarrassment, failure, or loss (Rasmussen et al., 2023). The psychological processes involved include emotions of hopelessness, mental shutdown, and a restricted outlook on the future. Emotional pain is characterized by significant intensity and is frequently persistent, often aggravated by perceived social limitations, including stigma, normative expectations, or unsupportive surroundings.

Unlike protests or negotiations, these suicides are mainly self-directed. The act is not meant to send a message or influence others, but instead represents the only feasible way to escape unbearable pain. Cultural and societal conventions, such as rigid family honor codes and widespread neglect of mental health, may exacerbate feelings of imprisonment (Shuvo et al., 2025). People who choose this path often carefully plan their death, showing a continuing and unavoidable sense of being trapped rather than acting impulsively or spontaneously.

2.4 Impulsive Suicide

Impulsive suicides occur suddenly without planning and are mainly driven by intense emotional distress or provocation (Beach et al., 2022). The decision to act may come from a brief moment of strong psychological pain triggered by personal loss, conflict, or humiliation. Poor emotion regulation, reduced inhibitory control, and hyper-arousal are cognitive and neurobiological factors that have been shown to worsen the shift from distress to suicidal behavior (Rasmussen et al., 2025). Unlike protest or negotiating suicides, impulsive suicides typically lack symbolic or relational motives. There is no goal to send a message or to bargain, but rather a reaction to the situation and an inability to cope. The availability of quick, lethal methods is an environmental factor that greatly influences how quickly the act is carried out (Arafat et al., 2021). Vulnerability may also increase due to cultural factors such as social restraint, limited emotional expression, or poor crisis support.

Interventions to reduce risk in this pathway focus on quickly decreasing risk through means restriction, improving coping skills, and enhancing crisis response services (Arafat, 2024). Overall, these pathways show the diversity of suicidal behavior after a traumatic life event. Even though they all result in self-harm, the causes, mental processes, and social contexts are quite different. Understanding these differences can help researchers and clinicians better understand suicidal behavior and develop culturally sensitive treatment and risk assessment for people facing psychological crises.

3 Conclusion

Suicidal behavior subsequent to an immediate negative life event should be comprehensively understood as a series of pathways rather than a singular procedure, either as a protest against injustice, a means to effect change, an escape from confinement, or an impulsive act driven by intense emotions. All four routes are evident in Bangladesh, shaped by the cultural and social realities of this Asian nation. The key lesson is that these suicides typically occur within minutes or hours, but never over months or years. In other words, prevention must be implemented promptly post-conflict by restricting access to lethal resources and providing viable support avenues. By seeing suicide as both an individual and as a societal indication, and by redirecting attention towards life-saving measures and the cultivation of compassionate, responsive communities, Bangladesh can implement transformative life-saving policies.

References

Ansloos, J. P., & White, J. H. (2025). Critical suicide notes: On witnessing and Prefigurative politics. *Social Sciences, 14*(3), 140. https://doi.org/10.3390/socsci14030140

Arafat, S. Y., Kar, S. K., & Rezaeian, M. (2025). War crisis and protest suicide. In *Ecological and social determinants of suicidal behavior* (pp. 205–212). Springer Nature Singapore. https://doi.org/10.1007/978-981-96-4028-7_11

Arafat, S. Y., Kar, S. K., Parvin, S., & Kabir, R. (2024). Protest suicide in South Asia: Cases and literature review. *South East Asian Journal of Suicide Prevention, 1*(1).

Arafat, S. Y. (2024). Suicidal behavior and suicide prevention in Bangladesh. In *Mental health in Bangladesh: From bench to community* (pp. 185–196). Springer Nature Singapore. https://doi.org/10.1007/978-981-97-0610-5_11

Arafat, S. M. Y., Mohit, M. A., Mullick, M. S. I., Kabir, R., & Khan, M. M. (2021). Risk factors for suicide in Bangladesh: Case–control psychological autopsy study. *BJPsych Open, 7*(1), e18. https://doi.org/10.1192/bjo.2020.152

Beach, V. L., Gissandaner, T. D., & Schmidt, A. T. (2022). The UPPS model of impulsivity and suicide: A systematic literature review. *Archives of Suicide Research, 26*(3), 985–1006. https://doi.org/10.1080/13811118.2021.1892002

Case 1. (2022). *Businessman who set himself on fire in front of press club dies, Prothomalo.* Prothomalo. Available at: Accessed July 9, 2023, from https://en.prothomalo.com/bangladesh/businessman-who-set-himself-on-fire-in-front-of-press-club-dies

Case 2. (2022). *Woman's bid to commit suicide at Press Club: AL leader sent to jail.* Daily Observer. Accessed July 9, 2023, from https://observerbd.com/news.php?id=390631

Case 3. (2025). *Worker 'commits suicide' in factory over Facebook post in Gazipur, holiday declared.* Prothom Alo. Accessed July 9, 2023, from https://www.prothomalo.com/bangladesh/district/0x6etr5mo9

Case 4. (2025). *I will commit suicide if Mamun doesn't marry me'.* Dhaka Post. Accessed July 9, 2023, from https://www.dhakapost.com/country/347982

Case 5. (2024). *Teenage girl attempts suicide to escape marriage.* Kalbela. Accessed July 9, 2023, from https://www.kalbela.com/country-news/129325

Cheah, D., Schmitt, G., & Pridmore, S. (2008). Suicide, misappropriation and impulsivity. *Australian & New Zealand Journal of Psychiatry, 42*, 544–546. https://doi.org/10.1080/00048670802050611

Dee, G., Ryznar, R., & Dee, C. (2023). Epigenetic changes associated with different types of stressors and suicide. *Cells, 12*(9), 1258. https://doi.org/10.3390/cells12091258

Deisenhammer, E. A., Ing, C. M., Strauss, R., Kemmler, G., Hinterhuber, H., & Weiss, E. M. (2009). The duration of the suicidal process: How much time is left for intervention between consideration and accomplishment of a suicide attempt? *The Journal of Clinical Psychiatry, 70*(1), 19–24.

Kirmayer, L. J. (2022). Suicide in cultural context: An ecosocial approach. *Transcultural Psychiatry, 59*(1), 3–12. https://doi.org/10.1177/13634615221076424

Macintyre, V. G., Mansell, W., Pratt, D., & Tai, S. J. (2021). The psychological pathway to suicide attempts: A strategy of control without awareness. *Frontiers in Psychology, 12*, 588683. https://doi.org/10.3389/fpsyg.2021.588683

Marsh, I., Winter, R., & Marzano, L. (2022). Representing suicide: Giving voice to a desire to die? *Health, 26*(1), 10–26. https://doi.org/10.1177/13634593211046843

Pollak, O. H., Guzmán, E. M., Shin, K. E., & Cha, C. B. (2021). Defeat, entrapment, and positive future thinking: Examining key theoretical predictors of suicidal ideation among adolescents. *Frontiers in Psychology, 12*, 590388. https://doi.org/10.3389/fpsyg.2021.590388

Rajkumar, R. P. (2025). Theoretical models of suicide. In *Ecological and social determinants of suicidal behavior* (pp. 1–46). Springer Nature Singapore. https://doi.org/10.1007/978-981-96-4028-7_1

Rasmussen, S., Cramer, R. J., Nascimbene, L., Robertson, R. A., Cacace, S., & Bowling, J. (2023). A qualitative assessment and short-term mediation analysis of defeat, entrapment, and suicide. *Suicide and Life-threatening Behavior, 53*(5), 880–892. https://doi.org/10.1111/sltb.12990

Rasmussen, S., Martin, B., & Cramer, R. J. (2025). Multidimensional impulsivity and suicidal behaviour: A partial test of the integrated motivational-volitional (IMV) model of suicide. *Archives of Suicide Research, 29*(1), 26–44. https://doi.org/10.1080/13811118.2024.2322118

Rezvi, M. R., Hasan, M. A., Islam, Z., & Ahmmed, M. K. (2025). Mental health impacts on protestors and victims' families of the July Movement-2024 in Bangladesh. *Mental Health: Global Challenges Journal, 8*(1), 102–111. https://doi.org/10.56508/mhgcj.v8i1.243

Shuvo, T. A., Hossain, K., & Dey, D. R. (2025). Suicide attempts in Bangladesh: Prevalence, trends, and disparities. *Journal of Medicine, Surgery and Public Health, 5*, 100170. https://doi.org/10.1016/j.glmedi.2024.100170

Syme, K. (2021). Bargaining model of suicidal behavior. In *Encyclopedia of evolutionary psychological science* (pp. 512–514). Springer International Publishing. https://doi.org/10.1007/978-3-319-19650-3_3839

Sikveland, R. O., Kevoe-Feldman, H., & Stokoe, E. (2022). *Crisis talk: Negotiating with individuals in crisis*. Routledge.

Simon, O. R., Swann, A. C., Powell, K. E., Potter, L. B., Kresnow, M. J., & O'Carroll, P. W. (2001). Characteristics of impulsive suicide attempts and attempters. *Suicide & Life-Threatening Behavior, 31*(Supplement 1), 49–59. https://doi.org/10.1521/suli.32.1.5.49.24212

Tapoi, C., Chancel, R., Baltzis, S., Cikrikcili, U., Cenci, D., & Castroman, J. L. (2024). Suicide across time and cultures: From a philosophical debate to network analysis. *European Psychiatry, 67*(S1), S779–S780. https://doi.org/10.1192/j.eurpsy.2024.1623

Tasfi, J. T., & Mostofa, S. M. (2024). Understanding complex causes of suicidal behaviour among graduates in Bangladesh. *BMC Public Health, 24*(1), 560. https://doi.org/10.1186/s12889-024-17989-x

Chapter 9
Non-suicidal Self-Injury in Bangladesh

S. M. Yasir Arafat

1 Introduction

Self-harm/self-injury is a hidden public health problem across the world. It is known in various names like 'non-suicidal self-injury (NSSI)', 'deliberate self-harm', 'self-harm', 'self-injurious behaviour' and 'non-suicidal self-injurious behaviour'. It is different from suicidal behaviour based on the intent before the attempt. In an NSSI attempt, there will not be any intent of dying by suicide. However, sometimes it is difficult to determine the intent due to the emotional status of the mind before an attempt. Additionally, a non-suicidal attempt may be fatal due to the consequences and unavailability of support. In contrast, a suicide attempt may be non-fatal due to several reasons, such as a change of mind during the attempt, abortive measures by friends and family members, adequate support after the attempt, or mechanical failure. NSSI is an important predictor of future suicide (Lowry et al., 2023). Although it has been noticed as distress behaviour for a long time, it has been considered a separate entity from suicidal behaviour since the early 2000s (Denton & Álvarez, 2024). I consider the definition of NSSI as 'deliberate self-inflicted destruction of body tissue that results in immediate damage, for purposes not culturally sanctioned and without suicidal intent' (Moloney et al., 2024). It is commonly prevalent in adolescents. One recent meta-analysis found the prevalence among 10–19 years of age was 17.7% (Moloney et al., 2024), while another meta-analysis of community-based studies found the rate ranged from 11.5% to 33.8% (Gillies et al., 2018). Another meta-analysis of studies among persons who did not attend for clinical services found the prevalence among adolescents 22% (Xiao et al., 2022).

S. M. Y. Arafat (✉)
Department of Psychiatry, Bangladesh Specialized Hospital, Dhaka, Bangladesh

Faculty of Medicine and Health Sciences, Department of Public and Community Health, Frontier University Garowe, Garowe, Somalia

S. M. Y. Arafat (ed.), *Suicidal Behavior in Bangladesh*, Mental Health Systems and Policy in Low- and Middle-Income Countries,
https://doi.org/10.1007/978-981-95-8321-8_9

South Asia is a suicide-dense region that caters to about one-fourth of the global population, where about 30% of global suicides happen (Arafat et al., 2025a). As an emerging entity, there is a limited number of articles in the region that determine various aspects of NSSI. One systematic review found the prevalence among the non-clinical population ranged between 21% and 33% in lifetime and 3.2 and 44.8% in a year, where it was between 2% and 27% in lifetime and 5% and 16.4% in a year, respectively, among the clinical population (Haregu et al., 2023). The reported rate denotes high variations that could be due to variations in methods of measuring, definition of self-harm, study samples, and time of the study conditions. Considering the socio-demography, NSSI is more common in females than males, and it is noted more among persons aged 14–35 years (Moloney et al., 2024; Haregu et al., 2023; Fernandez et al., 2024). While considering the methods, self-cutting, drug/medication-overdose, poisoning, head banging, and self-biting are noted as the common methods of NSSI in the region (Haregu et al., 2023). Among the various risk factors are individual factors such as emotional dysregulation, female sex and psychiatric disorders and environmental factors such as childhood trauma, familial disharmony and academic stress (Fernandez et al., 2024).

Bangladesh is one of the leading (8th) densely populated countries in the world with about 170 million population and lower-middle income background (Arafat et al., 2025b). Here, suicidality and NSSI are under-prioritized public health issues, like in other low- and middle-income countries (LMICs). Suicide attempt is a criminal offense according to the legal structure, which results in an enduring stigma and cultural prohibitions in disclosing NSSI and suicidal behaviour (both fatal and non-fatal) (Arafat, 2026). While considering suicide and suicidal behaviour, there is an increased trend of research articles since 2020 (Uddin & Arafat, 2026). Nevertheless, there are various challenges, such as lack of suicide data, as we do not know the rate of suicidal thoughts, plans and attempts among the general population (Arafat & Khan, 2024; Arafat, 2024a). In addition to that, little is known about the epidemiology, methods and mental illness among persons with NSSI, even though it is a predictor of future suicide death (Lowry et al., 2023). As suicide attempt is a criminal offense and there is low suicide literacy, NSSI attempts have also been stigmatised in Bangladesh, where there is neglect for health-seeking for it (Arafat, 2025). One recent narrative review was found that assessed ten published articles on NSSI in Bangladesh (Arafat et al., 2025b). This chapter aims to delve into NSSI in Bangladesh as a research as well as a clinical entity, focusing on epidemiology, methods and psychiatric morbidity, which is supposed to help the formulation of a national suicide prevention strategy in the country. I consider the recent narrative review as a baseline paper while organizing the contents. Additionally, I update the recent changes in this chapter.

2 Non-suicidal Self-Injury in Bangladesh

2.1 Available Studies

As per the methodology of the review, ten papers were identified after an extensive search in PubMed, Scopus, Google, Google Scholar, and BanglaJOL with search terms (for the detailed methodology, please check Arafat et al., 2025b). Among the 10 papers, nine papers have been published, and one was available as a preprint (Arafat et al., 2024; Bhattacharjee et al., 2023; Chowdhury et al., 2013; Fariduzzaman et al., 2025; Hussain et al., 2008; Motin et al., 2020; Mozumder, 2024; Mozumder et al., 2023; Mullick et al., 1994; Uddin et al., 2019) (Table 9.1). I included three additional papers (Imam & Biswas, 2023; Shimul et al., 2025; Haque, 2023) for this chapter (Table 9.1). I tried to include all the papers on it. However, based on the available mental health journals, their publication history, and indexing pattern, the chapter may exclude some papers (Arafat, 2024b). A similar challenge was also acknowledged in a recent review (Arafat et al., 2025b). The earliest identified research was published in 1984 (Mullick et al., 1994), and the latest paper was published in 2025 (Shimul et al., 2025). The sample size of the studies ranged from 51 to 480. Nine studies were conducted among clinical populations, that is persons with self-harm attended/hospitalized clinical services, two studies were conducted among sexual minorities (lesbian, gay, bisexual, and transsexual) populations, and one study was conducted among healthy university students (Table 9.1). Twelve studies were cross-sectional in design, and the remaining one study was case-control in nature (Motin et al., 2020). Only five studies included respondents with only NSSI without suicidal intent, while others did not mention any clear demarcation. Among the thirteen studies, five were conducted in Dhaka, two studies were conducted in multiple districts, two studies in Sylhet, and one study each was conducted in Rajshahi, Chottogram, Jamalpur, and Rangpur (Table 9.1).

2.2 Prevalence of NSSI in Bangladesh

The prevalence among community populations has not been determined yet. Only two studies assessed the rate in a specific population, that is, among university students (Fariduzzama et al., 2025) and the sexual minority group (gay) (Mozumdar et al., 2023). The lifetime prevalence of NSSI in Bangladesh ranged from 17% to 40.2%. This inadequate estimate indicates lack of proper academic attention, covert nature of the problem, and lack of awareness about NSSI.

Table 9.1 Research on NSSI in Bangladesh (Adapted from Arafat et al., 2025b)

Study	Sample characteristics	Data collection year	Domain	Intent	Population	Study place	Summary
Arafat et al. (2024)	$N = 100$, $M = 38$, mean age- 23.1 (±7.7), range 14–50 years	2022–2023	Mental illness, and life event	Mixed with suicidal intent	Patients attended for clinical services	Dhaka	The majority of the participants were females and unmarried. The prevalence of mental illness was 71%, and negative life events was 52% (48 h). Depression and borderline personality disorder (BPD) were the prominent disorders, and familial discord was the prominent factor.
Bhattacharjee et al. (2023)	$N = 100$, $M = 43$, mean age 23.6, range 14–65 years	2017	Psychosocial factors	Mixed with suicidal intent	Patients attended for clinical services	Sylhet	It measured the psychosocial factors of self-poisoning among patients admitted in hospital. The majority of the patients were unmarried, and females living in low socioeconomic conditions. The prevalence of mental illness was 30%. Depression was the most common diagnosis, and familial disharmony and relationship problems were the common psychosocial issues.
Chowdhury et al. (2013)	$N = 100$ $M = 94$, age 24–42 years	2009	Deliberate self-harm (DSH) among substance users	Non-suicidal self-injury (NSSI)	Patients attended for clinical services	Dhaka	It measured the methods of NSSI among patients with substance use disorder. Self-cutting (39%) was the most noted method.
Fariduzzaman et al. (2025)	$N = 200$ $M = 65.5\%$	2020	NSSI among university students	NSSI	University students	Dhaka	The prevalence of NSSI was 17%, which was fourfold higher among females.

Hussain et al. (2008)	$N = 66$ $M = 42.4\%$	2006	DSH in clinical patients	Mixed with suicidal intent	Patients attended for clinical services	Rajshahi	The majority of the participants were females. Poisoning and overdose were the most common methods (90%), and relationship problems (55%) and premarital affair rejection were the prominent risk factors.
Motin et al. (2020)	$N = 276$, 138 patients with self-harm mean age- 21.9 (±4.6), range 18-40 years	2016–2018	Personality disorder in DSH	NSSI	Patients attended for clinical services	Sylhet	The rate of personality disorders among participants with DSH was higher among the patient group compared to the control group (37.7 vs 11.6%). BPD was the most common disorder (18.8%).
Mozumder et al. (2024)	$N = 383$	2017	Self-harm among the LGBT community	NSSI	Sexual minorities	4 districts	NSSI was found more among lesbians.
Mozumder et al. (2023)	$N = 102$		Self-harm among gay	NSSI	Sexual minorities	Dhaka	It determined NSSI among gay populations. The prevalence of NSSI was 40.2%.
Mullick et al. (1994)	$N = 100$ mean age- 24.3 (±8.5), range 16–52 years	1992	Depression in DSH	Mixed with suicidal intent	Patients attended for clinical services	Dhaka	It measured depressive disorders in DSH among patients admitted at hospital. The rate of major depressive disorder (MDD) was 38%. Previous attempts and high suicidal intent were more common among persons with MDD.

(continued)

Table 9.1 (continued)

Study	Sample characteristics	Data collection year	Domain	Intent	Population	Study place	Summary
Uddin et al. (2019)	$N = 51$, $M = 5.9\%$	2017–2018	sociodemographic profile and risk factors	Mixed with suicidal intent	Patients attended for clinical services	Chittagong	The majority of the patients were females, under the age of 20 years, and of poor socioeconomic status. Sedative overdose was the commonest method (53%). It found that the relationship problems were the major factor, and 45% had mental illness, where depression (23.5%) and BPD (11.6%) were the leading diagnoses.
Imam and Biswas (2023)	$N = 100$, $M = 39$	2013–2014	Prevalence of DSH among persons with mental illness		Psychiatric patients	Jamalpur	The prevalence of DSH among psychiatric patients was 46%. It was more common among patients with depression.
Shimul et al. (2025)	480 mothers	2024	awareness about children's self-harm	NSSI	Mothers	Multiple regions	Awareness was higher in urban areas (30 vs 23.3%). Cutting and hitting were the common methods in both urban and rural areas. Emotional distress, academic pressures, and social media were the prominent triggers in urban areas, whereas family-related stressors were common in rural areas.
Haque (2023)	116	2010–2011	Physical morbidity		Patients with self-harm	Rangpur	The prevalence of general medical conditions among persons with DSH was 13%.

2.3 Methods of NSSI in Bangladesh

Methods of NSSI widely varied based on the intent of attempt and study populations. One study assessing the methods of NSSI among persons with substance abuse undergoing treatment (Bhattacharjee et al., 2023). It found that self-cutting (39%) and burning (26%) are prominent methods. It is important to consider that 94% of the participants were male, and they have additional substance use disorders. Other studies with undifferentiated intent and mixed sample revealed drug (medication) overdose, poisoning, and hanging as important methods (Arafat et al., 2024; Bhattacharjee et al., 2023; Hussain et al., 2008; Uddin et al., 2019).

2.4 Associated Factors

Risk factors are poorly identified for NSSI in Bangladesh. Like the suicidal behaviour, emotional and social factors are prominent issues (Arafat et al., 2025b). Family disharmony, marital conflict, premarital love relationship, extramarital love/sexual relationships, and negative life events were the prominent psychosocial associated factors (Arafat et al., 2024; Bhattacharjee et al., 2023; Hussain et al., 2008; Uddin et al., 2019). Mental illness is an important factor for NSSI. The prevalence of mental illness was 71% among patients with self-harm irrespective of suicidal intent (Arafat et al., 2024). Other studies found different rates, that is, 45% (Uddin et al., 2019) and 30% (Bhattacharjee et al., 2023). All the studies had participants from the clinical population with mixed intent. Therefore, I did not find any study assessing the psychiatric burden among NSSI in Bangladesh. It may be due to the evolving nature of the concept and lack of academic attention. Among the diagnoses, borderline personality disorder (BPD) (30%) was the commonest diagnosis, followed by depression (Arafat et al., 2024). One study found the prevalence of major depressive episodes was 38% among hospitalized patients with self-harm (Mullick et al., 1994). It also noted association with the severity of depression and suicidal intent. All these articles had respondents with mixed intent, that is, prevalence among self-harm without suicidal intent has not been identified.

2.5 Awareness of NSSI

As previously mentioned, suicidal behaviour and NSSI are covert issues in Bangladesh due to the enduring stigma, low suicide literacy, and lack of awareness. It receives academic attention. One study assessed the awareness of mothers about self-harm of children with a comparison between rural and urban areas (Shimul et al., 2025). It found that the awareness among mothers about self-harm among child(ren) was significantly higher in urban (30 vs. 23.3%) than rural areas. Mothers identified that cutting and hitting were the common methods in both urban and rural areas. While considering the associated factors, mothers noted that emotional distress, academic pressures, and social media were the prominent triggers in urban areas, whereas family-related stressors were common in rural areas.

3 Potential Challenges

3.1 Lack of Research

There is a limited number of studies on NSSI in Bangladesh. I found only five studies with participants who had no suicidal intent during self-harm. Almost all the studies followed a cross-sectional design, the majority of the studies were conducted in Dhaka, and the sample sizes were relatively small and among clinical populations. This can be due to the evolving nature of NSSI, lack of culturally validated measuring tools, lack of academic attention, and enduring high stigma.

3.2 Unmeasured Burden

The burden of NSSI among the community population has not been measured yet in Bangladesh. Two studies with specific groups of populations found a wide range of prevalence (17–40.2%). No nation-wide study among the general population has been identified.

3.3 Unmeasured Mental Health Burden

The mental health burden among persons with NSSI has not been revealed yet. The available studies measured the rates among participants with/without suicidal intent.

4 Ways Ahead

Based on the available evidence and identified challenges, Bangladesh urgently needs academic and public health attention and mental health service readiness for NSSI. Academic attention would foster augmented research and prioritize the areas aligning with the other mental health priorities. Validation of measuring instruments in Bangla and development of culturally tailored instruments would foster research on NSSI. Nation-wide studies among the general population are warranted to measure the country burden as well as the mental health burden. Longitudinal studies are warranted to identify the culturally tailored methods, potentially risk and culture driven resilience factors which are important for prevention.

5 Conclusions

Based on the available evidence, it is found that NSSI is a significant burden; however, under-researched and under-acknowledged public health, mental health, as well as research entity in Bangladesh. This chapter discussed the extent of studies published on NSSI in Bangladesh, the socio-demographic characteristics, and epidemiology of NSSI in the country. The lifetime prevalence is 17–40.2%, self-cutting is the commonest method, relationship problems with family members are associated with attempts, and psychiatric disorders are associated with NSSI. However, it is important to consider that the findings are obtained from potentially low-quality data irrespective of the intent of suicide. Further nationwide community-based studies are necessary to measure the problem and to consider preventive measures.

References

Arafat, S. M. Y. (2024a). Suicidal behavior and suicide prevention in Bangladesh. In S. M. Y. Arafat (Ed.), *Mental health in Bangladesh*. Springer. https://doi.org/10.1007/978-981-97-0610-5_11

Arafat, S. M. Y. (2024b). Psychiatric education and research system in Bangladesh. In S. M. Y. Arafat (Ed.), *Mental health in Bangladesh*. Springer. https://doi.org/10.1007/978-981-97-0610-5_12

Arafat, S. M. Y. (2025). Suicide prevention in Bangladesh: The role of police. *The Lancet. Psychiatry, 12*(3), 173. https://doi.org/10.1016/S2215-0366(24)00443-7

Arafat, S. M. Y. (2026). Law and suicide prevention in Bangladesh. In S. M. Y. Arafat (Ed.), *Suicidal behavior in Bangladesh*. Springer. https://doi.org/10.1007/978-981-95-8321-8_10

Arafat, S. M. Y., & Khan, A. R. (2024). Suicidal behavior in Bangladesh. In S. M. Y. Arafat, M. Rezaeian, & M. M. Khan (Eds.), *Suicidal behavior in muslim majority countries*. Springer. https://doi.org/10.1007/978-981-97-2519-9_4

Arafat, S. M. Y., Shormi, F. R., & Kibria, M. G. (2024). Psychiatric disorder and life-event in self harm: A cross-sectional study among clinical population in Bangladesh. *Heliyon, 10*(19), e38627. https://doi.org/10.1016/j.heliyon.2024.e38627

Arafat, S. M. Y., Rajkumar, R. P., & Kar, S. K. (2025a). *Trend of suicide research in South Asia: A bibliometric analysis of the last three decades*. Omega, 302228251323991. Advance online publication. https://doi.org/10.1177/00302228251323991.

Arafat, S. M. Y., Mali, B., & Mazumder, A. H. (2025b). Nonsuicidal self-injury in Bangladesh: A narrative review. *Health Science Reports, 8*(5), e70790. https://doi.org/10.1002/hsr2.70790

Bhattacharjee, B., Roy, S., Alam, M. M. J., Royle, R. K. S., Paul, S., Islam, M. S., Bari, M. S., & Chowdhury, F. R. (2023). Psychosocial factors behind deliberate self-poisoning in a tertiary care hospital of Bangladesh: A cross-sectional study. *Cureus, 15*(6), e39893. https://doi.org/10.7759/cureus.39893

Chowdhury, S. H., Rahman, M. S., Islam, M. A., Tabassum, R., Kamal, A. H. M. K. M., Al-Azad, M. A. S., & Islam, M. M. (2013). Deliberate self-harm in substance use disorder patients-a study at tertiary level hospitals in Bangladesh. *Journal of Armed Forces Medical College, Bangladesh, 9*(1), 63–74.

Denton, E. G., & Álvarez, K. (2024). The global prevalence of nonsuicidal self-injury among adolescents. *JAMA Network Open, 7*(6), e2415406. https://doi.org/10.1001/jamanetworkopen.2024.15406

Fariduzzaman, A. M., Al Azdi, Z., Kushal, S. A., Amin, Y. M., Roy, K., Datta, J., et al. (2025). Prevalence and pattern of self-harm among university students in Dhaka, Bangladesh. *Health Science Reports, 8*, e70911. https://doi.org/10.1002/hsr2.70911

Fernandez, J. A., Jaladin, R. A. M., & Lau, P. L. (2024). Nonsuicidal self-injury in Southeast Asia: A systematic literature review. *Millennial Asia, 15*(1), 160–183. https://doi.org/10.1177/09763996221095146

Gillies, D., Christou, M. A., Dixon, A. C., Featherston, O. J., Rapti, I., Garcia-Anguita, A., Villasis-Keever, M., Reebye, P., Christou, E., Al Kabir, N., & Christou, P. A. (2018). Prevalence and characteristics of self-harm in adolescents: Meta-analyses of community-based studies 1990-2015. *Journal of the American Academy of Child and Adolescent Psychiatry, 57*(10), 733–741. https://doi.org/10.1016/j.jaac.2018.06.018

Haque, T. (2023). Co-morbid general medical conditions among patients with deliberate self harm - A study in a tertiary care hospital, Rangpur. *Bangladesh. The Insight, 5*(02), 163–169. https://www.bdjournals.org/index.php/insight/article/view/288

Haregu, T., Chen, Q., Arafat, S. M. Y., Cherian, A., & Armstrong, G. (2023). Prevalence, correlates and common methods of non-suicidal self-injury in South Asia: A systematic review. *BMJ Open, 13*(11), e074776. https://doi.org/10.1136/bmjopen-2023-074776

Hussain, A. M., Ekram, A. S., Alim, M. A., Ahad, M. A., Qais, S., & Alam, M. (2008). Study on deliberate self harm in a tertiary hospital. *TAJ, 7*, 10–60.

Imam, S. M. A., & Biswas, A. (2023). Prevalence of deliberate self-harm in different psychiatric disorders: Insights from a study of 100 patients. *East African Scholars Journal of Medical Sciences, 6*(12), 408–412. https://doi.org/10.36349/easms.2023.v06i12.005

Lowry, N. J., Ryan, P. C., Mournet, A. M., Snyder, D. J., Claassen, C., Jobes, D., Harrington, C., Pao, M., Horowitz, L. M., & Bridge, J. A. (2023). Non-suicidal self-injury and suicide risk among adult medical inpatients. *Journal of Affective Disorders Reports, 11*, 100474. https://doi.org/10.1016/j.jadr.2023.100474

Moloney, F., Amini, J., Sinyor, M., Schaffer, A., Lanctôt, K. L., & Mitchell, R. H. B. (2024). Sex differences in the global prevalence of nonsuicidal self-injury in adolescents: A meta-analysis. *JAMA Network Open, 7*(6), e2415436. https://doi.org/10.1001/jamanetworkopen.2024.15436

Motin, M. A., Chowdhury, A. R., Royle, R. K. S., Azam, A. S., & Khan, M. M. (2020). Personality disorders in adult population with deliberate self-harm. *Achieves of NIMH, 3*, 18–23.

Mozumder, M. K. (2024). *Life under the rainbow: Self-harm and suicidality among LGBT community in Bangladesh.* Preprint.

Mozumder, M. K., Jasmine, U. H., Haque, M. A., & Haque, S. (2023). Mental health and suicide risk among homosexual males in Bangladesh. *PLoS One, 18*(8), e0289597. https://doi.org/10.1371/journal.pone.0289597

Mullick, M. S., Karim, M. E., & Khanam, M. (1994). Depression in deliberate self harm patients. *Bangladesh Medical Research Council Bulletin, 20*(3), 123–128.

Shimul, M. M. H., Baroi, O., & Khandker, S. (2025). Comparing rural and urban mothers' awareness of self-harm and associated risk factors among high school students in Bangladesh. *Preventive Medicine Reports, 103127*. https://doi.org/10.1016/j.pmedr.2025.103127

Uddin, M. S., & Arafat, S. M. Y. (2026). Suicide research in Bangladesh. In S. M. Y. Arafat (Ed.), *Suicidal behavior in Bangladesh*. Springer. https://doi.org/10.1007/978-981-95-8321-8_13

Uddin, M. G., Biswas, R. S. R., & Mamun, S. H. (2019). Sociodemographic profile and intention of deliberate self-harm among patients admitted in a tertiary care hospital, Chittagong, Bangladesh. *Journal of the Scientific Society, 46*(2), 53–56. https://doi.org/10.4103/jss.JSS_9_19

Xiao, Q., Song, X., Huang, L., Hou, D., & Huang, X. (2022). Global prevalence and characteristics of non-suicidal self-injury between 2010 and 2021 among a non-clinical sample of adolescents: A meta-analysis. *Frontiers in Psychiatry, 13*, 912441. https://doi.org/10.3389/fpsyt.2022.912441

Chapter 10
Law, Policy, and Strategies on Suicide Prevention in Bangladesh

S. M. Yasir Arafat

1 Introduction

Suicide is a global public health problem that kills more than 720,000 people in a year (World Health Organization, 2025). It is the outcome of a complex interaction among multiple factors, starting from biology to wider ecological and environmental variables (Zalsman et al., 2016). Risk factors vary widely from country to country, culture to culture, and time to time (Cho et al., 2016; Favril et al., 2022). Prevention strategies vary widely based on the risk factors, considering the country, culture, and evidence of effectiveness (Zalsman et al., 2016; Mann et al., 2005). Strategies have been considered in three categories: that is, universal strategies for the general population, selected strategies for persons at risk, and indicated strategies for persons with suicidal behavior (World Health Organization, 2014). They range from psychiatric treatment for individuals to legal changes in a country or society for the general population. Pack size restriction of paracetamol, ban of hazardous pesticides, and change of criminal status are the prominent examples of law and policy-level impact on suicide prevention globally.

Bangladesh is a lower-middle-income country with 170 million people, a dual burden of diseases, and a negligible mental health budget (Bangladesh Bureau of Statistics, 2024; Arafat et al., 2024a). Due to its disease burden, income category, and budgetary allocation, suicide prevention is less prioritized in the country. Additionally, the country does not have publicly available data, a national suicide surveillance system, or a national suicide prevention program (Arafat, 2025a). Available evidence suggests that the ban of category I pesticides, which is one of the

S. M. Y. Arafat (✉)
Department of Psychiatry, Bangladesh Specialized Hospita, Dhaka, Bangladesh

Faculty of Medicine and Health Sciences, Department of Public and Community Health, Frontier University Garowe, Garowe, Somalia

S. M. Y. Arafat (ed.), *Suicidal Behavior in Bangladesh*, Mental Health Systems and Policy in Low- and Middle-Income Countries,
https://doi.org/10.1007/978-981-95-8321-8_10

few suicide prevention measures in Bangladesh, resulted in a reduction of suicides by poisoning (Chowdhury et al., 2018). For an effective suicide prevention strategy, Bangladesh needs to modify the legal framework. This chapter discusses the legal structure and its role in suicide prevention in Bangladesh. It highlights the current legal status of suicide attempts, its impact, expected legal modification and their speculated impact, and consideration of suicide prevention in the current Mental Health Act, Policy, and Strategy.

2 Legal Status of Suicide Attempt in Bangladesh

Bangladesh is bearing the legacy of criminal laws of the British Raj, formulated more than 160 years ago (Islam & Islam, 2003). Like many other countries, a suicide attempt is a criminal offence in Bangladesh (World Health Organization XE "World Health Organization (WHO)" , 2023; United for Global Mental Health, 2021; Mishara & Weisstub, 2016). Among 192 countries and states, suicide is still illegal in 23 countries, and it is punishable with jail sentences in an additional 20 countries that implement Islamic or Sharia law (World Health Organization, 2023; Mishara & Weisstub, 2016). Individuals who attempt to take their own lives risk severe penalties for themselves and even their families. Punishments vary, with penalties ranging from 1–3 years' imprisonment and fines (United for Global Mental Health, 2021). In Bangladesh, Chap. XVI, Section 309 of the Penal Code (1860) criminalizes a suicide attempt. The law is as follows: "whoever attempts to commit suicide and does any act towards the act of commission of such offence, shall be punished with simple imprisonment for a term which may extend to one year, or with fine, or with both" (The Penal Code, 1860). On the legal aspect, a suicide attempt is considered a criminal offence, and punishment is imprisonment extending up to one year with or without a fine. Nevertheless, there is no record of giving punishment to any of the nonfatal attempts. It should be borne in mind that criminalization, along with social stigma, makes suicidal attempts underreported, and even the deaths are attributed to other causes. Therefore, the data on the suicide rate and non-fatal attempts available in Bangladesh do not depict the actual picture. Logically, the question comes: if you don't know the real picture of a problem, then how is it possible to formulate a solution to the event?

2.1 Mental Health Act

Bangladesh passed the latest Mental Health Act in 2018, replacing the Lunacy Act of 1912. The Act mentioned some major areas of mental health services like the establishment of hospitals for psychiatric patients, hospitalization and treatment guidelines, legal rights of psychiatric patients, and guardianship of properties of persons with mental illness (Laws of Bangladesh, n.d.). The law does not include any aspects on the prevention of suicidal behavior in Bangladesh (Arafat, 2025b).

2.2 National Mental Health Policy

The National Mental Health Policy (NMHP) was approved in 2022. It includes 15 objectives and areas of action where suicide prevention has been considered (Government of Bangladesh, 2022). Reduction of sick for suicide and suicide attempts has considered covering the areas: (i) formulation of a national suicide prevention strategy, (ii) awareness creation, formulation of an emergency response system, and gatekeeper training, and (iii) improvement of suicide data quality.

2.3 National Mental Health Strategic Plan (2020–2030)

The National Mental Health Strategic Plan (NMHSP) was approved in 2022. Suicide prevention has been placed under general objective 3 (*to implement strategies for mental health promotion and risk reduction for mental health conditions*), where the reduction of suicide deaths has been attempted by 5% by 2025 (Government of the People's Republic of Bangladesh, 2022). The strategy prioritized several areas for suicide prevention: (i) augmented research, (ii) referral to health services for suicidal behavior, (iii) formulation of a national strategy for substance use and suicidality, (iv) emergency services for suicidal behavior, (v) means restrictions (hazardous pesticides), (vi) decriminalization, (vii) national program for suicide prevention, (viii) provision of training for gatekeepers, (ix) emergency telephone lines, (x) postvention, (xi) preparation of suicide and self-harm registry, (xii) suicide surveillance, and (xiii) formulation of culture-appropriate media guidelines (Government of The People's Republic of Bangladesh, 2022).

3 Criminal Legal Status and Suicidal Behavior

Criminal legal status deters persons with suicidal behavior from seeking care and help due to the fear of legal consequences (World Health Organization, 2023). It also deters health services from providing care for the same reason. Due to their criminal legal status, persons with suicidal behavior are avoided by public hospitals and referred to public hospitals, which are sometimes far from residences. These people are kept in the veranda of the public hospitals in a neglected state when they need psychological support (Arafat, 2026).

Criminal legal status endures higher stigma and lower literacy about suicide and suicidal behavior (World Health Organization, 2023; Ochuku et al., 2022). Studies indicate a similar finding in Bangladesh, indicating a high stigma towards suicide among those with literacy status (Arafat & Ali, 2026). Due to the stigma and criminal legal status, there may be marginalization and seclusion while performing the funeral, and burial of the deceased may face problems (World Health Organization, 2023).

Although it has been considered that criminal legal status may deter from suicide attempts, ecological studies identified that countries with criminal status have a higher suicide rate than others (Wu et al., 2022).

Decriminalization affects suicide prevention in various ways. First, it helps people to open up and share their distress about mental health and suicidal behavior, which will help in suicide prevention (World Health Organization, 2023). Second, it helps a person with suicidal behavior to take necessary clinical services without social fear, harassment, or stigma. It reduces social stigma and shame associated with mental disorders and suicidal behaviors. It also improves data quality and reduces the challenges for collecting data on suicidal behavior (World Health Organization, 2023).

4 Law and Suicide Prevention in Bangladesh

4.1 Legislative Body and Suicide Prevention

The legislative body has an important and decisive role in suicide prevention in Bangladesh. Policy-level changes are expected in several areas, such as decriminalization of suicide attempts, and banning pesticides and commonly used medications like Benzodiazepines with a satisfying prescription as means restrictions. Changes in the criminal legal status are expected to increase help-seeking and access to health care after a nonfatal attempt, as there will not be fear of legal harassment. It will also remove the stigma of being assigned as "police case," and there will not be any barrier to admitting the patients to the nearby private hospitals. It is expected to reduce underreporting and misclassification of suicide deaths (Arafat, 2025c).

4.2 Law Enforcement Agency

The law enforcement agency has a prominent role in suicide prevention. First, the police could be a readily available source of data in the absence of a national suicide database as the legal structure entitles the police as the first responder, as well as to decide the mode of death (Arafat, 2025c; Bose & Arafat, 2026). The challenges of suicide data have been discussed in Chap. 1 of this book (Arafat & Kabir, 2026). Second, the national emergency helpline (999) is coordinated by the Home Ministry when the police handle emergencies raised from suicide attempts (Arafat et al.,

2025). Evidence indicates that the helpline prevented many suicide attempts in the country.

4.3 *Means Restriction and Law*

Bangladesh has implemented the ban of category I pesticides, which resulted in a reduction of suicide by poisoning (Chowdhury et al., 2018). In addition to that, the country needs the implementation of restricted sales of benzodiazepines, which is one of the major methods of suicide attempts (Arafat et al., 2024c). One report indicated a suicide attempt by collecting benzodiazepines from foodpanda/online dispensing, which needs regulatory attention (Arafat, 2025d).

5 Decriminalization of Suicide Attempt in Bangladesh

The World Health Organization (WHO) recommended decriminalizing suicide attempts and suggested stepwise guidance for helping decriminalization (World Health Organization, 2023, Box 10.1). Nowadays, keeping and addressing these problems in mind, academicians have started to raise their concern and demand decriminalization of suicidal behavior, which in turn will encourage the help-seeking by the victim for mental support without any legal harassment (Arafat, 2019; Arafat et al., 2019). However, 50.6% of Islamic religious leaders (Imams) opined that decriminalization would not prevent suicide in Bangladesh (Arafat et al., 2024b). Imams are the important stakeholders for the decriminalization of suicide attempts in Bangladesh, as more than 90% of the people are Muslims (Bangladesh Bureau of Statistics, 2024).

Now we may have to face the question of whether the decriminalization of suicide is equivalent to the legalization of suicide. Bhatti et al. describe it fantastically by differentiating decriminalization and legalization (Bhatti et al., 2021). Something being decriminalized doesn't indicate it as a legal entity. Referring to the perspective of mental health professionals, the article upholds it in a way that decriminalization would not legalize suicidal behavior; instead, it will inhibit the legal steps for persons with suicidal behavior.

Another question may arise, whether decriminalization should create a positive impact on lowering suicide or not (Wu et al., 2022). This sort of question is just a model of argument rather than a solution. Because a person attempting suicide is already suffering mental pain and agony, and punishment sanctioned on him/her would change nothing but to prevent the said accused from seeking help from others. As we know, mental support, psychiatric evaluation, and counseling are important steps in order to prevent further attempts to die by suicide. Readily available and easily accessible mental health support to distressed and indicated persons has proven the preventive role in suicide prevention (Zalsman et al., 2016).

Decriminalization would facilitate it. Hence, it is a hard time to take necessary steps to adjust or change the laws on a timely basis, making it decriminalized, which would create a space to seek consultation from others without fear of jail.

In the Southeast Asia region, suicide attempt is not a criminal offense in Bhutan, Indonesia, the Maldives, Nepal, Sri Lanka, and Thailand (Arafat et al., 2020). Now we could get a look at the legal framework related to suicide that exists in South Asia, including countries such as Bangladesh, India, and Pakistan. In India, Section 309 the Penal Code (1860) criminalizes attempted suicide. This is the same as in Pakistan and Bangladesh, described in Sections 325 and 309, respectively. Ranjan et al. mentioned a judgment of 1985 by the Delhi High Court as a landmark judgment (Ranjan et al., 2014; Behere et al., 2015). The court commented, "*The continuance of Section 309 I.P.C. (criminalizing suicide) is an anachronism unworthy of a human* society *like ours.*" The Indian Penal Code was commenced during the British Empire in 1860, and it has persisted in India, albeit suicide has been decriminalized in the United Kingdom in 1961 (Ranjan et al., 2014). Suicide was criminalized in Pakistan as per Sect. 325 of the Pakistan Penal Code, 1860. It criminalizes attempted suicide with punishment (Mehtab et al., 2022; Pakistan Penal Code Act, 1860). After a long battle, India stopped the effects of the law that criminalized attempted suicide in 2017 by formulating the Mental Healthcare Act. Yet, further steps are warranted to remove the Penal Code Act in India. Likewise, in India, decriminalization of suicide was done in Pakistan in December 2022 (Sibghatullah et al., 2025). Examples of decriminalizing suicide in Muslim-majority countries such as Malaysia and Pakistan could be considered while prioritizing it in Bangladesh (Chan et al., 2024).

Box 10.1 WHO's recommendations related to decriminalization of suicide attempts (World Health Organization, 2023)

A. Identification and repealing the legal structure that criminalize suicide attempts.
B. Engaging the stakeholders to understand and dispel moral, cultural, or religious justifications for criminalization or those based on the notion of punishment as a deterrent to suicide.
C. Organizing advocacy campaigns to make to decriminalize suicide attempts.
D. Capitalizing on global events and opportunities for advocacy, such as World Suicide Prevention Day (10 September) and World Mental Health Day (10 October).
E. Building and budgeting for a "postdecriminalization"/"transition" awareness program specifically to train first responders, including police, emergency health care providers, mental health professionals, peer supporters, and other relevant persons who encounter persons at risk of suicide.
F. Developing a comprehensive national suicide prevention strategy.
G. Establishing rights-oriented, community-based mental health services.
H. Reforming or developing new mental health-related laws, policies, and strategic plans that promote the rights of persons with mental health conditions and psychosocial disabilities.

6 Conclusions

This chapter discussed the current legal framework and its impact on suicidal behavior and suicide prevention in the country. It also highlights potential areas of legal reformation for suicide prevention in Bangladesh. Decriminalization could be an immediate measure while subsequent changes would be attempted, like a national suicide prevention program, a national suicide surveillance system, and quality data on suicidal behavior.

References

Arafat, S. M. Y. (2019). Current challenges of suicide and future directions of management in Bangladesh: A systematic review. *Global Psychiatry, 2*(1), 9–20. https://doi.org/10.2478/gp-2019-0001

Arafat, S. M. (2025a). Suicide is criminal, data is silent: Reimagining suicide surveillance in Bangladesh—From police reports to public health action. *International Journal of Mental Health and Addiction, 1–3* .https://doi.org/10.1007/s11469-025-01514-1

Arafat, S. M. Y. (2025b). Suicide prevention in Bangladesh: Critical analysis of mental health law, policy and strategy. *BJPsych International, 22*(4), 138–141. https://doi.org/10.1192/bji.2025.10042

Arafat, S. M. Y. (2025c). Suicide prevention in Bangladesh: The role of police. *The Lancet. Psychiatry, 12*(3), 173. https://doi.org/10.1016/S2215-0366(24)00443-7

Arafat, S. M. Y. (2025d). Online dispensing of benzodiazepines can be an emerging threat for suicide prevention in Bangladesh: A case and potential preventive measures. *Asian Journal of Psychiatry, 106*, 104446. https://doi.org/10.1016/j.ajp.2025.104446

Arafat, S. M. Y. (2026). Mental health and suicidal behavior in Bangladesh. In S. M. Y. Arafat (Ed.), *Suicidal behavior in Bangladesh*. Springer. https://doi.org/10.1007/978-981-95-8321-8_3

Arafat, S. M. Y., & Ali, S. A. Z. (2026). Literacy and stigma of suicidal behavior in Bangladesh. In S. M. Y. Arafat (Ed.), *Suicidal behavior in Bangladesh*. Springer https://doi.org/10.1007/978-981-95-8321-8_12

Arafat, S. M. Y., & Kabir, R. (2026). Data is silent, epidemiology is blur: Suicidal behavior in bangladesh-what is known and what needs to improve. In S. M. Y. Arafat (Ed.), *Suicidal Behavior in Bangladesh*. Springer. https://doi.org/10.1007/978-981-95-8321-8_1

Arafat, S. M. Y., Mali, B., & Akter, H. (2019). Quality of online news reporting of suicidal behavior in Bangladesh against World Health Organization guidelines. *Asian Journal of Psychiatry, 40*, 126–129. https://doi.org/10.1016/j.ajp.2018.10.010

Arafat, S. Y., Kar, S. K., Marthoenis, M., Cherian, A. V., Vimala, L., & Kabir, R. (2020). Quality of media reporting of suicidal behaviors in South-East Asia. *Neurology, Psychiatry and Brain Research, 37*, 21–26. https://doi.org/10.1016/j.npbr.2020.05.007

Arafat, S. M. Y., Giasuddin, N. A., & Mazumder, A. H. (2024a). Access to mental health care in Bangladesh—Current status, potential challenges, and ways out. In S. M. Y. Arafat & S. K. Kar (Eds.), *Access to mental health care in South Asia*. Springer. https://doi.org/10.1007/978-981-99-9153-2_3

Arafat, S. Y., Islam, M. K., Khan, M. A. S., & Amin, R. (2024b). The perception of imams (Islamic religious leaders) on the legal status and decriminalization of suicide attempts in Bangladesh: A cross-sectional study. *Global Psychiatry Archives, 7*(1), 7–12. https://doi.org/10.52095/gpa.2023.7115.1077

Arafat, S. M. Y., Shormi, F. R., & Kibria, M. G. (2024c). Psychiatric disorder and life-event in self harm: A cross-sectional study among clinical population in Bangladesh. *Heliyon, 10*(19), e38627. https://doi.org/10.1016/j.heliyon.2024.e38627

Arafat, S. M. Y., Mourin, C., & Jahan, R. (2025). Crisis help line and suicide prevention in Bangladesh: Challenges and ways ahead. *Asian Journal of Psychiatry, 109*, 104565. https://doi.org/10.1016/j.ajp.2025.104565

Bangladesh Bureau of Statistics. (2024). *Population & housing census 2022*. https://bbs.gov.bd/site/page/47856ad0-7e1c-4aab-bd78-892733bc06eb/Population-&-Housing (accessed on 28 September 2024).

Behere, P. B., Sathyanarayana Rao, T. S., & Mulmule, A. N. (2015). Decriminalization of attempted suicide law: Journey of Fifteen Decades. *Indian Journal of Psychiatry, 57*(2), 122–124. https://doi.org/10.4103/0019-5545.158131

Bhatti, M., Ansari, A., & Khan, B. (2021). Is it time to decriminalize suicide in Pakistan? A critical review. *Annals of Allied Health Sciences, 7*(1), 27–33. https://aahs.kmu.edu.pk/index.php/aahs/article/view/166

Bose, P. K., & Arafat, S. M. Y. (2026). Forensic medicine, post-mortem and suicide in Bangladesh. In S. M. Y. Arafat (Ed.), *Suicidal behavior in Bangladesh*. Springer. https://doi.org/10.1007/978-981-95-8321-8_2

Chan, L. F., Ibrahim, N., Khamal, N. R., Panirselvam, R. R., Pereira, E. J., & Khan, M. (2024). A global call for decriminalization of attempted suicide. *Crisis, 45*(6), 383–388. https://doi.org/10.1027/0227-5910/a000974

Cho, S. E., Na, K. S., Cho, S. J., Im, J. S., & Kang, S. G. (2016). Geographical and temporal variations in the prevalence of mental disorders in suicide: Systematic review and meta-analysis. *Journal of Affective Disorders, 190*, 704–713. https://doi.org/10.1016/j.jad.2015.11.008

Chowdhury, F. R., Dewan, G., Verma, V. R., Knipe, D. W., Isha, I. T., Faiz, M. A., Gunnell, D. J., & Eddleston, M. (2018). Bans of WHO class i pesticides in Bangladesh-suicide prevention without hampering agricultural output. *International Journal of Epidemiology, 47*(1), 175–184. https://doi.org/10.1093/ije/dyx157

Favril, L., Yu, R., Uyar, A., Sharpe, M., & Fazel, S. (2022). Risk factors for suicide in adults: Systematic review and meta-analysis of psychological autopsy studies. *Evidence-Based Mental Health, 25*(4), 148–155. https://doi.org/10.1136/ebmental-2022-300549

Government of Bangladesh. (2022). *National Mental Health Policy*, Bangladesh, 2022. https://nimh.gov.bd/english/wp-content/uploads/2023/04/Bangladesh-National-Mental-Health-Policy-2022.pdf (accessed on 2 July, 2025).

Government of The People's Republic of Bangladesh. (2022). *National mental health strategic plan, 2020–2030*. https://old.dghs.gov.bd/index.php/bd/home/6171-nmu-2020-2030 (accessed on 2 July, 2025).

Islam, M. N., & Islam, M. N. (2003). Forensic medicine in Bangladesh. *Legal Medicine (Tokyo, Japan), 5*(Suppl 1), S357–S359. https://doi.org/10.1016/s1344-6223(02)00132-3

Laws of Bangladesh. (n.d.). *Mental Health Act 2018*. http://bdlaws.minlaw.gov.bd/act-1273.html (accessed on 01 July 2025).

Mann, J. J., Apter, A., Bertolote, J., Beautrais, A., Currier, D., Haas, A., Hegerl, U., Lonnqvist, J., Malone, K., Marusic, A., Mehlum, L., Patton, G., Phillips, M., Rutz, W., Rihmer, Z., Schmidtke, A., Shaffer, D., Silverman, M., Takahashi, Y., Varnik, A., et al. (2005). Suicide prevention strategies: A systematic review. *JAMA, 294*(16), 2064–2074. https://doi.org/10.1001/jama.294.16.2064

Mehtab, F. H., Mahmud, A., Riaduzzaman, R., Alam Khan, M. U., & Hossen, F. (2022). Right to commit suicide in India: A comparative analysis with suggestion for the policymakers. *Cogent Social Sciences, 8*(1), 2017574. https://doi.org/10.1080/23311886.2021.2017574

Mishara, B. L., & Weisstub, D. N. (2016). The legal status of suicide: A global review. *International Journal of Law and Psychiatry, 44*, 54–74. https://doi.org/10.1016/j.ijlp.2015.08.032

Ochuku, B. K., Johnson, N. E., Osborn, T. L., Wasanga, C. M., & Ndetei, D. M. (2022). Centering decriminalization of suicide in low - and middle - income countries on effective suicide prevention strategies. *Frontiers in Psychiatry, 13*, 1034206. https://doi.org/10.3389/fpsyt.2022.1034206

Pakistan Penal Code Act. (1860). *Pakistan Penal Code Act 1860 ch. XLV (PK). 21*. https://www.pakistani.org/pakistan/legislation/1860/actXLVof1860.html (accessed on 18 August, 2022).

Ranjan, R., Kumar, S., Pattanayak, R. D., Dhawan, A., & Sagar, R. (2014). (De-)criminalization of attempted suicide in India: A review. *Industrial Psychiatry Journal, 23*(1), 4–9. https://doi.org/10.4103/0972-6748.144936

Sibghatullah, M., Dayani, K., Zia, M., & Sabri, T. (2025). Perspectives on the decriminalisation of suicide in Pakistan: Historical context, societal impacts, and the way forward. *The Lancet Regional Health. Southeast Asia, 35*, 100568. https://doi.org/10.1016/j.lansea.2025.100568

The Penal Code. (1860). *Penal Code1860. Chapter XVI*. http://bdlaws.minlaw.gov.bd/act-11/section-3140.html (accessed on 2 July, 2025).

United for Global Mental Health. (2021). *Decriminalising suicide: Saving lives, reducing stigma*. https://www.iasp.info/2021/09/08/decriminalising-suicide-reducing-stigma-saving-lives/ (accessed on 2 July, 2025).

World Health Organization. (2014). *Preventing suicide: A global imperative*. World Health Organization. https://www.who.int/publications/i/item/9789241564779 (accessed on 2 July, 2025).

World Health Organization. (2023). *WHO policy brief on the health aspects of decriminalization of suicide and suicide attempts*. World Health Organization. https://www.who.int/publications/i/item/9789240078796 (accessed on 31 August, 2025).

World Health Organization. (2025). *Suicide*. WHO. Available online: https://www.who.int/news-room/fact-sheets/detail/suicide (accessed on 02 July 2025).

Wu, K. C., Cai, Z., Chang, Q., Chang, S. S., Yip, P. S. F., & Chen, Y. Y. (2022). Criminalisation of suicide and suicide rates: An ecological study of 171 countries in the world. *BMJ Open, 12*(2), e049425. https://doi.org/10.1136/bmjopen-2021-049425

Zalsman, G., Hawton, K., Wasserman, D., van Heeringen, K., Arensman, E., Sarchiapone, M., et al. (2016). Suicide prevention strategies revisited: 10-year systematic review. *The Lancet. Psychiatry, 3*(7), 646–659. https://doi.org/10.1016/S2215-0366(16)30030-X

Chapter 11
Media and Suicidal Behavior in Bangladesh

S. M. Yasir Arafat and Asibul Islam Anik

1 Introduction

Suicide is a preventable public health issue with wide-ranging social, emotional, and economic consequences. Every year, over 727,000 people die by suicide across the world (World Health Organization, 2025). Southeast Asia had a higher suicide rate (10.2 per 100,000) than the global average (9.0 per 100,000 (World Health Organization, 2021). In 2019, nearly 6000 persons died by suicide in Bangladesh (World Health Organization, 2021).

The risk factors for suicide include mental health issues, financial strain, poverty, trauma, abuse, unemployment, life crises, chronic physical ailments, lack of support, lack of access to treatment, and so on. On the other hand, access to mental healthcare, family and community support, socioeconomic possibilities, ethical and responsible media coverage, awareness-raising, and stigma reduction could be considered as the protective factors (Zalsman et al., 2016; World Health Organization, 2014). Hence, the contributing and preventing factors of suicide are complicated and not completely understood, but scientific evidence from numerous global experiments demonstrates that media coverage of suicide can occasionally result in contagion, with higher suicide rates across a population (Niederkrotenthaler et al., 2010; Stack, 2020). After analyzing 31 studies around the world, Niederkrotenthaler and his team (2020) found that media coverage on celebrity suicide tends to

S. M. Y. Arafat (✉)
Department of Psychiatry, Bangladesh Specialized Hospital, Dhaka, Bangladesh

Faculty of Medicine and Health Sciences, Department of Public and Community Health, Frontier University Garowe, Garowe, Somalia

A. I. Anik
Epidemiology and Applied Health Research, School of Epidemiology and Public Health, University of Ottawa, Ottawa, Canada

S. M. Y. Arafat (ed.), *Suicidal Behavior in Bangladesh*, Mental Health Systems and Policy in Low- and Middle-Income Countries,
https://doi.org/10.1007/978-981-95-8321-8_11

accelerate the overall suicide rate in the general population by 8% to 18% within the next 30 to 60 days, and if the coverage explicitly mentions the suicide method used by the celebrity, the likelihood of applying the same suicide method increases by 18% to 44%. But such types of incidents or associations with suicide were not observed in general suicide reporting (Niederkrotenthaler et al., 2020). On the other hand, the likelihood of imitative (copycat) suicide may be reduced by offering beneficial educational material and coping mechanisms.

In Bangladesh, suicide has been widely publicized in online news portals and vividly dramatized in Bangla films, resulting in an unprecedented impact of media on suicide among the mass population. Given the foregoing, the WHO has recommended several guidelines for media reporting on suicide, particularly for use in countries where national standards do not already exist (World Health Organization, 2023). This chapter discusses how suicide is portrayed in Bangladeshi media, what are the media guidelines reporting suicides in Bangladesh, and what are the challenges of implementing these guidelines, along with further recommendations.

2 Role of Media on Suicidality

The impact of mass media reporting on suicide has always been a controversial issue for a long time (Niederkrotenthaler et al., 2010). Goethe's novel *Die Leiden des jungen Werthers* (*The Sorrows of Young Werther*), published in 1774, was one of the earliest acknowledged documents that gave rise to the connections between the media and suicide. In the novel, Werther shoots himself with a revolver after he has been rejected by the woman he loves, and soon after the publication of this novel, several suicidal events of young men were reported using a similar technique to kill themselves in acts of hopelessness. Hence, the concept "Werther effect" was developed, and later it was used in the technical literature to designate "copy-cat" suicides (Myers, 2012). On the contrary, it has also been observed that media discourse sometimes supports suicide preventive efforts by educating society about the management of mental illness and suicidality. Such protective approaches had been termed the "Papageno effect" (Niederkrotenthaler et al., 2010), which refers to Mozart's opera *The Magic Flute* (1791), where a boy in love became suicidal, but survived owing to the intervention of his friends.

The suicidal tendency influenced by the media descriptions is potentially more far-reaching than direct person-to-person propagation. Social scientists and psychologists have developed several theories that can explain both the direct and indirect roles of media behind these suicidal tendencies and/or ideation. According to the *Behavioral Contagion* theory, behavioral contagion in a society refers to the spread of a particular behavior through a group of people or a medium, and the propensity of an individual to copy that behavior is motivated by those (group of) people who are either nearby or to what (medium) they have been exposed (Wheeler, 1966). Though this theory was originally employed to explain unpleasant features of crowd behavior, behavioral contagion is now also concerned with the spread of media circulation and online information. *Social learning theory*, another platform for understanding parts of suicide contagion, is shaped by imitating or modeling others' behavior (Bandura, 1969). Imitative learning is influenced by several factors, including the behaviors and norms of the model (e.g., any celebrity) and rewarding outcomes or consequences associated with the observed behaviors observe the positive outcomes (e.g., public attention) that others receive from such behaviors. Additionally, suicide contagion can also be conceptualized using a public health or infectious illness model of contagion. In this model, the role of agent (i.e., the model), host (i.e., vulnerable individual), and environmental characteristics (e.g., mental health disorder or social anxiety from parental and/or peer pressure) play in the overall transmission process (i.e., suicidal ideation or suicide) (Gould, 2001). However, based on the interactions of these three theories, the following discussions will depict the impact of media on suicide contagion.

Both print media and broadcast media frequently report suicide by glorifying the death, describing in stories and/or in graphic details. Such irresponsible reporting to augment the news worthiness and sensationalization of the event could be a grave risk for people who have already attempted suicide in the past. These editorial tactics might be ok for most of the people, but the few people who are struggling with depression or being mentally vulnerable and contemplating suicide might be encouraged by these descriptions and then take the action (i.e., suicide), since someone else has already done it. Additionally, if a celebrity suicide is published along with the means of suicides and sensationalized in reporting style, then there might be an increase in the suicide rate. From the analyses of 42 research articles, it was found that studies that measured the influence of a celebrity suicide narrative were nearly 14 times more likely to identify a copycat effect than those that did not (Stack, 2002). This finding might explain the dramatic increase in suicide hotline calls in the month of Chester Bennington's suicide (in 2017), a world-renowned singer. For this situation, several mental health experts have blamed media reporting, since journalists prominently highlighted the method of his suicide, even in the headlines of the newspapers (Schonfeld, 2017).

When newspapers, films, and television portray the report of a suicidal event, and a child or a mentally vulnerable person is reading the details of that event, that particular child or person is indirectly learning another method of suicide. In this way, copycat suicide is mostly accountable on the media, and people learn suicide manuals from the newspaper and television reports of actual suicides. Consequently, after hearing or reading about a suicide in the media, people who are vulnerable consider the incident as a glorified example, one of the simplest methods to find relief from all the existing issues, and self-assume that they also have the permission to do it.

The *Werther effect* not only forecasts an increase in suicide, but it also predicts that the majority of suicides would occur in the same or a similar manner as the one reported. The effect gets amplified if people find that the publicized suicide was committed by someone in a position similar to their own. Most of the people who have already attempted to kill themselves are ambivalent, and they just want relief from their surrounding pressure. For example, in the US state of New Jersey, a 12-year old student who had been continuously bullied at school died by suicide.

And immediately after this incident, the higher authority of that school took strict and adaptive measures to stop bullying at any level (BBC News, 2018). However, seeing this publicized incident with a detailed background on television and/or newspapers, other teenagers or students who are also experiencing bullying at their schools could relate to the story and be more likely to see themselves going down the same path. They see that suicide is bringing a glamorous end with an appropriate solution, along with the deceased getting sympathy and attention that they did not receive at school.

Surprisingly, a specific age group and timing were found to be influenced significantly by such suicide contagion. Younger and older people, but not middle-aged adults, appeared to be the most vulnerable group to this effect. It was found that in Western countries, there's a 1–2% variance in suicide rates and 5% for adolescents, which occurred due to media reporting (Sanger-Katz, 2014). The numbers may be small, but some quick calculations might clarify it better. For example, globally in 2016, an estimated 817,000 people died by suicide (Naghavi, 2019). Here, even a change to 2% or 5% would have been associated with a reduction of 16,340 to 40,850 deaths, respectively. Again, in terms of timing, most of the suicidal actions tend to happen in the days and sometimes weeks following the suicide of a celebrity, and in exceptional cases, an extended degree of suicidal thinking may remain for up to 1 year (Sisask & Värnik, 2012). For example, after Marilyn Monroe died from a suspected suicide in 1962, the national suicide rate increased by more than 10% in the year following her death.

Nevertheless, news stories focusing on the adverse effect of suicidal ideation, but not accompanied by a suicide attempt or completion, may have a protective effect, which is the "Papageno effect". But such protective reporting mostly comes in "Thematic frame" (i.e., in editorial or op-ed pages), and eventually reduces the quantities of sensationalist reporting and so-called news-worthiness. It has been found that in newspapers, a presentation or a true story of how individuals had overcome suicide thoughts may increase and emphasize on the concept of "going on living" (Niederkrotenthaler et al., 2010). Simultaneously, self-motivating and "think it again"-based approaches become more successful when newspapers, televisions, and films portray the stories on people who avoided suicide thoughts and instead used practical mechanisms to cope with difficult life situations.

3 Media and Suicidal Behavior in Bangladesh

In Southeast Asia, one of the world's most densely populated regions, media reporting of suicide is imbalanced. In Bangladesh, the situation is considerably worse due to poor and irresponsible inspection before publishing such incidents (Arafat et al., 2020a). Both print media and online media are widely seen as popular means of disseminating information (Azad, 2025). The total circulation of Bangla newspaper is about 1.5 million, and English newspaper is around 70,000 (Azad, 2025). The top 10 Bangla newspapers contain 90% of circulations, and a single English newspaper contains 77% of the market share. There is always an explicit difference between the newspaper circulation in urban and rural areas of Bangladesh, depending on the literacy rate and purchasing capability. Again, compared to the previous two decades, the overall newspaper (print version) circulation throughout the country has decreased because of 24-h television news broadcast, easily accessible internet service, and faster news availability on online news portals and social media. The readership rates have also been declining since the last decade, that is, readership rates were 26.9% in 2011, 25.6% in 2015, and 23.8% in 2016, with a dramatic decline after 2018 (nearly 15%, Azad, 2025). Online media, online news portals, and social media use could be the potential reasons for declining circulation.

Since the circulation of some leading newspapers is stable and still significant, the print press is considered the most influential and traditional media of information sharing and plays a crucial role in opinion-building throughout the society. Based on this fact, social scientists, media experts, and policy makers have recently investigated the quality and style of these media reporting on suicide or any other socially sensitive events. According to these investigations, it was found that misinformation can be spread by the poor media reporting style; for example, by providing simplified, mono-causal explanations that indicate suicide is a solution to immediate triggers rather than being associated with a complex array of proximal and distal risk factors (e.g., psychiatric disorder and social/religious attitudes toward suicide, Hawton & Heeringen, 2009).

In the last decade, several studies using data from newspaper reports (Arafat et al., 2019, 2020a, 2020b, 2020c, 2020d) have assessed the quality of media coverage on suicidal behavior in Bangladesh (including print and online platform) for suicidal behavior among the general population (Table 11.1). Also, the quality of reporting has been assessed in online news portals for celebrity suicide (Arafat et al., 2025a). One study reported the depiction of suicidal behavior in Bangla motion picture, that is, movie and drama (Arafat et al., 2025b). The studies of suicide among the general population considered the most circulated daily national newspapers (both Bangla and English) of Bangladesh. While assessing the quality of suicide reporting in terms of print media, online news portal, Bangla vs. English media, and movies and/or dramas, these studies focused on the likelihood and/or presence of revealing the identity of the suicide victims (such as names and addresses) and their occupations, mentioning the details of suicide methods, indicating the occurrence places and time, discussing the leading factors and life events, describing about suicide notes, mono-causality, using the term "suicide" in headline, and printing the pictures of the events.

On the other hand, due to the unavailability of a suicide central database in Bangladesh, many of the social scientists conduct suicide related research based on the media-reported suicide data (Arafat et al., 2021a). The reported suicide rates and characteristics of suicidal behaviors in the media are not entirely representative of actual suicides in the broader population (Armstrong et al., 2019). Studies showed that suicides involving women, aged under 30 years, divorced or widowed males, unmarried females, students, and those using lethal suicide methods were significantly overreported in print media, relative to their occurrence in the broader

Table 11.1 Characteristics of media reporting of suicidal behavior in Bangladesh

Variable	Arafat et al. (2019)	Arafat et al. (2020b)	Arafat et al. (2020c)	Arafat et al. (2020d)	Arafat et al. (2025a)*	Arafat et al. (2025b)**
Sample size	320	327	403	199	163	71
Name stated	308 (96.3)		371 (92.1)	196 (98.5)	162 (99.4)	
Occupation mentioned	309 (96.6)		332 (82.4)	149 (74.9)	162 (99.4)	49 (69.0)
Method stated	307 (95.9)	322 (98.4)	285 (70.7)	168 (84.4)	116 (71.2)	71 (100)
Life events mentioned	222 (69.4)		85 (21.1)		86 (52.8)	
Public site	10 (3.1)	19 (5.8)	54 (13)	5(2.5)		
Monocausality	205 (64.1)	147 (44.7)	66 (16.4)	9 (4.5)		
Suicide note	24 (7.5)	20 (6.1)	17 (4.2)	18 (9)		
Suicide in headline	301 (94.1)	133 (40.6)	187 (46.4)	124 (62.3)	29 (17.8)	
Method in headline	60 (18.7)	35 (10.7)	128 (31.8)	62 (31.2)	11 (6.7)	
Life events in headline	102 (31.9)		12 (3)		7 (4.3)	
Photo of deceased	46 (14.4)	11 (3.4)	12 (3)	108 (54.3)	146 (89.6)	
Mental illness	9 (2.81)	20 (6.1)	11 (2.7)	0	94 (57.7)	4 (5.6)
Drug abuse	1 (0.3)		2 (0.5)	0		
Expert opinion	0	0	0	0	10 (6.1)	
Research finding	0	0	0	0	4 (2.5)	
Any statistics	0	0	0	0	9 (5.5)	
Prevention program	0	0	0	0	2 (1.2)	3 (4.2)
Educative information	0	0	0	0	2 (1.2)	
Any contact identity	0	0	0	0	0	

Values expressed as number of reports *n* (%), * = celebrity suicide; ** = movie and drama population (Armstrong et al., 2019). These types of discrepancies may lead the mass population to develop misunderstandings about current suicidal behavior in their society. Therefore, the accuracy of newspapers' suicide reporting, as well as studies that have been done using media-based suicide data, must be viewed with caution.

3.1 *Quality of Suicidal Behavior Reporting in Print Media*

In order to determine the newspaper representation on suicidal behavior, Arafat et al. (2020b) assessed the content quality of suicide cases reported in six daily newspapers in Bangladesh. Their study found that, on average, these newspapers publish at least two suicide cases daily, and the mean length of those articles was 11.3 sentences. In the story details, almost all the articles mentioned suicide methods, and more than three-fourths of the articles reported how those methods were employed during the act. Another study (Arafat et al., 2020c) showed that among the 403 suicide reports of six daily Bangladeshi newspapers, 92% stated the name of the deceased person and 82% mentioned their occupation. Additionally, description of suicidal method (71%), "suicide" in headline (46%), mention of life events (21%), and report on mono-causality (16%) were also prominently stated in the news stories (Arafat et al., 2020c). None of the studies mentioned any potentially helpful reporting practices, such as expert opinion from a mental health professional, thematic reporting/statistics related to suicide, mentioning a suicide prevention program/support service, or any contact details for a suicide support service, etc., among their selected suicide news stories (Arafat et al., 2020b, 2020c). Such reporting approaches are unintentionally conveying the message that suicide execution methods to vulnerable populations may be experiencing suicide ideation, while missing opportunities to educate and raise awareness of the public against suicide.

3.2 *Quality of Suicidal Behavior Reporting in Online News Portals*

Due to the rapid digitization in Bangladesh, a recent boom of online media portals has been observed. A few studies have analyzed the quality of suicide coverage in online news portals. Arafat et al. (2019) analyzed published contents of eight Bangla online news portals that focused on the availability of suicide news, and found that nearly 85% of the reports were related to suicide, with 93% reporting a single suicide. 95% of the stories mentioned the means and methods of suicide, and about 70% highlighted the deceased person's life circumstances that led them to the ultimate decision. Approximately 20% of the news portals mentioned the means and methods of suicide in the headlines, and 32% described the life events of the deceased person in the headline. 14% news portals presented the photo of suicide victims, which was rare in print media. Another study from Bangladesh reviewed among four online news portals (Arafat et al., 2020d). It was observed that there was significant nonadherence to WHO-recommended suicide reporting guidelines and potentially detrimental and harmful aspects, such as the deceased's identity and occupation, the method used, and the deceased's pictures were explicitly disclosed (Arafat et al., 2020a). Both studies (Arafat et al., 2019, 2020d) showed that there was no inclusion of expert comment, stress coping strategies, preventative programs, educative information for people, or help-seeking contact information (i.e., address or phone number of a help center) provided in any of the news stories. Therefore, one can imagine how poorly and unethically the online news portals are continuously reporting on suicidal behavior in Bangladesh, if compared with any standard suicide reporting guidelines.

3.3 Bangla vs. English Daily Newspapers

In Bangladesh, apart from the number of circulation and readership rates, there are some distinguishing features and qualities between Bangla- and English-language newspapers, regarding suicide. Bangla-language newspapers usually publish more suicide-related stories on a daily basis compared to the English-language newspapers (Arafat et al., 2019, 2020b, 2020c). For example, in 2017, nearly 40% suicide articles were reported in just *The Daily Jugantor* (Bangla-language newspaper), whereas one of the leading English-language newspapers (*The Daily Star*) published only 6.1% (Arafat et al., 2020b). Additionally, Bangla-language newspapers tend to publish particular suicide cases repeatedly or more than once, which is rarely found in English-language newspapers. However, there are some other underlying factors which make a significant difference between the qualities of Bangla- and English-language newspaper coverage style. Firstly, we can consider the relationship between readability and readers of a newspaper agency. In Bangladesh, the newspaper content quality and business success are not linearly correlated (Genilo et al., 2016). Again, the Bangla and English newspapers have separate readership bases (Azad, 2025). People from all socioeconomic statuses, both rural and urban, with minimum literacy, read Bangla newspapers; whereas English-language papers are read by educated urban readers. So when a journalist and/or an editor from an English newspaper tries to report sensitive issues (such as suicide), they become more concerned and rigorous about the quality of the content and try to follow any relevant guidelines. That is why English newspapers in Bangladesh might have small circulation, but most importantly, they have educative value and a big impact on the social development (Genilo et al., 2016). On the other hand, the number of circulation matters for most of the Bangla news agencies. It is well known that story sensationalization increases newsworthiness, which ultimately increases the overall readability. Since a small amount of readability augmentation can greatly increase the circulation of a newspaper, most of the journalists and news agencies just focus on the quantity of episodic news coverage, rather than the quality and thorough evaluation of their reporting style. That is why, in sensitive cases such as suicide, Bangla newspapers frequently try to create a false hype and sensation of that event by publishing the unethical details of the incident (Arafat et al., 2019). Second, although WHO has proposed some general guidelines on suicide reporting for journalists, none of the news organizations in Bangladesh have established their own code of conduct or guidelines on how suicide reporting should be. Additionally, a considerable proportion of local journalists are unaware that there are any suicide reporting guidelines for media professionals. But there is a plausible reason behind the fact. Training and regular basis, short courses can help journalists, editors, and gatekeepers to become well-informed regarding the existing suicide prevention activities in Bangladesh. Where most of the English news organizations offer training and workshops to their journalists to upgrade their credentials and globalize their reporting style, such proactive approaches are rarely found among local newspaper agencies (Hossain & Islam, 2012). So a large number of local journalists remain unaware of the suicide reporting guidelines, and eventually they report suicidal behavior in a careless and sensational manner. For these reasons, unlike English newspapers, Bangla newspapers tend to report suicide cases with unnecessary and terrible details and fail to adhere to preventive approaches to educate the population about suicide.

3.4 *Suicide Depiction in Bangla Motion Pictures*

Suicidal behavior has commonly been depicted in Bangla movies and dramas. Arafat et al. (2025b) recently conducted a study where Bangla movies and dramas with suicidal scenes and scripts were searched on YouTube. They found that in movies and dramas, younger adults were the prominent victims; suicidal attempts (both fatal and nonfatal) were commonly depicted in the leading roles (i.e., heroes and heroines); hanging followed by jumping in front of train was frequently shown as the suicide method; home was the commonest place of attempts; and females played the roles of taking most suicide attempts. Bangla movies showed that premarital/extramarital affairs and sexual harassment were the most prominent causes of suicide. Some movies depicted the scene of attempts being carried out, and a quarter of contents normalized or justified the suicide attempts in their stories. None of the movies/dramas educated the public about the preventive aspects of suicide, a negligible number of contents featured anecdotes on coping techniques with life difficulties or suicidal ideas, and how to get support from a psychologist or any tele-counseling centers (Arafat et al., 2025b).

3.5 Quality of Suicide Reporting for Celebrity Suicide

The quality of reporting of online news portals was assessed after the suicide of a singer, Sadi Mohammad, who died on 13 March 2024 (Arafat et al., 2025a). The study assessed 163 news reports published in 96 news outlets; 72.4% published in Bangla, and 27.6% of reports were published in English. It indicates the attention span of the media, as about one-third of the reports were published within the day of death, three-fourths of the reports were published within 48 h, and about 95% of the reports were published within a week. It also indicates the extent of coverage that the news was published in about 100 news outlets. The reporting was irresponsible compared to WHO media guidelines for suicide reporting, with the presence of potentially harmful characteristics and absence of potentially helpful characteristics.

4 Media Reporting Guidelines

WHO has stressed positive and responsible coverage of suicide cases, which encourages help-seeking behavior, raises awareness of suicide prevention, provides experiences of people who have overcome suicidal thoughts, or promotes coping methods, and can help reduce suicides and suicidal behavior (World Health Organization, 2023). Recently, both general and country-specific media guidelines have been developed for the concerned bodies of media organizations and professionals, which are applicable to reporting across all types of media. Along with the general guidelines provided by WHO and other similar organizations, the Samaritans and the American Foundation for Suicide Prevention have their own guidelines.

4.1 WHO Guidelines

The suicide reporting guidelines, recommended by WHO (in 2023), are generally designed in terms of any form of media coverage. But, particularly, some recommendations are more applicable to print media or digital platforms. And, as a limitation, these guidelines do not practically address issues concerning websites, movies, dramas, or stage plays. The following box represents the WHO-recommended dos and don'ts (as guidelines) for media professionals and editors while reporting on suicide events in the media (Table 11.2).

Table 11.2 Major excerpts from WHO media guidelines

Dos	Don'ts
• Do provide accurate information about where and how to seek help for suicidal behavior. • Do educate the public about the facts of suicide and suicide prevention based on facts. • Do report stories of how to cope with life stressors or suicidal thoughts, and necessity of seeking help. • Do apply particular caution when reporting celebrity suicides. • Do apply caution when interviewing bereaved family or friends or persons with lived experience of suicide. • Do recognize that media professionals themselves may be affected by stories about suicide.	• Don't report the details of suicide notes. • Don't oversimplify the reason for a suicide or reduce it to a single factor. • Don't place stories about suicide prominently and don't unduly repeat such stories. • Don't use language/content which sensationalizes, romanticizes or normalizes suicide, or that presents it as a viable solution to problems. • Don't explicitly describe the method used. • Don't provide details about the site/location. • Don't use sensational headlines. • Don't use photographs, video footage, audio recordings, or digital or social media links.

4.1.1 Brief Descriptions of WHO Guidelines

Provide Accurate Information About Where to Seek Help

Suicide-supportive information (such as counseling centers and helplines, suicide prevention and/or awareness centers, 24/7 emergency helplines, official contact address of mental health and welfare professionals, and self-help groups) should be mentioned at the end of all suicide coverage. Most importantly, the mentioned address or contact information should be regularly checked to ensure accuracy. Also, one phone number or one contact address/website should be provided rather than a long list of potential resources, since it could be counter-productive.

Educate the Public About the Facts of Suicide and Suicide Prevention, Without Spreading Myths

Media reports that repeatedly publish misconceptions and/or myths about suicide can trigger imitative behavior among the mass population (Table 11.3). So, along with leading the facts about suicide while discussing suicide, it is also important to report on how to prevent suicide, and how suicidal people and/or their families can seek help, about the accessibility of that help.

Report Stories of How to Cope with Life Stressors or Suicidal Thoughts, and How to Get Help

Reporting on the personal accounts of individuals who overcame adversity and suicidality may inspire others in challenging and stressful life situations to follow similar positive coping mechanisms. Stories that integrate educative materials typically help people to focus on the positive sides of their lives, to overcome their suicidal thoughts, and to find ways to get help for those suicidal.

Apply Particular Caution When Reporting Celebrity Suicides

Reporting on celebrity suicides increases the newsworthiness and the readership for a specific point of time. But these reports induce vulnerable people towards

Table 11.3 Myths of suicidal behavior (Adapted from WHO, 2023)

Myth	Fact
Talking about suicide can encourage suicidal behavior.	Talking about suicidal behavior can give a person the time to rethink the decision, thereby preventing suicide. It does not lead to someone taking their life.
Someone who is suicidal is determined to die	People who are suicidal are often ambivalent about living or dying, and they just want relief from their pain. Access to emotional support at the right time may prevent suicide.
Suicidal behavior is easy to explain.	Suicidal behavior is not easy to explain. It is extremely complex.
People who talk about suicide do not really intend to do it.	Speaking about suicidal thoughts and feelings needs to be taken seriously, as some persons might proceed to act on their suicidal feelings.
Most suicides happen suddenly without warning	Some suicides occur without warning; however, most have been preceded by warning signs, whether verbal (e.g., by saying "I will kill myself") or behavioral (e.g., by buying the means to take one's life).
Only people with mental health conditions are suicidal.	Many people who are suicidal do not have a mental health condition, and many people with mental health conditions do not have a wish to die.

copycat suicides. Hence, while reporting on celebrity suicides, specific points need to be taken care of. For instance, reporting style should not glamorize the suicide, avoid descriptions of the suicide method, and avoid misinterpreting the cause of suicide/death before postmortem. Instead of that, the focus should be on how that celebrity contributed to the community and how their departure negatively affected others.

Apply Caution When Interviewing Bereaved Family or Friends and Persons with Lived Experience

Several key considerations should be cautiously followed when collecting information from family, friends, and others who have been bereaved by suicide and/or who may be in a grieving situation. For example, respect for the privacy of the relatives and friends of the deceased person, instead of dramatizing the actual story, and disclosure of personal information or description of suicide notes (that might be unknown to the bereaved friends and families) should be avoided.

Recognize That Media Professionals Themselves May Be Affected by Stories About Suicide

As a human being, it is not uncommon that journalists from any setting can be resonated by their own experiences while reporting a suicide story. It is one of the obligations of media organizations to ensure the necessary supports (such as debriefing opportunities) and mentoring arrangements (could be psychological counselling too) for the media professionals.

Do Not Place Stories About Suicide Prominently and Do Not Unduly Repeat Such Stories

In terms of print and online news media, suicidal stories should be presented in the inside pages, rather than on the front page, with highlighting the term "suicide" in the headlines. On the other hand, for broadcast stories, news on suicide should be allocated either in the second or third break of television news, rather than as the lead item. Again, news editors and gatekeepers should be cautious during publication or broadcasting regarding the repetition or updating of the original story.

Do Not Use Language That Sensationalizes or Normalizes Suicide, or Presents It as a Constructive Solution to Problems

The presentation style and the reporting language have a significant influence on a society's suicidal behavior. That is why reports on "suicide rates" for a specific time period (thematic frame) are more preferable than reports on specific suicide details (episodic frame). Suicide reports using thematic frames help people to convey the message that suicide is a public health problem, and indicate the risk factors, along with educating the public on suicide prevention mechanisms. On the other hand, usage of "successful suicide" or "unsuccessful suicide" should be avoided, since they imply that suicide is a desirable outcome. Additionally, the term "committed suicide" implies criminality, though suicide is not a criminal offence in most countries worldwide. In such cases, terms like "died by suicide" or "took his/her life" could be a better fit.

Do Not Explicitly Describe the Method Used

Any types of description or discussion of the method, such as the name and number of the drugs taken for suicide, used tool (towel, knife, or blade, etc.), or any novel method that was applied for taking life, should be avoided in the coverage. Because this type of information might trigger a susceptible individual to follow and accelerate the suicidal behavior.

Do Not Provide Details About the Site/Location

Similar to the description of the suicide method, indicating the suicide occurrence place, sometimes titled as "suicide site" (e.g., a bridge, a tall building, a residential well, a cliff, or a railway station or crossing where suicidal acts have occurred) can influence the vulnerable person to imitate the act. Hence, media professionals should carefully report about the locations (if necessary) by not using sensationalist language to describe them or without mentioning the number of incidents that occurred at that location.

Do Not Use Sensational Headlines

Since news headlines are aimed to attract the readers' attention by providing the abstract of a story in as few words as possible, the application of words like "suicide" should not be used in the headlines. At the same time, applying detailed reference to the method or site of the suicide should be discouraged.

Do Not Use Photographs, Video Footage, or Digital Media Links

In terms of suicidal deaths, photographs, video footage, and social media or YouTube links of the suicide scenes, along with the suicide location and/or method, should not be reported in newspapers and/or TV. And, the disclosure of the deceased person (by suicide) should be discouraged or handled with great caution; that is, placing the picture obscurely within the text, or not glamorizing the individual or suicidal act. And, suicide notes, final text messages, call records, social media posts, or emails of the deceased persons should be kept hidden from the public.

5 Initiatives to Improve Quality of News Reporting in Bangladesh

In a critical review study, where media coverage on suicide across some countries (Bangladesh, Canada, India, Ireland, Netherlands, Slovenia, South Korea, Sri Lanka, and UK) was investigated, it was revealed that there was no help-seeking information and contact address (0%) available in the Bangladeshi and Sri Lankan suicide news stories (Stack, 2020). And based on the recent findings (Arafat et al., 2019, 2020a, 2020b, 2020c), none of the newspapers were found to follow the WHO guidelines while reporting suicide cases in the newspapers, regardless of the print and/or online media. However, to improve the quality of media coverage of suicide cases in accordance with WHO guidelines, during the last decade, media experts, policymakers, and mental health experts from both government and nongovernmental organizations have been organizing training sessions and workshops targeting the media professionals of Bangladesh.

In September 2017, a 3-h training was conducted in Cox's Bazar among the local journalists regarding media reporting of suicide conducted by Humanity and Inclusion, an international NGO under the *Mental Health and Psychosocial Support (MHPSS)* program. In the training session, general physicians, mental health experts, counsellors, and other health govt, and NGO professionals were the moderators who trained the local media professionals to assess and manage the mental health condition and suicidal behavior reporting in using the Mental Health Gap Action Programme intervention guidelines (Momotaz et al., 2019).

In 2018, to motivate the Bangladeshi journalists and encourage them on responsible reporting of suicide, WHO and the *National Institute of Mental Health* (NIMH, Bangladesh) conducted several workshops where media professionals, especially journalists and editors, from printed, electronic, and TV media channels (WHO Bangladesh, 2018). In those workshops, the organizers trained media professionals on the WHO suicide prevention guidelines (World Health Organization, 2023), that is, the "Dos" and "Don'ts," to ensure safe and responsible media coverage of suicides in Bangladesh. This initiative was repeated again in 2022 among more than 60 media professionals at NIMH, Dhaka (WHO Bangladesh, 2022).

Again, in 2022, WHO with the collaboration of Directorate General of Health Services (DGHS), and the NIMH conducted three workshops (3–5 July 2022) with the media professionals from more than 60 print, electronic, and online media of Bangladesh (WHO Bangladesh, 2022). The prime agenda of the workshops was to enhance the awareness and capacity building of media professionals for the appropriate reporting style of suicide news stories. Specifically, media professionals from the national English dailies (e.g., *The Daily Star*, *The Daily Sun*, *The New Age*, and *The Financial Express*), Bangla dailies (e.g., *Daily Prothom Alo, Bhorer Kagoj, Shmokaal*, *Bangladesh Protidin*, *Kaler Kantha*, *Jugantar*, and *Shangbad*), Bangla online news portals (e.g., *Bangla Tribune*, *BD News 24.com*, *Barta 24*, and *Jagonews 24*), and the electronic media (e.g. *Bangladesh National TV*, *71 TV*, *Nagorik*,

Boishakhi, *ATN News*, *Ekkator TV*, *Banglavision TV*, *RTV*, and *GTV*) participated in the training workshop (WHO Bangladesh, 2022).

In 2025, one dissemination program was arranged involving the motion picture producers in the country, explaining the WHO guidelines of suicide reporting (Correspondent, 2025).

6 Challenges of Sensible Media Reporting in Bangladesh

Implementation of media guidelines while reporting suicide cases could be one of the effective approaches to reduce the possibility of copycat suicide in Bangladesh. Apart from the suicide reporting guideline implementation, there are several reasons in countries like Bangladesh behind such sensationalized and careless media coverage of suicide. However, the challenges faced by media professionals in reporting suicide cases with proper guidelines are outlined below.

6.1 No National Suicide Database

Though global database such as *World Population Review*, *World Bank*, *World Life Expectance*, WHO, etc. record country-specific suicide rates, till date in Bangladesh, there is no central suicide database which could record suicide rates as well as causes, means, age and sex specific suicidal behavior, number of suicide attempts, etc. at community level (Arafat, 2025a). That is why it is hard for Bangladeshi media professionals to write statistics or evidence-based suicide reports in a thematic framework. Since most of the details of the suicide reports we read are gathered from the family members, neighbors, and workmates of the deceased, or police personnel, the news is portrayed from sociocultural, personal, and legal perspectives rather than psychological information (Arafat et al., 2021b).

6.2 No Established Suicide Prevention Policies

Bangladesh also lacks any suicide prevention strategies. Existing government and nongovernment intervening programs for suicide prevention are extremely restricted, fragmented, and nearly invisible. Though a few suicide prevention action plans have been proposed, they are not officially established and validated (Arafat, 2018, 2025b). Again, most of the suicide incidents are covered by criminal reporters. So, it would be a questionable approach if any reporter provides suicide prevention measurements by his/her own style.

6.3 Lack of Collaboration with Mental Health Professionals

Because of the shortage of mental health specialists in comparison to the population's mental health requirements, regular collaboration and discussion of media personnel with mental health professionals appears to be difficult while producing any suicide coverage (Arafat, 2024). At the same time, due to limited motivation, unavailability, and disinclination of mental health professionals, the scope of research in suicidal behavior is becoming narrower. Consequently, media professionals remain in the dark about how to convey the suicide preventive strategies, coping mechanisms, and help-seeking messages while reporting suicide in print media and Television.

6.4 Negligence of Applying Suicide Reporting Guidelines in Local Media

Suicide reporting guidelines, recommended by WHO, are not properly reflected in national dailies, let alone in local newspapers. Though there have been a few workshops to provide training on how to report suicidal cases in media, the participants were mostly from the media platforms at the national level. Hardly any journalists from the local newspaper (either online or print version) participated in such workshops. That is why in Bangladeshi local newspapers, the quality of suicide news coverage is very low, indicating the frequent negligence of WHO reporting guidelines (Arafat et al., 2020b).

6.5 Underestimation of Suicide Rates in Media

Similar to other developing nations, suicide rates are under-estimated in Bangladesh due to the lack of adequate statistics and a central suicide database (Arafat, 2019; Armstrong et al., 2019). That is, the actual rate of suicide in Bangladesh is yet to come out, and quality data remains a real challenge for the media experts, policy makers, researchers, and journalists to conduct scientific analyses using the actual data, to write suicide cases in a thematic frame, and to propose sustainable suicide reporting policies (Arafat, 2019).

6.6 Criminalized Legal Status

Since the act of suicide or suicide attempts is considered a punishable criminal act in Bangladesh (The Penal Code, 1860; Act no. XLV, Chap. 309), crime reporters mostly cover suicide news stories in print and online media platforms (Arafat et al.,

2020b). As a result, suicide is stigmatized, neglected, and the reporting style of suicidal behavior is overlooked from the mental health perspectives, as well as the suicide reporting guidelines in media.

6.7 *Ignoring the Social Variables Influencing Suicidality*

In terms of suicide provoking socioeconomic factors in Bangladesh (i.e., younger age, failure in examinations, family history of suicide, substance usage, problem in workplace, financial debts, one-sided affair and/or break-ups, domestic violence, divorce, and mental illness), media should place a greater emphasis on the social reasons that led to the individual's suicide (Arafat et al. 2021a, 2021b; Arafat, 2019; Arafat & Saleem, 2025). This will also shift suicide from the sphere of mental disease to that of a "social sickness," perhaps de-stigmatizing help-seeking. On the other hand, the media should highlight the relevance of locally protective factors in lowering the risk of suicidal behavior. For example, it is believed that religious affiliation could be one of the important protective factors, particularly in Muslim countries, to discourage any attempt or act of suicide. But, this circumstance might also be contradictory (Hendin & World Health Organization, 2008). Hence, the public should be informed by the media about local study findings on suicide that are relevant to their area.

7 Recommendations

In the National Mental Health Strategic Plan (2020–2030) of Bangladesh, the Ministry of Health and Family Welfare's Department of Non-Communicable Diseases has proposed to take action on the development of the "National Suicide Prevention Program" and the establishment of the "National Suicide Registry" (Government of the People's Republic of Bangladesh, 2022; Arafat, 2025a, 2025b). Hence, the following recommendations might be worth considering while developing the National Suicide Prevention Policy, along with the improvements and expansions based on the feedback from media professionals and experts.

7.1 *Adaptation of Suicide Reporting Guidelines*

Journalists should cover the suicide stories following the WHO-provided guidelines. At the same time, there are three considerations which journalists should keep in mind (Sinyor et al., 2018): (a) weighing the newsworthiness of the story against the public's need to be warned about possible contagion risk; (b) taking into account the impact of the report on those mentally vulnerable individuals who are thinking of suicide or potentially at-risk for suicide; and (c) using a long-form reporting approach to cover the issue since it gives journalists the chance to engage in nuanced conversation and may help them to avoid oversimplifying the leading factors of suicide.

7.2 *Multisectoral Collaboration*

Since journalists are the experts in their area, they must take the lead in responsible suicide reporting. But media organizations and authorities should have frequent meetings, roundtable discussions, and forums to discuss suicide and its reporting style in collaboration with mental health professionals at a regular basis. At the same time, multisectoral collaboration should be established by media professionals, along with clinicians, social scientists, researchers, donors, social workers, voluntary organizations, nongovernmental organization, government, and/or any local organization connected with suicidality in Bangladesh.

7.3 *Decriminalization*

Decriminalization of suicide would help to destigmatize the existing problem, encourage appropriate care-seeking behaviors for suicidality, and eliminate unnecessary legal harassment. Because, already in many Asian countries, there have been changes in the legal system to decriminalize suicide, and it has been considered an immediate priority (Arafat, 2025b, 2026). Finding out the appropriate prevention strategy, along with decriminalization of suicide, is immediately necessary to formulate, initiate, implement and evaluate its effectiveness.

7.4 *Health Reporters, Not Crime Reporters, Should Cover Suicide Stories*

Since crime reporters exclusively use unnecessary details, including photos and description of the method and/or situation of the event, health reporters are more suitable to cover suicide stories by avoiding the glorification of a suicide (especially for the celebrity cases) and the content of suicide notes (Sinyor et al., 2018). Additionally, health reports are aware of the public health issues, and they are most likely to report suicidal behaviors with help-seeking measures. Hence, this practice will minimize the possibility of detrimental suicide reporting practices, and, contrarily, it can make a positive contribution to the suicide prevention of a country.

7.5 *Training for the Journalists*

Journalism schools and media organizations should incorporate teaching and training sessions on how to report about suicide responsibly and respectfully, with an emphasis on ethics and social justice. Additionally, to make these ethical reporting practices sustainable, such training sessions and workshops should be conducted both for national and local (district level) journalists.

8 Conclusion

In this chapter, the role of media on suicidality, the quality of current suicide reporting style in media, utilization of suicide reporting guidelines by the media professionals, and the challenges of suicide reporting in media, along with some recommendations, have been discussed. While reporting on suicide cases, media professionals frequently revealed the identity of the suicide victims; mentioned the details of suicide methods; indicated the occurrence places and time; discussed the leading factors and life events; mono-causality; and used the term "suicide" in headlines, etc. to sensationalize and/or glorify the suicidal deaths. Such reporting approaches are unintentionally enhancing the likelihood of contagion suicides. Surprisingly, there were no expert comments, stress coping strategies, preventative programs, educational information for people, or help-seeking contact information, etc. provided in any of the news stories, which could effectively reduce the suicide rates and suicidal thoughts among the vulnerable individuals. Additionally, none of the newspapers (either print or online) followed the WHO guidelines while reporting suicide cases. Again, due to the lack of adequate statistics and a central suicide database, the actual rate of suicide in Bangladesh is yet to come out, and quality data remains a real challenge for media researchers, psychologists, and policymakers. However, these efforts indeed warrant the proactive and multisectoral collaboration within the country so that an appropriate prevention strategy can be developed and implemented to ensure the responsible suicide reporting in the media.

References

Arafat, S. (2018). Suicide prevention activities in Bangladesh. *Asian Journal of Psychiatry, 36*, 38. https://doi.org/10.1016/j.ajp.2018.06.009

Arafat, S. M. Y. (2019). Current challenges of suicide and future directions of management in Bangladesh: A systematic review. *Global Psychiatry, 2*(1), 09–20. https://doi.org/10.2478/gp-2019-0001

Arafat, S. M. Y. (2024). Mental health services in Bangladesh. In S. M. Y. Arafat (Ed.), *Mental health in Bangladesh*. Springer. https://doi.org/10.1007/978-981-97-0610-5_3

Arafat, S. Y. (2025a). Suicide is criminal, data is silent: Reimagining suicide surveillance in Bangladesh—From police reports to public health action. *International Journal of Mental Health and Addiction, 1–3*. https://doi.org/10.1007/s11469-025-01514-1

Arafat, S. M. Y. (2025b). Suicide prevention in Bangladesh: Critical analysis of mental health law, policy and strategy. *BJPsych International, 22*(4), 138–141. https://doi.org/10.1192/bji.2025.10042

Arafat, S. M. Y. (2026). Law, policy, and strategies on suicide prevention in Bangladesh. In S. M. Y. Arafat (Ed.), *Suicidal Behavior in Bangladesh*. Springer. https://doi.org/10.1007/978-981-95-8321-8_10

Arafat, S. M. Y., & Saleem, T. (2025). Suicide in Bangladesh: An ecological systems analysis. *Brain and Behavior, 15*(1), e70233. https://doi.org/10.1002/brb3.70233

Arafat, S. M. Y., Mali, B., & Akter, H. (2019). Quality of online news reporting of suicidal behavior in Bangladesh against World Health Organization guidelines. *Asian Journal of Psychiatry, 40*, 126–129. https://doi.org/10.1016/j.ajp.2018.10.010

Arafat, S. M. Y., Kar, S. K., Marthoenis, M., Cherian, A. V., Vimala, L., & Kabir, R. (2020a). Quality of media reporting of suicidal behaviors in South-East Asia. *Neurology, Psychiatry and Brain Research, 37*, 21–26. https://doi.org/10.1016/j.npbr.2020.05.007

Arafat, S. M. Y., Khan, M. M., Niederkrotenthaler, T., Ueda, M., & Armstrong, G. (2020b). Assessing the quality of media reporting of suicide deaths in Bangladesh against World Health Organization guidelines. *Crisis, 41*(1), 47–53. https://doi.org/10.1027/0227-5910/a000603

Arafat, S. M. Y., Mali, B., & Akter, H. (2020c). Is suicide reporting in Bangla online news portals sensible? A year-round content analysis against World Health Organization guidelines. *Asian Journal of Psychiatry, 49*. https://doi.org/10.1016/j.ajp.2020.101943

Arafat, S. M. Y., Mali, B., & Akter, H. (2020d). Do Bangladeshi newspapers educate public while reporting suicide? A year round observation from content analysis of six national newspapers. *Asian Journal of Psychiatry, 48*, 101920. https://doi.org/10.1016/j.ajp.2019.101920

Arafat, S. M. Y., Hussain, F., Jakaria, K. M., Itu, Z. T., & Islam, M. A. (2021a). Empirical studies on suicide in Bangladesh in a decade (2011-2020). *Global Psychiatry Archives, 4*(1), 109–122. https://doi.org/10.52095/gp.2021.10692

Arafat, S. M. Y., Menon, V., & Kar, S. K. (2021b). Media and suicide prevention in Southeast Asia: Challenges and directions. *Journal of Public Health, 43*(1), e123–e124. https://doi.org/10.1093/pubmed/fdaa084

Arafat, S. M. Y., Sultana, Y., & Akter, H. (2025a). Quality of News Reporting of Celebrity Suicide in Bangladesh against World Health Organization Guidelines. *Global Psychiatry Archives, 8*(1), 1–7. https://doi.org/10.52095/gpa.2025.7579.1100

Arafat, S. M. Y., Jalil, S. B., Alam, M. S., Sultana, N., Ahmed, M. I. U., Abedin, M. M., & Armstrong, G. (2025b). Suicide in bangla movie and drama: A content analysis. *Omega, 91*(2), 1058–1071. https://doi.org/10.1177/00302228221148286

Armstrong, G., Vijayakumar, L., Pirkis, J., Jayaseelan, M., Cherian, A., Soerensen, J. B., Arya, V., & Niederkrotenthaler, T. (2019). Mass media representation of suicide in a high suicide state in India: An epidemiological comparison with suicide deaths in the population. *BMJ Open, 9*(7), e030836. https://doi.org/10.1136/bmjopen-2019-030836

Azad, M. A. K. (2025). *Media landscapes—Bangladesh*. Media Landscapes. https://medialandscapes.org/country/pdf/bangladesh

Bandura, A. (1969). Social-learning theory of identificatory processes. *Handbook of Socialization Theory and Research, 213*, 262.

BBC News. (2018, June 20). *New Jersey school sued over bullied girl's suicide*. https://www.bbc.com/news/world-us-canada-44552864.

Correspondent, S., (2025). Suicide prevention needs multi-pronged efforts: experts. *The Daily Star*. https://www.thedailystar.net/news/bangladesh/news/suicide-prevention-needs-multi-pronged-efforts-experts-4019706 (accesed October 27, 2025).

Genilo, J. W., Asiuzzaman, M., & Osmani, M. M. H. (2016). Small circulation, big impact: English language newspaper readability in Bangladesh. *Advances in Journalism and Communication, 4*(4), 4. https://doi.org/10.4236/ajc.2016.44012

Gould, M. S. (2001). Suicide and the media. *Annals of the New York Academy of Sciences, 932*, 200–221.; discussion 221–224. https://doi.org/10.1111/j.1749-6632.2001.tb05807.x

Government of the People's Republic of Bangladesh. (2022). *National mental health strategic plan, 2020–2030. Government of the People's Republic of Bangladesh* (https://old.dghs.gov.bd/index.php/bd/home/6171-nmu-2020-2030 [cited 21 Dec 2024]).

Hawton, K., & van Heeringen, K. (2009). Suicide. *The Lancet, 373*(9672), 1372–1381. https://doi.org/10.1016/S0140-6736(09)60372-X

Hendin, H., & World Health Organization. (2008). *Suicide and suicide prevention in Asia*. World Health Organization. https://www.who.int/publications/i/item/9789241596893

Hossain, M. A., & Islam, M. S. (2012). Information-seeking by print media journalists in Rajshahi, Bangladesh. *IFLA Journal, 38*(4), 283–288.

Momotaz, H., Ahmed, H. U., Uddin, M. M. J., Karim, R., Khan, M. A., Al-Amin, R., Anwar, N., & Kessaram, T. (2019). Implementing the Mental health gap action programme in Cox's Bazar, Bangladesh. *Intervention, 17*(2), 243. https://doi.org/10.4103/INTV.INTV_14_19

Myers, D. (2012). *Social psychology* (11th ed.). McGraw-Hill Education.

Naghavi, M. (2019). Global, regional, and national burden of suicide mortality 1990 to 2016: Systematic analysis for the Global Burden of Disease Study 2016. *BMJ, 364*, 194. https://doi.org/10.1136/bmj.l94

Niederkrotenthaler, T., Voracek, M., Herberth, A., Till, B., Strauss, M., Etzersdorfer, E., Eisenwort, B., & Sonneck, G. (2010). Role of media reports in completed and prevented suicide: Werther v. Papageno effects. *The British journal of psychiatry, 197*(3), 234–243. https://doi.org/10.1192/bjp.bp.109.074633

Niederkrotenthaler, T., Braun, M., Pirkis, J., Till, B., Stack, S., Sinyor, M., Tran, U. S., Voracek, M., Cheng, Q., & Arendt, F. (2020). Association between suicide reporting in the media and suicide: Systematic review and meta-analysis. *BMJ, 368*. https://doi.org/10.1136/bmj.m575

Sanger-Katz, M. (2014). The science behind suicide contagion. *The New York Times*. https://www.nytimes.com/2014/08/14/upshot/the-science-behind-suicide-contagion.html

Schonfeld, Z. (2017). *After Chester Bennington's death, suicide experts fear a contagion effect*. Newsweek https://www.newsweek.com/chester-bennington-suicide-linkin-park-chris-cornell-639940

Sinyor, M., Schaffer, A., Heisel, M. J., Picard, A., Adamson, G., Cheung, C. P., Katz, L. Y., Jetly, R., & Sareen, J. (2018). Media guidelines for reporting on suicide: 2017 update of the Canadian Psychiatric Association policy paper. *The Canadian Journal of Psychiatry, 63*(3), 182–196. https://doi.org/10.1177/0706743717753147

Sisask, M., & Värnik, A. (2012). Media roles in suicide prevention: A systematic review. *International Journal of Environmental Research and Public Health, 9*(1), 123–138. https://doi.org/10.3390/ijerph9010123

Stack, S. (2002). Media coverage as a risk factor in suicide. *Injury Prevention, 8*(Suppl 4), iv30–iv32. https://doi.org/10.1136/ip.8.suppl_4.iv30

Stack, S. (2020). Media guidelines and suicide: A critical review. *Social Science and Medicine, 262*, 112690. https://doi.org/10.1016/j.socscimed.2019.112690

Wheeler, L. (1966). Toward a theory of behavioral contagion. *Psychological Review, 73*(2), 179–192. https://doi.org/10.1037/h0023023

WHO Bangladesh. (2018, November 4). *Workshops for journalists on responsible reporting of suicide*. https://www.who.int/bangladesh/news/detail/04-11-2018-workshops-for-journalists-on-responsible-reporting-of-suicide

WHO Bangladesh. (2022, July 25). *Workshop on responsible reporting on suicide!*. https://www.who.int/bangladesh/news/detail/25-07-2022-workshop-on-responsible-reporting-on-suicide (accessed September 03, 2025).

World Health Organization. (2014). *Preventing suicide: A global imperative*. WHO. https://apps.who.int/iris/handle/10665/131056 (accessed on July 15, 2022).

World Health Organization. (2021). *Suicide worldwide in 2019: Global health estimates*. https://www.who.int/publications/i/item/9789240026643 (accessed 31 August, 2025).

World Health Organization. (2023). *Preventing suicide: A resource for media professionals: Update 2023*. https://www.who.int/publications-detail-redirect/9789240076846 (accessed on April 17, 2024).

World Health Organization. (2025). Suicide. WHO. Available online: https://www.who.int/news-room/fact-sheets/detail/suicide (accessed on 27 May 2025).

Zalsman, G., Hawton, K., Wasserman, D., van Heeringen, K., Arensman, E., Sarchiapone, M., et al. (2016). Suicide prevention strategies revisited: 10-year systematic review. *The Lancet. Psychiatry, 3*(7), 646–659. https://doi.org/10.1016/S2215-0366(16)30030-X

Chapter 12
Literacy and Stigma of Suicide in Bangladesh

S. M. Yasir Arafat and Syeda Ayat-e-Zainab Ali

1 Literacy, Stigma, and Suicide Prevention

Suicide is a preventable behaviour, notwithstanding the concerning suicide statistics (World Health Organization, 2025). Suicide prevention and help-seeking for suicidal behaviour depend on several factors, including cultural representation, a higher level of stigma associated with suicidal behaviour, and a lack of literacy connected to suicide or mental health (Aldalaykeh et al., 2020; Jahan et al., 2023). While literacy encompasses knowledge about mental disorders or suicidality, including signs and symptoms, risk factors, and prevention and treatment approaches, it can also help with identification and appropriate help-seeking (Calear et al., 2022, 2024). Stigma is defined as negative attitudes or beliefs towards an individual or group based on specific characteristics (Subu et al., 2021).

Research indicates that those with mental health issues who experience stigma and prejudice may be more likely to consider suicide (Pierantonelli et al., 2024; Ali et al., 2025). The short- and long-term mediating factors in this association are self-stigma, according to a study by Oexle et al. (2018). It has been determined that knowledge regarding suicide may both promote help-seeking behaviours (Calear et al., 2024) and lessen the consequences of stigma (Takahashi et al., 2023). Among other characteristics, educational attainment, gender, age, prior exposure to intimate encounters, and cultural background are all strongly associated with this notion, which relates to public understanding about this issue (i.e., causes, risk factors)

S. M. Y. Arafat (✉)
Department of Psychiatry, Bangladesh Specialized Hospital, Dhaka, Bangladesh

Faculty of Medicine and Health Sciences, Department of Public and Community Health, Frontier University Garowe, Garowe, Somalia

S. Ayat-e-Zainab Ali
Department of Clinical Psychology, Shifa Tameer-e-Millat University, Islamabad, Pakistan

S. M. Y. Arafat (ed.), *Suicidal Behavior in Bangladesh*, Mental Health Systems and Policy in Low- and Middle-Income Countries,
https://doi.org/10.1007/978-981-95-8321-8_12

(Batterham et al., 2013; Jorm, 2000). Similarly, peer support networks with higher suicide literacy tend to promote professional help-seeking instead of self-help (Cruwys et al., 2018).

Higher literacy lowers stigmatising attitudes, which in turn increases help-seeking behaviours, according to studies that clearly reveal a negative association between stigma and literacy (Jahan et al., 2023). For instance, among students, more positive attitudes on seeking psychological support are correlated with better knowledge about suicide (Güler et al., 2025). Therefore, increasing suicide literacy is an essential preventative measure because it normalises conversations about suicidal thoughts, reduces stigma, and encourages early intervention—all of which are critical for saving lives.

2 Literacy and Stigma of Suicide in Bangladesh

The sociodemographic profile and cultural background of Bangladesh have a major impact on the prevalence and trends of suicidal behaviour (Arafat, 2019). Bangladesh probably has far higher suicide rates than are officially recorded, mostly as a result of widespread stigma, cultural taboos, and inadequate reporting procedures. To comprehend and address this significant public health issue, it is imperative to address these difficulties (Arafat & Kabir, 2026). There is growing evidence that suicide behaviour is an unaddressed issue that requires thorough research (Arafat, 2024). Existing research shows that suicide rates in Bangladesh vary greatly, with rural communities and women experiencing greater rates (Arafat et al., 2025; Arafat & Khan, 2024; Arafat & Kabir, 2026).

In Bangladesh, stigma is still a major obstacle to prevention, and there is still a lack of knowledge about suicide. Recent research assessing stigma and suicide literacy in young adults revealed a negative correlation between stigmatising views and suicide literacy. Suicide literacy was lower and stigmatising attitudes were more prevalent among male subjects, respondents with chronic mental illness, smokers, those who were single, divorced, or bereaved, and those with lower levels of education (below HSC) (Jahan et al., 2023). While stigma was significantly lower among female university students and those with a history of past attempts, Arafat et al. (2022a) found that suicide literacy was significantly higher among female students, medical students, those with a family history of suicidal attempts, and those with a history of non-fatal student attempts. The study by Arafat et al. (2022b) also assesses the suicide stigma and suicide literacy of Bangladeshi medical students. A higher level of suicidal behaviour and a history of prior mental health care use indicated the efficacy of mass media initiatives in lowering stigma and increasing awareness.

In Bangladesh, validation studies of the Literacy of Suicide Scale (LOSS) and Stigma of Suicide Scale (SOSS) scales revealed gaps in basic knowledge and associated higher stigma with a decreased willingness to recommend professional help. These findings suggest that low suicide literacy reduces the recognition of warning signs and delays the seeking of professional help (Arafat et al., 2022a; Maruf et al.,

2022; Islam et al., 2024). According to the WHO's 2019 National Mental Health Survey, about 17% of Bangladeshi adults experience mental health issues. About 92.3% of them do not seek medical help; this statistic is partly explained by stigma, low mental health knowledge, and a lack of resources (Ministry of Health & Family Welfare, 2021; Ahmed & Sifat, 2021).

The official mortality statistics probably undercount suicides because of cultural taboos and legal complications that discourage accurate reporting and disclosure, despite epidemiological work showing significant suicidal ideation and attempts across community and student samples (Arafat et al., 2025, 2018). Interventions must work on several levels because stigma is social and internalised. These levels include identifying and referring at-risk individuals, improving population suicide literacy through mass media and school campaigns, and reforming legal and policy barriers that maintain secrecy (Arafat, 2025a).

3 Literacy and Stigma: Current Status and Challenges of Suicide Prevention in Bangladesh

In Bangladesh, suicide and suicide prevention receive insufficient attention (Arafat, 2019). According to Hoque and Arafat (2026), the main obstacles to suicide prevention in the nation are the absence of a national suicide database and suicide prevention programme, the criminal legal status of suicide, stigma, subpar media coverage, a lack of clinical services for suicidal behaviour, and a lack of funding (Haque & Arafat, 2026; Arafat, 2025b, 2025c). Despite an increase in suicide research in Bangladesh in recent years, few studies have examined the prevalence of suicide stigma and related factors in the general population, as well as literacy levels.

Suicide literacy among various groups, including young adults, medical students, doctors, religious leaders, and other community stakeholders, has been the subject of several recent studies conducted in Bangladesh. Suicide literacy levels range from modest to low, according to the findings. The mean literacy score, according to Jahan et al. (2023), was 3.86 on a scale of 0–12. These findings also showed that respondents with chronic mental illness, smokers, unmarried/divorced/widowed male subjects, and those with lower levels of education had higher stigmatising attitudes and lower suicide literacy. Maruf et al. (2022) found that doctors with a family history of suicide, those who were single, and those who had experienced suicidal thoughts both in their lifetime and within the previous year had higher suicide literacy. In the SOSS-B stigma subscale, respondents with a history of mental illness scored much lower on stigma than Muslims and city dwellers. According to Arafat et al. (2022b), stigma was significantly lower among female students, those with mental disorders, those with a family history of suicide attempts, and those who had suicidal thoughts in the past year and throughout their lives. Meanwhile, literacy was significantly higher among married students, students with psychiatric disorders and chronic physical illnesses, and students who had suicidal thoughts in the past year. Although they frequently exhibit higher levels of literacy than the general population, discrepancies nevertheless exist even among medical professionals and trainees (Jahan et al., 2023).

The degree of schooling, living in an urban area, and having previously encountered mental health information are all factors that influence literacy. While formal education and mental health training enhance awareness of risk factors and where to get assistance, they may not always result in a decrease in stigma or the desire for help, particularly when cultural and religious beliefs prevent people from talking about self-harm in public. Overall, a lack of suicide literacy across large populations hinders community-level prevention, prompt help-seeking, and early detection.

In Bangladesh, there are several facets to the stigma associated with mental illness and suicide. Suicide is often framed as wicked, shameful, or dishonourable by cultural and religious traditions, which leads to social exclusion, familial secrecy, and a reluctance to talk about suicidal thoughts. Local responses are frequently shaped by religious leaders and community elders, whose opinions can either reinforce stigma or, when involved, serve as a resource for compassionate outreach (Islam et al., 2024). According to a recent study by Islam et al. (2024), suicide literacy among Bangladesh's Imams (Islamic religious leaders) is poor and comparable to that of undergraduates. High levels of public stigma are documented by empirical studies on individuals who attempt suicide, and stigmatising views can exist among healthcare professionals as well, impeding the provision of compassionate care (Faruk et al., 2023).

The criminalisation of attempted suicide and the involvement of law enforcement and medico-legal processes in suspected self-harm fatalities have historically deterred families from reporting attempts and survivors from seeking medical attention, which exacerbates societal stigma (Arafat, 2025a). Punitive post-attempt processes, the lack of confidential reporting channels, and criminalisation all work together to stifle surveillance, skew official statistics, and impede prevention, as recent policy analysis and commentary have shown. As a first step towards de-stigmatization and improved surveillance, legal framework reform is frequently advised (Arafat, 2025a).

The risk of suicide and the ability to prevent it are influenced by both stigma and literacy. While high stigma deters disclosure and help-seeking even in cases when recognition is present, low literacy makes it possible to overlook symptoms and warning indicators. Improved literacy, on the other hand, may raise awareness but discourage individuals from taking action if it is not accompanied by initiatives to lessen stigma. If societal views discourage disclosure, for instance, a young person who notices suicidal thoughts in a peer may not have the information or the courage to intervene. Information campaigns alone are less likely to result in behaviour change than interventions that target both knowledge and attitudes, such as integrating psychoeducation with community conversations conducted by reliable local personalities (Jahan et al., 2023).

In Bangladesh, social and religious elements continue to have a significant impact on all facets of life, including the laws governing suicide, diagnosis registration, and stigma. Additionally, the families fear police persecution, societal humiliation, and religious ramifications, so they do not reveal the actual nature of the death

(Bose & Arafat, 2026). Bangladesh's health system and policy framework for suicide prevention show both growing awareness of the problem and significant inadequacies that impede advancement (Arafat, 2019). Although suicide has been acknowledged as a major public health concern, Bangladesh still lacks a comprehensive, fully resourced national suicide prevention strategy consistent with the World Health Organization's (WHO) recommended framework (Arafat, 2024).

According to the psychological autopsy study in Bangladesh, 87% of the suicides did not reach mental health care (Arafat et al., 2021), while according to the National Mental Health Survey, only 10% of people with mental illnesses sought mental health treatment (Ministry of Health & Family Welfare, 2021). A person's decision to seek treatment for a mental illness might be influenced by a variety of socioeconomic variables. Compared to people from the least developed nations, where average education and awareness levels are lower, those from developed nations with greater average education are more likely to seek mental healthcare treatments. Other variables that influence the behaviour of people seeking mental health care include geography, gender, age, and prior experience with mental diseases, according to mental health literature. Rural residents typically have less access to mental health care services than their urban counterparts (Huque et al., 2025).

Suicide risk in Bangladesh is influenced by factors other than the health system, such as social expectations, gender roles, family dynamics, and economic burdens. Epidemiological and qualitative research frequently identifies family conflict, intimate partner violence, academic pressure, and unemployment as proximal stressors (Huque et al., 2025).

According to numerous community surveys, women and teenagers seem to be especially at risk, while male suicides go unreported due to different methods of death and reporting customs. Other structural factors include poverty, debt, agricultural hardship, and access to pesticides, which is a major cause of suicides in rural areas. A multisectoral approach that addresses social determinants in addition to mental health care is therefore necessary for any prevention plan (Arafat, 2025a).

Notwithstanding these difficulties, there has been substantial development. Calls for decriminalisation, more public discussion, and the inclusion of mental health in Bangladesh's universal health care goal all point to a change in priorities. Current initiatives, however, will continue to be dispersed and inadequate in the absence of a cohesive national strategy, strong surveillance, legislative reform, and a methodical integration of suicide prevention into the primary healthcare system.

4 Ways Forward for Suicide Prevention in Bangladesh

Suicidal thoughts have preceded the suicide attempt in those who attempt suicide. An attempt at suicide is therefore a sign of extreme mental pain. Early intervention is a cornerstone of the WHO's global suicide prevention programme. According to Ali et al. (2025), early intervention is crucial in preventing poor consequences, including suicide death, when it comes to suicidal ideation. Research indicates that many who are contemplating suicide have benefited from getting the right help. However, a major obstacle to accomplishing this fundamental tenet of suicide prevention is that people frequently put off getting help for mental health issues until they are in a very bad situation (Thomás et al., 2024).

The general public's mental health literacy has been found to be low (Thomás et al., 2024), but mental health literacy is important when it comes to getting help for mental health issues because knowing that help is available and how to get it influences action (Wei et al., 2015). Furthermore, the public's unfavourable perceptions of those who struggle with mental health issues can have a lasting effect on such individuals, perhaps facilitating or impeding their ability to rehabilitate (Thomás et al., 2024).

A multifaceted strategy that tackles both widespread stigma and low suicide literacy is necessary for effective suicide prevention in Bangladesh. Increasing public awareness is an important first step. According to research, suicide literacy is low in Bangladesh, where there are many misunderstandings that suicide is only related to moral failings or sin, as well as a lack of knowledge about warning signals and available treatments (Arafat et al., 2022b). To debunk myths and normalize help-seeking, national awareness campaigns—displayed through educational institutions, religious organisations, the media, and schools—should be culturally tailored. While community gatekeeper training for educators, medical professionals, and religious leaders can improve early diagnosis and referral routes, school-based mental health education can give youth coping skills.

The reduction of stigma is equally important. According to studies, stigma contributes to underreporting of suicide and delays disclosure and treatment (Arafat et al., 2022a, 2022b). Interventions must involve powerful community members, especially religious leaders, to combat this and present suicide prevention in a sympathetic, faith-sensitive manner. Another crucial step is to decriminalise suicide because punitive laws discourage people from getting help and perpetuate stigma (Arafat et al., 2022b). Services can be made more accessible by incorporating suicide prevention within the *National Mental Health Strategic Plan* (2020–2030), which is backed by primary care funding and task shifting to non-specialist clinicians (Arafat, 2025a; Spottswood et al., 2022). Additionally, since families are frequently the first to respond in emergency circumstances, family-centred programmes ought to be given priority. Isolation and recurrence risks can be decreased by education and post-attempt support for families. Bangladesh may transition to a more efficient, humane, and community-based suicide prevention paradigm by concurrently increasing literacy, eliminating stigma, changing legislation, and extending access to care (Arafat et al., 2022c).

One of the most effective ways to address the issue of suicide is through suicide prevention programmes, which are frequently at the forefront of suicide prevention initiatives. These programmes teach the general public how to recognise and effectively intervene with people who are at risk for suicide (Platt & Niederkrotenthaler, 2020). As a result, public awareness of the factors that encourage and hinder help-seeking may be crucial in promoting early intervention, which informs suicide prevention legislation. Understanding mental health literacy and its relationship to attitudes and beliefs regarding suicide could help South Asian communities, such as Bangladesh, by giving policymakers insight into evidence-based tactics that support early intervention for suicide prevention. Thus, encouraging early intervention for suicide prevention through evidence-based measures.

Therefore, increasing suicide literacy can assist people and communities in recognising and addressing suicide risk more effectively. Furthermore, by combating the stigma associated with suicide, people and communities can foster a more welcoming and encouraging atmosphere for those who are experiencing suicidal thoughts, lowering the chance of social isolation and raising the chances that they will seek treatment. Not much research has been done on the young generation's lack of suicide literacy. By increasing suicide literacy, communities and individuals may be able to recognise persons who could be at risk for suicide based on their behaviour, feelings, and other risk factors. This may result in early assistance and intervention, which may help prevent suicidal thoughts and actions.

5 Conclusions

Suicide prevention in Bangladesh requires a concerted approach that increases awareness, decreases stigmatising attitudes, increases the number of resources available, and fortifies surveillance. Enhancing suicide literacy is a practical, research-based measure that can lessen stigma and encourage getting help earlier, two important factors in reducing suicide risk across the country.

References

Ahmed, F., & Sifat, R. I. (2021). Strategic assessment of mental health and suicide amid COVID-19 pandemic in Bangladesh. *The International Journal of Health Planning and Management, 36*(3), 980–985. https://doi.org/10.1002/hpm.3121

Aldalaykeh, M., Dalky, H., Shahrour, G., & Rababa, M. (2020). Psychometric properties of two Arabic Suicide Scales: Stigma and literacy. *Heliyon, 6*(4), e03877. https://doi.org/10.1016/j.heliyon.2020.e03877

Ali, S. A. E. Z., Saleem, T., & Arafat, S. Y. (2025). Risk factors for suicide in Pakistan: A mixed methods study of psychological autopsies and perspectives of health professionals. *Archives of Suicide Research, 29*(4), 891–910. https://doi.org/10.1080/13811118.2024.2436635

Arafat, S. M. Y., & Kabir, R. (2026). Data is silent, epidemiology is blur: Suicidal behavior in Bangladesh-what is known and what needs to improve. In S. M. Y. Arafat (Ed.), *Suicidal behavior in Bangladesh*. Springer. https://doi.org/10.1007/978-981-95-8321-8_1

Arafat, S. M. Y., Baminiwatta, A., Amin, R., Akter, H., & Kabir, R. (2025). Prevalence of suicidal behavior in Bangladesh: A systematic review and meta-analysis. *Health Science Reports, 8*(8), e71200. https://doi.org/10.1002/hsr2.71200

Arafat, S. Y. (2025a). Suicide prevention in Bangladesh: Critical analysis of mental health law, policy and strategy. *BJPsych International, 22*(4), 138–141. https://doi.org/10.1192/bji.2025.10042

Arafat, S. M. Y. (2025b). Suicide prevention in Bangladesh: The role of police. *The Lancet. Psychiatry, 12*(3), 173. https://doi.org/10.1016/S2215-0366(24)00443-7

Arafat, S. M. Y. (2025c). Suicide is criminal, data is silent: Reimagining suicide surveillance in Bangladesh—From police reports to public health action. *International Journal of Mental Health and Addiction*. https://doi.org/10.1007/s11469-025-01514-1

Arafat, S. M. Y. (2024). Suicidal behavior and suicide prevention in Bangladesh. In S. M. Y. Arafat (Ed.), *Mental health in Bangladesh*. Springer. https://doi.org/10.1007/978-981-97-0610-5_11

Arafat, S. M. Y., & Khan, A. R. (2024). Suicidal behavior in Bangladesh. In S. M. Y. Arafat, M. Rezaeian, & M. M. Khan (Eds.), *Suicidal behavior in muslim majority countries*. Springer. https://doi.org/10.1007/978-981-97-2519-9_4

Arafat, S. M. Y., Hussain, F., Hossain, M. F., Islam, M. A., & Menon, V. (2022a). Literacy and stigma of suicide in Bangladesh: Scales validation and status assessment among university students. *Brain and Behavior, 12*(1), e2432. https://doi.org/10.1002/brb3.2432

Arafat, S. Y., Maruf, M. M., & Hossain, M. F. (2022b). Literacy and stigma of suicide among medical students of Bangladesh: Status and associated factors. *Bangladesh Medical Research Council Bulletin, 48*(3), 225–230. https://doi.org/10.3329/bmrcb.v48i3.62430

Arafat, S. M. Y., Saleem, T., Edwards, T. M., Ali, S. A., & Khan, M. M. (2022c). Suicide prevention in Bangladesh: The role of family. *Brain and Behavior, 12*(5), e2562. https://doi.org/10.1002/brb3.2562

Arafat, S. M. Y., Mohit, M. A., Mullick, M. S. I., Kabir, R., & Khan, M. M. (2021). Risk factors for suicide in Bangladesh: Case-control psychological autopsy study. *BJPsych Open, 7*(1), e18. https://doi.org/10.1192/bjo.2020.152

Arafat, S. M. Y. (2019). Current challenges of suicide and future directions of management in Bangladesh: A systematic review. *Global Psychiatry, 2*(1), 9–20. https://doi.org/10.2478/gp-2019-0001

Arafat, S. M. Y., Mali, B., & Akter, H. (2018). Demography and risk factors of suicidal behavior in Bangladesh: A retrospective online news content analysis. *Asian Journal of Psychiatry, 36*, 96–99. https://doi.org/10.1016/j.ajp.2018.07.008

Batterham, P. J., Calear, A. L., & Christensen, H. (2013). Correlates of suicide stigma and suicide literacy in the community. *Suicide and Life-Threatening Behavior, 43*(4), 406–417. https://doi.org/10.1111/sltb.12026

Bose, P. K., & Arafat, S. M. Y. (2026). Forensic medicine, post-mortem and suicide in Bangladesh. In S. Y. Arafat (Ed.), *Suicidal behavior in Bangladesh*. Springer. https://doi.org/10.1007/978-981-95-8321-8_2

Calear, A. L., Batterham, P. J., Trias, A., & Christensen, H. (2022). The literacy of suicide scale. *Crisis, 43*(5), 385–390. https://doi.org/10.1027/0227-5910/a000798

Calear, A. L., Morse, A. R., Christensen, H., McCallum, S., Werner-Seidler, A., Alexander, R., & Batterham, P. J. (2024). Evaluating suicide attitudes and suicide literacy in adolescents. *Journal of Mental Health, 33*(3), 312–319. https://doi.org/10.1080/09638237.2023.2245883

Cruwys, T., An, S., Chang, M. X. L., & Lee, H. (2018). Suicide literacy predicts the provision of more appropriate support to people experiencing psychological distress. *Psychiatry Research, 264*, 96–103. https://doi.org/10.1016/j.psychres.2018.03.039

Faruk, M. O., Khan, A. H., Chowdhury, K. U. A., Jahan, S., Sarker, D. C., Colucci, E., & Hasan, M. T. (2023). Mental illness stigma in Bangladesh: Findings from a cross-sectional survey. *Global Mental Health (Cambridge, England), 10*, e59. https://doi.org/10.1017/gmh.2023.56

Güler, C., Kaya, K., & Acu, B. G. (2025). Self-stigma to psychological help-seeking among university students in the health sciences: The role of suicide literacy, suicide stigma, and other predictors. *BMC Psychology, 13*(1), 779. https://doi.org/10.1186/s40359-025-03005-3

Hoque, M. B., & Arafat, S. M. Y. (2026). Suicidal behavior in Bangladesh: The preventive measures. In S. Y. Arafat (Ed.), *Suicidal behavior in Bangladesh*. Springer. https://doi.org/10.1007/978-981-95-8321-8_14

Huque, R., Azad, A. K., Islam, K., Ahmed, H. U., & Amin, M. R. (2025). Mental health care seeking behavior in Bangladesh: Determinants and treatment gaps. *BMC Psychiatry, 25*(1), 779. https://doi.org/10.1186/s12888-025-06813-4

Islam, M. K., Maruf, M. M., Saeed Khan, M. A., & Arafat, S. M. Y. (2024). Literacy and stigma of suicide among Islamic religious leaders (Imams) in Bangladesh: A cross-sectional study. *International Review of Psychiatry (Abingdon, England), 36*(4–5), 535–542. https://doi.org/10.1080/09540261.2023.2252507

Jahan, I., Sharif, A. B., & Hasan, A. B. M. N. (2023). Suicide stigma and suicide literacy among Bangladeshi young adults: A cross-sectional study. *Frontiers in Psychiatry, 14*, 1160955. https://doi.org/10.3389/fpsyt.2023.1160955

Jorm, A. F. (2000). Mental health literacy: Public knowledge and beliefs about mental disorders. *The British Journal of Psychiatry, 177*(5), 396–401. https://doi.org/10.1192/bjp.177.5.396

Maruf, M. M., Shormi, F. R., Sajib, M. W. H., Acharjee, P., Ara, H., Roy, S., et al. (2022). Level and associated factors of literacy and stigma of suicide among Bangladeshi physicians: A cross-sectional assessment. *Mental Illness, 2022*(1), 9914388. https://doi.org/10.1155/2022/9914388

Ministry of Health & Family Welfare. (2021). *National Mental Health Survey 2019*. Retrieved March 29, 2023, from http://nimh.gov.bd/wp-content/uploads/2021/11/Mental-Health-Survey-Report.pdf

Oexle, N., Waldmann, T., Staiger, T., Xu, Z., & Rüsch, N. (2018). Mental illness stigma and suicidality: The role of public and individual stigma. *Epidemiology and Psychiatric Sciences, 27*(2), 169–175. https://doi.org/10.1017/S2045796016000949

Platt, S., & Niederkrotenthaler, T. (2020). Suicide prevention programs: Evidence base and best practice. *Crisis: The Journal of Crisis Intervention and Suicide Prevention, 41*(Suppl 1), S99–S124. https://doi.org/10.1027/0227-5910/a000671

Pierantonelli, M., Mira, A., Zamora, Á., Desdentado, L., Diego-Pedro, R., González Hernández, E., Bretón-López, J., García-Palacios, A., & Baños, R. M. (2024). Levels and predictors of suicide literacy and suicide stigma in Spanish-speaking individuals. *Brain and Behavior, 14*(11), e70125. https://doi.org/10.1002/brb3.70125

Spottswood, M., Lim, C. T., Davydow, D., & Huang, H. (2022). Improving suicide prevention in primary care for differing levels of behavioral health integration: A review. *Frontiers in Medicine, 9*, 892205. https://doi.org/10.3389/fmed.2022.892205

Subu, M. A., Wati, D. F., Netrida, N., Priscilla, V., Dias, J. M., Abraham, M. S., & Al Yateem, N. (2021). Types of stigma experienced by patients with mental illness and mental health nurses in Indonesia: A qualitative content analysis. *International Journal of Mental Health Systems, 15*(1), 77. https://doi.org/10.1186/s13033-021-00502-x

Takahashi, A., Tachikawa, H., Takayashiki, A., Maeno, T., Shiratori, Y., Matsuzaki, A., & Arai, T. (2023). Crisis-management, anti-stigma, and mental health literacy program for university students (CAMPUS): A preliminary evaluation of suicide prevention. *F1000Research, 11*, 498. https://doi.org/10.12688/f1000research.111002.2

Thomás, M., Ciara, M., Laura, M., & Richéal, B. (2024). Promoting early-intervention for suicide prevention: The role of mental health literacy and attitudes towards suicide: a quantitative study in Ireland. *Health Policy, 149*, 105150. https://doi.org/10.1016/j.healthpol.2024.105150

Wei, Y., Kutcher, S., & LeBlanc, J. C. (2015). Hot Idea or Hot Air: A Systematic Review of Evidence for Two Widely Marketed Youth Suicide Prevention Programs and Recommendations for Implementation. *Journal of the Canadian Academy of Child and Adolescent Psychiatry = Journal de l'Academie canadienne de psychiatrie de l'enfant et de l'adolescent, 24*(1), 5–16.

World Health Organization. (2025). *Suicide*. WHO. Accessed May 27, 2025, from https://www.who.int/news-room/fact-sheets/detail/suicide

Chapter 13
Suicide Research in Bangladesh

Md Saleh Uddin and S. M. Yasir Arafat

1 Introduction

Suicide is one of the predominant causes of mortality compared to other conditions such as malaria, human immunodeficiency virus (HIV) infection and breast carcinoma or even events such as war or homicide; in 2019, nine people died per 100,000 population worldwide (World Health Organization, 2021a, 2021b). The diverse epidemiological characteristics of suicide in Asia represent the complex interaction among cultures or customs, the transformation toward urban life, easy access to measures to commit suicide, and social permission or limitations. Following African nations (11.2/100,000 age-standardized), Southeast Asian countries are at the top of the list of suicide rates (10/100,000, age-standardized) (World Health Organization, 2021a). Bangladesh is one of the low- and middle-income countries (LMIC) with about 170 million people, where in 2018, 572,600 deaths were caused by non-communicable diseases or NCDs (cardiovascular diseases, cancer, chronic respiratory diseases, diabetes, and others), which contributes 67% of total mortality of the country (Health Bulletin, 2020). Unfortunately, the existing NCD data lacks suicide information, which may change the overall NCD-related mortality scenario in Bangladesh and will be helpful to approach towards developing a national suicide prevention strategy. This compilation of research findings also revealed that national suicide studies on education, awareness or literacy, epidemiology, psychopathology, prevention, and impact (or

M. S. Uddin
Department of Psychiatry, Bangladesh Medical University, Dhaka, Bangladesh

S. M. Y. Arafat (✉)
Department of Psychiatry, Bangladesh Specialized Hospital, Dhaka, Bangladesh

Faculty of Medicine and Health Sciences, Department of Public and Community Health, Frontier University Garowe, Garowe, Somalia

S. M. Y. Arafat (ed.), *Suicidal Behavior in Bangladesh*, Mental Health Systems and Policy in Low- and Middle-Income Countries,
https://doi.org/10.1007/978-981-95-8321-8_13

burden) have yet to be explored, without which an effective suicide prevention policy or strategy would not be possible to formulate in the future. Prioritizing the research domains and capacity building could be the main issues without which authentic nationwide suicide data may not be revealed. This chapter aims to assess the overall suicide research in Bangladesh and enable the reader to know what has been done following the independence (1972–2025) of Bangladesh in the field of suicide research.

2 Suicide Research in Bangladesh

2.1 1972–1999

In the early decades of Bangladesh (1971–1999), a few studies on suicide research were noted that provide important information about local characteristics of suicide. A retrospective study of death reports (due to injuries and induced abortion) review conducted from 1976 to 1986 among women of 15–44 years in *Matlab*, a sub-district of Bangladesh, found that 4.9% of total death (n=1139) happened due to suicide (n=56), where the methods of suicide were poisoning (39) and hanging (n=17) (Fauveau & Blanchet, 1989). In another study in the same geographical area, data were collected longitudinally from 1982 to 1998 to observe deaths due to violence regardless of gender among people aged 15–44 years and revealed that the female suicide rate was higher among females than males (1.3 vs. 0.8 per 10,000 person-years) (Ahmed et al., 2004). It reported a total of 160 suicides among 1297 deaths due to violence. A study of autopsy findings at the *Forensic Medicine Department* of *Sir Salimullah Medical College (SSMC)*, Dhaka, was conducted over a decade (1988–1997) to review the cause of unnatural death. It reported that apart from other reasons (accidents and homicide) for death, 18% of the deaths happened due to suicide (Islam & Islam, 2003). Another study attempted to explore the risk factors of violent death in rural Bangladesh, where researchers followed the population of nearly 62,000 in 10 districts of the country during 1990–1999. The study revealed that there were significant differences in the sociodemographic context where the probability of victim of violent death was 61.2 per 10,000 if the person is very young, male, poor, illiterate, and Muslim (Hadi, 2005). Finally, another study was conducted all over the country and collected data from 60 districts from 3702 public health facilities to identify the characteristics of injury-related death among women aged 10–50 years from the 1996 to 1997 and found that among them, there were a total of 28,998 deaths. It reported that 23% of deaths were due to intentional or unintentional injury, and among them, half (3317) were due to suicide. Regarding suicide information, poisoning and hanging were the most common methods, and among all the suicide victims, 71% were below 30 years of age, predominantly married, with rural and low economic background, and 6% of them were pregnant (Yusuf et al., 2000).

2.2 *2000–2019*

2.2.1 Community Study

In an observational study, researchers aimed to review the changes in the pattern of death among females aged 15–49 years by using the information from nationally representative surveys of 2001 and 2010. Three physicians explored the medical cause of death by verbal autopsy (VA) and found that the cause of death had shifted from communicable to non-communicable disease (NCD). Among NCDs, suicide and deaths due to violence were the prominent causes of death among teenage girls (Nahar et al., 2015). Another community-based survey was carried out from December 2009 to March 2010 at Mominpur union under Sadar Upazilla of the district *Chuadanga*, where 12,422 people were interviewed from 3551 residences. The study revealed that the suicide rate was 128.8 per 100,000 population, where victims were predominantly female (male: female 1:4), below 30 years of age (20–29 years) (42.9%), low-income group (45.7%), married and had family discord (Feroz et al., 2012). In another study, according to Khan et al. (2020), the rate of suicide attempts and suicide in *Jhenaidah*, during 2010–2018, was 136.35/100,000 and 20.6/100,000 consecutively, and poisoning was the most common method of suicide attempt or suicide among victims (Khan et al., 2020). Another census was conducted in June–November 2013 in the rural area (51 unions) to evaluate the reason for death related to injury, and it was found that most of the suicide cases were female and fell in the 15–24 age group (Alonge et al., 2017). Sharmin Salam et al. (2017) conducted similar research for 6 months (June–November 2013) in rural areas to assess fatal and non-fatal suicide. They found that fatal and non-fatal suicide rates were 3.29 and 9.86 per 100,000 person-years (PY), respectively. Among the deceased, married adolescents were 22 times more likely to die by suicide compared to unmarried people, and illiterate daily workers were 16 times more likely to die by suicide than educated or students. Most importantly, the common methods of suicide were hanging and poisoning (Sharmin Salam et al., 2017). In a recent study, it was revealed that there is a high incidence of acute poisoning in *Jashore* with a significant amount of death toll, where *organophosphorus compound* (OPC) is the most common agent of poisoning due to its easy availability (Acherjya et al., 2020). Unfortunately, the financial burden (on family and government) of poisoning case treatment has not been estimated on a large scale, although a cross-sectional study conducted in *Chattogram Medical College* (CMC) *Hospital* in 2016 assessed the agrochemical poisoning treatment expenditure by patients and the cost analysis by Verma et al. (2017). The study noted that it takes three times more money than their monthly expenses (Verma et al., 2017).

2.2.2 Medicolegal Autopsy Report Review

Due to the lack of a national suicide data-keeping system, autopsy report review becomes one of the feasible ways to explore suicide information in Bangladesh. In 2005, an autopsy review of a total of 557 cases was conducted in the *Mymensingh*

Medical College (MMC) mortuary to assess typical and atypical hanging (Talukder et al., 2008). Such findings of hanging knots could be helpful data in the future to resolve cases in a forensic context, whether it's homicidal or suicidal. Another review was conducted at the MMC morgue, from January 2007 to December 2008. It was found that among 1862 autopsy cases, 692 (37.16%) were identified as OPC poisoning cases, which were the main cause of suicide apart from other outcomes, and the 21–30 years age group was the highest in number, and suicide victims were predominantly 401 (57.8%) males (Quader et al., 2010). One retrospective study was done at the *CMC* morgue from January 2014 to December 2016 which reveal the causative factors and injury pattern of cutthroat wounds. It assessed 106 cases of cutthroat wounds from 7300 medico-legal autopsies, where most of the victims were male (74 cases), the most affected age groups were 21–30 years (both male & female), and homicides (91) and suicide (13) were the major causes of death (Akber et al., 2021). In another study, a total of 114 organophosphorus poisoning cases autopsied at the *SSMC* morgue were analyzed during the period from January 2016 to December 2017. Male predominance was noted to account for 75% of total cases compared to females' 25% of cases, and the most common age group involved was 21–30 years 31% and lower socio-economic status (Sumon et al., 2021).

2.2.3 Injury Death Record Review

An epidemiological study conducted among 819,429 people of all ages to identify the characteristics of injury-related death in 2003 found that adolescent females (10–19 years) are the most vulnerable age group. The overall suicide rate found in this huge sample was 7.3 per 100,000 per year, which was 17 times higher in rural people compared to urban setups. The majority of the suicide victims were from low socio-economic backgrounds, illiterate, and had poisoned themselves (Mashreky et al., 2013). Other death report reviews (2001–2017) found that among 3433 dowry-related deaths, 231 were suicides, and among 750 deaths (2014–2017), 31 were due to suicide (Rahman, 2018). A nationwide cross-sectional survey on injury death was conducted between March and June 2016 and identified suicide as the leading cause of injury deaths in Bangladesh, and every year, an estimated 23,868 people die due to suicide in Bangladesh (14.7/100,000 population per year). The incidences were peaking in late adolescents, females predominantly, mostly in residences (71%), and poisoning (73.9%) and hanging were the methods of suicide (Chowdhury et al., 2018a). An unnatural death review of *Thakurgaon* district conducted from 2014 to 2018 revealed that 840 suicidal deaths occurred during this period, where the mean suicide rate was 12.17 per 100,000 per year. Most of the victims were below 30 years of age (57.02%), and 55.12% were females. Hanging was found to be the most commonly used method (73.1%), followed by poisoning (25.15%), jumping in front of the train, and burning. Interestingly, incidents would peak in March and August of a calendar year (Arafat & Karmakar, 2019).

2.2.4 Case-Control Study

In 2013, a case-control study to find the risk factors of suicide in the southwest part of rural Bangladesh found that young, married females, from unitary families, with low economic backgrounds are more vulnerable to dying by suicide or parasuicide (Reza et al., 2014).

2.2.5 Case Reports

A report of copper sulphate poisoning was published in 1994 based on cases from the southern region of the country (Ahasan et al., 1994). A case of nine members of a family who died by suicide reported in 2007, which was due to their shared delusion of anti-religious faith, according to experts' analysis of their story and suicidal notes (Selim, 2010). Another case of suicide was of a 30-year-old unmarried female medical graduate who died by intravenous kerosene (a volatile hydrocarbon, used as fuel during cooking or lamp in rural areas), along with a sedative (midazolam) and antidepressant (amitriptyline). Probably pre-existing factor could be her introverted personality, her boyfriend's betrayal, and chronic *Major Depressive Disorder* diagnosed by a psychiatrist, though she didn't adhere to medications or psychotherapy (Arafat, 2018). Five more cases of suicide in the University of Dhaka in November 2018 were reported, where four of them were female students, and the recent stressors were: love affairs relationships, and academic issues (Arafat & Al Mamun, 2019). A case of suicide was reported 6 years after the Rana Plaza disaster (that happened in 2013), in which a young adult male survivor committed suicide, and following the psychological autopsy of that case, post-traumatic stress disorder was found to be associated (Mamun & Griffiths, 2020a). Another case of suicide of a college student by Gunshot where experts mentioned the student's mental health condition (depression), game addiction, academic stress, and bully could be the possible correlates (Mamun & Griffiths, 2020b).

2.2.6 Media Report Analysis

In a study conducted in 2019, researchers reviewed the social media responses to suicide and found that people express their feelings in nine different ways; these are: "angry, sadness, surprise, irony, ridicule, judgmental, justification, speculation, and miscellaneous" (Al-Zaman & Or Rashid, 2022). In a report analysis (01 November 2018 to 31 October 2019) of a total of 199 reports, 91% (181) reported about suicides where the identity and image of the deceased and method of suicide were mentioned in detail. Moreover, none of the reports contained any educational content or expert opinion regarding suicide information (prevalence, cause, prevention, intervention) (Arafat et al., 2020a). Similar findings (such as unavailable awareness-building contents) were also observed in another content analysis of 403 reports (01 November 2018 to 31 October 2019) (Arafat et al., 2020b). Other studies also found a similar status of quality of media reporting of suicide (Arafat et al., 2019, 2020c).

A news report analysis conducted between November 2016 and April 2017 found that most of the deceased (61%) are young adults (below 30 years and females (58%). Moreover, similar to other studies, rural background and family discord were the two most common social factors associated with these suicides, and hanging was the most common method of suicide (Shah et al., 2017). Following this study, other analysis findings showed aligned directions regarding age, sex, stressors, and the type of methods. For example, an online news portal suicide report analysis revealed that most of the victims are below 30 years, female, students, unmarried, hanged (60%), and having stressors such as relational issues, marital and family discords, and their own residence was a place of incidence (Arafat et al., 2018). A similar trend of findings was also observed in another 12-month study, where the author added new information on the timing of incidences as two peaks of cases were reported in April and November (Arafat et al., 2018).

2.2.7 Suicide Prevention

Currently, there is no suicide prevention programme nationwide, which is vital to reducing the negative impact on the community. Pesticide poisoning is one of the commonest methods in Bangladesh, and the ban on WHO Class I toxicity of highly hazardous pesticides (HHPs) from agriculture in 2000 has significantly reduced the mortality rate of suicide due to pesticide intake (Chowdhury et al., 2018b). Another initiative of the crisis phone helpline (Ears to listen) analyzed their 5-year call characteristics (N=14,344) and found that among the callers, about 50% are male, predominantly between the ages of 20 and 39, and most of them do not have suicidal ideation or thoughts. It was revealed that the most common cause of calls is crises due to relational problems, mental health conditions or addiction, and emotional issues. Though a small portion of callers mentioned clearly suicidal thoughts, there was no follow-up data analysis to compare whether such phone intervention reduced or prevented suicidal rate or suicidality (Iqbal et al., 2019). In correspondence, the author proposed the use of Facebook to predict suicidal intention, and provide intervention after detecting the issue through such social media (Facebook) based suicide prevention intervention, yet not been designed and applied to test its effectiveness by the researcher (Soron, 2019).

2.3 2020–2025

2.3.1 Case-Control Study

The first case-control psychological autopsy study in Bangladesh was published in 2020 by Arafat et al. (2021a). The study, conducted in Dhaka city, interviewed the next of kin of 100 individuals who had died by suicide and 100 age- and sex-matched controls to identify associated risk factors. Findings revealed that pre-existing psychiatric disorders, previous suicide attempts, adverse life events, social isolation, sexual harassment, unemployment, and substance abuse were significant determinants of suicide in the Bangladeshi context.

2.3.2 Prevalence

Meta-analytic evidence in Bangladesh indicates a high burden of suicidality, with lifetime suicidal thoughts affecting 24.2% of individuals and suicide plans or attempts ranging from 4% to 7%, with half of the population studied being students (Arafat et al., 2025c). Another systematic review reported a 4.25% prevalence of suicide attempts, higher among females and adults aged 18 and above, with an increasing trend from 2010 to 2023 (Shuvo et al., 2025). Together, these findings highlight that females and young adults are particularly vulnerable, and suicidal behaviours are rising over time. Supporting this, another systematic review and meta-analysis of six studies including 1625 Bangladeshi medical students found a pooled lifetime prevalence of suicidal behaviours at 25%, with suicidal ideation at 25%, plans at 6%, and attempts at 8%; female gender, depression, family history of suicide, and drug addiction were associated with ideation, while depression and drug addiction were linked to attempts (Rahman et al., 2025).

2.3.3 Case Report

During the COVID-19 pandemic, several case reports and news accounts highlighted diverse psychosocial stressors contributing to suicide in Bangladesh. Bhuiyan et al. (2021) described six cases linked to financial hardship, while Mamun et al. (2020) reported the suicide of a hospitalized woman allegedly denied treatment due to fears of COVID-19. Other reports included the joint suicide of a student and his mother following family conflict over examination modalities (Mamun et al., 2023a) and the suicide of a man socially ostracized for suspected infection despite testing negative postmortem (Mamun & Griffiths, 2020c). These cases reflect how financial strain, healthcare neglect, familial disputes, and stigma heightened suicide risk during the pandemic. A case report describes a 28-year-old Bangladeshi woman who admitted to killing her 32-day-old infant, revealing the under-researched issue of filicide in the country (Arafat et al., 2023). During COVID-19, after a heated dispute over the father arranging broadband so his 22-year-old son had to sit an online exam at home while the son wanted to attend campus, the son and his 47-year-old mother formed a suicide pact and died by ingesting poisonous gas tablets on 11 June 2020 in Bogra, Bangladesh (Mamun et al., 2023a).

2.3.4 Media and News Report Analysis

Media-based reviews during the COVID-19 lockdown in Bangladesh revealed rising suicides linked to family discord, financial stress, abuse, and stigma, with students identified as a particularly vulnerable group (Ashraf et al., 2021; Mamun et al., 2023b). Most student cases involved adolescents, females, and hanging as the predominant method, with relational and academic stressors frequently reported.

Analysis of 13 Bangladeshi newspapers revealed that suicide was more common among individuals under 30 and those who were employed. Regional variations were noted, with Khulna reporting higher rates and Chittagong the lowest. Among women, hanging, poisoning, and jumping were the most frequent methods, while family conflicts and blackmail emerged as the primary risk factors (Sharmin & Saha, 2024). A news report analysis of student suicides in Bangladesh during the COVID-19 pandemic revealed that females and adolescents aged 14–18 years were most affected, with hanging as the predominant method. Key stressors included relationship issues, being emotional, unfulfilled desires, family conflicts, academic failure, mental health problems, sexual complexities, and parental scolding. ArcGIS mapping showed that cases were concentrated in Dhaka and northern districts, highlighting regional variations in methods and stressors (Mamun et al., 2023b). A newspaper content analysis (2014–2024) of suicides in Bangladeshi prisons found hanging to be the predominant method, with roughly one-third of the deceased showing signs of psychiatric illness (Arafat, 2025).

Analysis of Bangla movies and dramas revealed that suicidal behaviour was predominantly depicted among young, unmarried adults, with hanging as the most common method and premarital/extramarital relationships and sexual harassment as key risk factors. Most portrayals contained potentially harmful elements, while content aligned with preventive guidance was minimal (Arafat et al., 2025a). A study of Bangladeshi media found that celebrity suicide reports emphasized demographic details and life events, underscoring their heightened public impact and the need for responsible reporting (Arafat et al., 2025b).

2.3.5 Medico-legal Autopsy Review

Retrospective autopsy-based studies in Bangladesh consistently identify hanging and organophosphorus (OPC) poisoning as the predominant methods of suicide, each showing distinct demographic and contextual patterns.

Hanging deaths are most common among young adults. At Dhaka Medical College (2017–2018), rope was the most frequently used ligature (58%), followed by dupatta, lungi, and saree, with atypical complete hanging predominating and most victims being male (Akhter et al., 2023). Another Dhaka study (Jan–Dec 2022) found hanging more prevalent among females, individuals under 33 years, and Muslims, with family disharmony as a leading precipitant (Ferdous et al., 2024). In Sylhet (2015–2018), 62.1% of hanging deaths involved adolescents and young adults, predominantly females (Sultana et al., 2024). In Sirajganj (2022–2023), hanging accounted for 58.9% of suicidal deaths, primarily among females aged 21–30 years, while poisoning, burns, falls, drowning, and firearms constituted the remainder (Talukdar et al., 2024).

OPC poisoning similarly contributes substantially to suicide mortality. Rangpur (2005–2007) reported 21% of deaths due to OPC poisoning, with females (52%) and individuals aged 21–30 years most affected, and married individuals constituting 80% of cases (Mili & Samad, 2024). In Manikganj (2019–2020), 21.8% of autopsied deaths were due to OPC poisoning, predominantly males (59%), with housewives and agricultural workers most affected; financial stress was the leading motive (Nahida et al., 2023). Sylhet (2016–2017) reported 58.7% of OPC poisoning victims were female, 76% were under 40 years, and respiratory failure was the main cause of death, with Companygonj, Kotwali, and Gowainghat being the most affected areas (Rahman et al., 2023).

These findings from retrospective autopsy reviews highlight that hanging and OPC poisoning are the principal methods of suicide in Bangladesh, disproportionately affecting adolescents, young adults, and females, and underscore the need for targeted preventive strategies.

2.3.6 Geographical Distribution

Region-specific evidence on suicide in Bangladesh is scarce, with only two studies identified. The southern district of Jhenaidah, shows that interpersonal conflicts, family tensions, financial strain, and societal attitudes towards mental health are the key contributors (Faruk et al., 2025). In northern Bangladesh, suicide attempters frequently presented with comorbid psychiatric disorders, including adjustment disorder, major depression, personality disorders, anxiety, and schizophrenia (Uddin et al., 2025). The forensic autopsy reviews also provide regional characteristics of suicide, which have been conducted in Dhaka, Manikganj, Sylhet, Sirajganj, and Rangpur (Akhter et al., 2023; Ferdous et al., 2024; Sultana et al., 2024; Talukdar et al., 2024). These limited findings underscore the need for targeted, region-specific research and prevention strategies addressing both psychosocial and psychiatric risk factors.

2.3.7 Others

In several studies, it was proved that mental health literacy or awareness increased help-seeking behaviour among people, though in Bangladesh such domain in suicide research not explored yet. Recently, Arafat and his colleagues validated the

Literacy of Suicide Scale (LOSS-B) and the *Stigma of Suicide Scale* (SOSS-B) in Bangla, which could be helpful to assess people's awareness about suicide and related stigma in the future (Arafat et al., 2022).

3 Bibliometric Analysis

Bibliometric analysis is a quick and brief method of analyzing research-related information regarding a particular topic. In a recent review of 44 empirical studies in Bangladesh over the last two decades (2001–2020), Arafat et al. (2021b) found that, most of the research adopted applied interview (34.1%) technique and secondary data analysis (31.8%) along with few qualitative researches (6.8%) (Arafat et al., 2021b). There are very few databases that have an in-built option to observe the bibliometric analysis, and among them the most popular database is Scopus. The authors aimed to review the suicide related publications in Bangladesh and searched this database by the keywords: "suicide" AND "Bangladesh" to review the research trend in terms of the researcher, type of researches, affiliations, and citations. The analysis found that the total number of research articles published is 568 from the year 1991 to 2025 (mid-September), and the first research explored the death of Bangladeshi rural women due to injuries and violence.

Though suicide research done irregularly, it started to rise significantly from 2016 onwards and surprisingly after 2020 (Fig. 13.1). In terms of research types conducted in Bangladesh, 58.8% are original research, 14.4% is letter to the editor, 9.2% is review work, and 12.9% are conference papers. Among the top three researchers found are: Arafat, S.M.Y. (n=104), Mamun, M.A. (n=59), and Kar SK

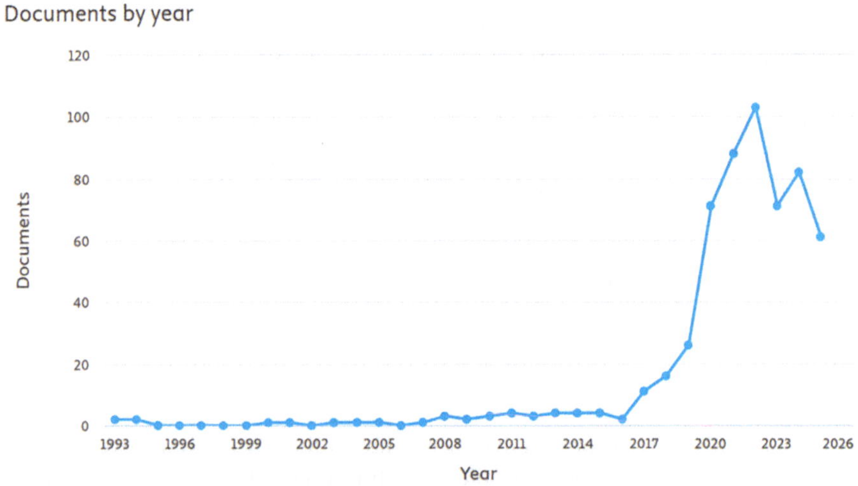

Fig. 13.1 Trend of published articles on suicide in Bangladesh found in Scopus

Table 13.1 Summary of research designs that focused on suicidal behaviour in Bangladesh (1972–2025)

Period	Research design
1971–1999	Forensic autopsy review
2000–2019	1. Case-control study 2. Forensic autopsy review 3. Injury death report review
2020–2025	1. Systematic review, meta analysis (SR, MA) 2. Cross-sectional study (qualitative, quantitative) 3. Case-control study 4. Scale validation study, machine learning prediction 5. Forensic autopsy review 6. Narrative review (article, book, book chapter) 7. Case reports 8. Content analysis of reports (media and news) 9. Letter to editor, correspondence

(n=38), who showed collaboration with each other. The top five organisations involved in the relevant research are: Jahangirnagar University (n=95), Enam Medical College and Hospital (n=80), CHINTA Research Bangladesh (n=68), the University of Dhaka (n=47), and International Centre of Diarrhoeal Disease Research, Bangladesh (ICDDR, B) (n=40).

4 Research Gaps of Suicide in Bangladesh

This depiction of Bangladeshi suicide research shows that studies conducted in different zone, timeline with diverse research designs (Table 13.1). It shows that the method of suicide has changed over the last 5 years (from poisoning to hanging), though other factors such as female, young adult, low economic background, and life events remain constant. Suicide researches related to magnitude, psychopathology, burden, and preventive interventions need to be explored in future.

5 Challenges of Suicide Research in Bangladesh

Although being a developing nation with lack of research resources (financial and infrastructural), interestingly, many researchers have contributed significantly regarding suicide issues in Bangladesh from a very early period to recent time. According to Arafat (2021), as an individual researcher, four challenges have been identified during case-control study in Bangladesh, and these are: (a) getting the list of suicides (as there is no national directory); (b) interviewing proxy respondents (as suicide considered crime here, people hesitate to disclose information); (c) getting documents (medical records, autopsy reports); and (d) poor help-seeking from mental health professionals (Arafat, 2021). It proves that developing a smart suicide directory, electronic medical record (EMR) system, a liaison between police and health departments, and awareness of mental health among the community are important areas that will facilitate suicide research in the future. Apart from these, suicide researchers themselves need a vibrant platform to set a specific suicide research plan and at the same time stakeholders need to involve different ministries (home, law, health, science and technology, information and broadcasting, education, sports, religion, cultural affairs, etc.) to formulate work plan to extract suicide findings and develop an effective suicide prevention measure.

6 Conclusion

The trajectory of suicide research in Bangladesh shows clear shifts over time: from 1971 to 1999 it relied mainly on autopsy report reviews, while during the COVID-19 period (2020–2022), a similar trend reappeared, dominated by descriptive reports and only a few case-control studies; since 2023, however, research has expanded in both volume and methodological rigor, with more original studies, systematic reviews, and advanced approaches such as machine learning–based suicidality assessment, alongside continued focus on risk factors, vulnerable groups, interventions, and policy.

References

Acherjya, G. K., Ali, M., Alam, A., Rahman, M. M., & Mowla, S. (2020). The scenario of acute poisoning in Jashore, Bangladesh. *Journal of Toxicology, 2020*, 2109673. https://doi.org/10.1155/2020/2109673

Ahasan, H. N., Chowdhury, M. J., Azhar, M. A., & Rafiqueuddin, A. K. M. (1994). Copper sulphate poisoning. *Tropical Doctor, 24*(2), 52–53. https://doi.org/10.1177/004947559402400020

Ahmed, M. K., van Ginneken, J., Razzaque, A., & Alam, N. (2004). Violent deaths among women of reproductive age in rural Bangladesh. *Social Science & Medicine (1982), 59*(2), 311–319. https://doi.org/10.1016/j.socscimed.2004.01.020

Al-Zaman, M. S., & Or Rashid, M. H. (2022). Social media users' reactions to suicide. *Journal of Loss and Trauma, 27*, 746–760. https://doi.org/10.1080/15325024.2022.2044701

Alonge, O., Agrawal, P., Talab, A., Rahman, Q. S., Rahman, A. F., Arifeen, S. E., & Hyder, A. A. (2017). Fatal and non-fatal injury outcomes: Results from a purposively sampled census of seven rural subdistricts in Bangladesh. *The Lancet. Global Health, 5*(8), e818–e827. https://doi.org/10.1016/S2214-109X(17)30244-9

Akber, E. B., Nowshin, I., & Jahan, I. (2021). Forensic profiling of cut throat wounds. *Mymensingh Medical Journal, 30*(1), 106–110.

Akhter, S. S., Salim, A., Hossain, M. M., Razib, S. J. U., & Karmakar, P. (2023). Retrospective study of ligature material on suicidal hanging. *Eastern Medical College Journal, 8*(1), 12–14. https://doi.org/10.3329/emcj.v8i1.66721

Arafat, S. M. Y. (2025). Prison suicide in Bangladesh: A news content analysis. *Health Science Reports, 8*(6), e70951. https://doi.org/10.1002/hsr2.70951

Arafat, S. M. Y., Jalil, S. B., Alam, M. S., Sultana, N., Ahmed, M. I. U., Abedin, M. M., & Armstrong, G. (2025a). Suicide in Bangla movie and drama: A content analysis. *Omega, 91*(2), 1058–1071. https://doi.org/10.1177/00302228221148286

Arafat, S. M. Y., Sultana, Y., & Akter, H. (2025b). Quality of news reporting of celebrity suicide in Bangladesh against World Health Organization guidelines. *Global Psychiatry Archives, 8*(1), 1–7. https://doi.org/10.52095/gpa.2025.7579.1100

Arafat, S. M. Y., Baminiwatta, A., Amin, R., Akter, H., & Kabir, R. (2025c). Prevalence of suicidal behavior in Bangladesh: A systematic review and meta-analysis. *Health Science Reports, 8*(8), e71200. https://doi.org/10.1002/hsr2.71200

Arafat, S. M. Y., Monira, S., & Lily, S. A. (2023). Filicide in Bangladesh: A case indicating the need for psychosocial support among mothers during peripartum. *Journal of General and Family Medicine, 24*(4), 254–256. https://doi.org/10.1002/jgf2.624

Arafat, S., Hussain, F., Hossain, M. F., Islam, M. A., & Menon, V. (2022). Literacy and stigma of suicide in Bangladesh: Scales validation and status assessment among university students. *Brain and Behavior, 12*(1), e2432. https://doi.org/10.1002/brb3.2432

Arafat, S., Mohit, M. A., Mullick, M., Kabir, R., & Khan, M. M. (2021a). Risk factors for suicide in Bangladesh: Case-control psychological autopsy study. *BJPsych Open, 7*(1), e18. https://doi.org/10.1192/bjo.2020.152

Arafat, S. M. Y., Hussain, F., Jakaria, K. M., Itu, Z. T., & Islam, M. (2021b). Empirical studies on suicide in Bangladesh in a decade (2011-2020). *Global Psychiatry, 4*(1), 109–122. https://doi.org/10.52095/gp.2021.10692

Arafat, S. M. Y. (2021). Challenges of conducting psychological autopsy study in Bangladesh: Data enumerator's view. *Asian Journal of Psychiatry, 63*, 102760. https://doi.org/10.1016/j.ajp.2021.102760

Arafat, S. M. Y., Mali, B., & Akter, H. (2020a). Is suicide reporting in Bangla online news portals sensible? A year-round content analysis against World Health Organization guidelines. *Asian Journal of Psychiatry, 49*, 101943. https://doi.org/10.1016/j.ajp.2020.101943

Arafat, S., Mali, B., & Akter, H. (2020b). Do Bangladeshi newspapers educate public while reporting suicide? A year round observation from content analysis of six national newspapers. *Asian Journal of Psychiatry, 48*, 101920. https://doi.org/10.1016/j.ajp.2019.101920

Arafat, S. M. Y., Khan, M. M., Niederkrotenthaler, T., Ueda, M., & Armstrong, G. (2020c). Assessing the quality of media reporting of suicide deaths in Bangladesh against World Health Organization guidelines. *Crisis, 41*(1), 47–53. https://doi.org/10.1027/0227-5910/a000603

Arafat, S., Mali, B., & Akter, H. (2019). Quality of online news reporting of suicidal behavior in Bangladesh against World Health Organization guidelines. *Asian Journal of Psychiatry, 40*, 126–129. https://doi.org/10.1016/j.ajp.2018.10.010

Arafat, S., & Karmakar, S. (2019). Seasonality of suicide in Thakurgaon district, Bangladesh, 2014-2018. *Asian Journal of Psychiatry, 44*, 119–120. https://doi.org/10.1016/j.ajp.2019.07.042

Arafat, S., & Al Mamun, M. A. (2019). Repeated suicides in the University of Dhaka (November 2018): Strategies to identify risky individuals. *Asian Journal of Psychiatry, 39*, 84–85. https://doi.org/10.1016/j.ajp.2018.12.014

Arafat, S., Mali, B., & Akter, H. (2018). Demography and risk factors of suicidal behavior in Bangladesh: A retrospective online news content analysis. *Asian Journal of Psychiatry, 36*, 96–99. https://doi.org/10.1016/j.ajp.2018.07.008

Arafat, S. (2018). Suicide by intravenous kerosene: A case report in Bangladesh. *Asian Journal of Psychiatry, 33*, 126–127. https://doi.org/10.1016/j.ajp.2017.11.010

Ashraf, M. N., Jennings, H., Chakma, N., Farzana, N., Islam, M. S., Maruf, T., Uddin, M., Uddin Ahmed, H., McDaid, D., & Naheed, A. (2021). Mental health issues in the COVID-19 pandemic and responses in Bangladesh: View point of media reporting. *Frontiers in Public Health, 9*, 704726. https://doi.org/10.3389/fpubh.2021.704726

Bhuiyan, A., Sakib, N., Pakpour, A. H., Griffiths, M. D., & Mamun, M. A. (2021). COVID-19-related suicides in Bangladesh due to lockdown and economic factors: Case study evidence

from media reports. *International Journal of Mental Health and Addiction, 19*(6), 2110–2115. https://doi.org/10.1007/s11469-020-00307-y
Chowdhury, S. M., Mashreky, S. R., & Rahman, A. F. (2018a). PA 20–4–2021 suicide in Bangladesh: Unfolding the epidemiological burden from a nationwide survey. *Injury Prevention, 24*, A46. https://doi.org/10.1136/injuryprevention-2018-safety.123
Chowdhury, F. R., Dewan, G., Verma, V. R., Knipe, D. W., Isha, I. T., Faiz, M. A., Gunnell, D. J., & Eddleston, M. (2018b). Bans of WHO Class I Pesticides in Bangladesh-suicide prevention without hampering agricultural output. *International Journal of Epidemiology, 47*(1), 175–184. https://doi.org/10.1093/ije/dyx157
Faruk, O., Awal, A., & Chowdhury, K. U. A. (2025). Factors contributing to the higher prevalence of suicide in Jhenaidah, Bangladesh: A qualitative exploration. *BMJ Open, 15*(6), e089985. https://doi.org/10.1136/bmjopen-2024-089985
Fauveau, V., & Blanchet, T. (1989). Deaths from injuries and induced abortion among rural Bangladeshi women. *Social Science & Medicine (1982), 29*(9), 1121–1127. https://doi.org/10.1016/0277-9536(89)90025-7
Ferdous, J., Tasnim, Z., Aziz, M., & Sumon, M. S. R. (2024). One-year case study of autopsy of hanging in a tertiary teaching hospital at Dhaka City of Bangladesh. *Journal of Monno Medical College, 10*(2), 72–76. https://doi.org/10.3329/jmomc.v10i2.78115
Feroz, A., Islam, S. N., Reza, S., Rahman, A. M., Sen, J., Mowla, M., & Rahman, M. R. (2012). A community survey on the prevalence of suicidal attempts and deaths in a selected rural area of Bangladesh. *Journal of Medicine, 13*(1), 3–9. https://doi.org/10.3329/jom.v13i1.10042
Hadi, A. (2005). Risk factors of violent death in rural Bangladesh, 1990-1999. *Death Studies, 29*(6), 559–572. https://doi.org/10.1080/07481180590962695
Health Bulletin. (2020). *Ministry of Health and Family Welfare, Governement Republic of Bangladesh*. Accessed September 17, 2025, from https://old.dghs.gov.bd/images/docs/Publicaations/Health%20Bulletin%202019%20Print%20Version%20(2)-Final.pdf
Iqbal, Y., Jahan, R., & Matin, M. R. (2019). Descriptive characteristics of callers to an emotional support and suicide prevention helpline in Bangladesh (first five years). *Asian Journal of Psychiatry, 45*, 63–65. https://doi.org/10.1016/j.ajp.2019.09.005
Islam, M. N., & Islam, M. N. (2003). Forensic medicine in Bangladesh. *Legal Medicine (Tokyo, Japan), 5*(Suppl 1), S357–S359. https://doi.org/10.1016/s1344-6223(02)00132-3
Khan, A. R., Ratele, K., Arendse, N., Islam, M. Z., & Dery, I. (2020). Suicide and attempted suicide in Jhenaidah District, Bangladesh, 2010-2018. *Crisis, 41*(4), 304–312. https://doi.org/10.1027/0227-5910/a000631
Mamun, M. A., & Griffiths, M. D. (2020a). PTSD-related suicide six years after the Rana Plaza collapse in Bangladesh. *Psychiatry Research, 287*, 112645. https://doi.org/10.1016/j.psychres.2019.112645
Mamun, M. A., & Griffiths, M. D. (2020b). A rare case of Bangladeshi student suicide by gunshot due to unusual multiple causalities. *Asian Journal of Psychiatry, 49*, 101951. https://doi.org/10.1016/j.ajp.2020.101951
Mamun, M. A., & Griffiths, M. D. (2020c). First COVID-19 suicide case in Bangladesh due to fear of COVID-19 and xenophobia: Possible suicide prevention strategies. *Asian Journal of Psychiatry, 51*, 102073. https://doi.org/10.1016/j.ajp.2020.102073
Mamun, M. A., Bodrud-Doza, M., & Griffiths, M. D. (2020). Hospital suicide due to non-treatment by healthcare staff fearing COVID-19 infection in Bangladesh? *Asian Journal of Psychiatry, 54*, 102295. https://doi.org/10.1016/j.ajp.2020.102295
Mamun, M. A., Mamun, M. A., Hosen, I., Ahmed, T., Rayhan, I., & Al-Mamun, F. (2023b). Trend and gender-based association of the Bangladeshi student suicide during the COVID-19 pandemic: A GIS-based nationwide distribution. *The International Journal of Social Psychiatry, 69*(1), 38–46. https://doi.org/10.1177/00207640211065670
Mamun, M. A., Chandrima, R. M., & Griffiths, M. D. (2023a). Mother and son suicide pact due to COVID-19-related online learning issues in Bangladesh: An unusual case report.

International Journal of Mental Health and Addiction, 21(2), 687–690. https://doi.org/10.1007/s11469-020-00362-5
Mashreky, S. R., Rahman, F., & Rahman, A. (2013). Suicide kills more than 10,000 people every year in Bangladesh. *Archives of Suicide Research, 17*(4), 387–396. https://doi.org/10.1080/13811118.2013.801809
Mili, N. A., & Samad, M. A. (2024). Epidemiology of fatal poisonings from organophosphorus compounds in Rangpur District, Bangladesh. *International Journal of Forensic Expert Alliance, 1*(1), 55–60. https://doi.org/10.70818/ijfea.v01i01.08
Nahar, Q., El Arifeen, S., Jamil, K., & Streatfield, P. K. (2015). Causes of adult female deaths in Bangladesh: Findings from two National Surveys. *BMC Public Health, 15*, 911. https://doi.org/10.1186/s12889-015-2256-6
Nahida, N. N., Rahman, M. Z., & Ahamed, B. U. (2023). Organophosphorus compound as suicidal poison in rural areas of Bangladesh: A medicolegal study. *Journal of Monno Medical College, 9*(1), 7–10. https://doi.org/10.3329/jmomc.v9i1.69019
Quader, M., Rahman, M. H., Kamal, M., Ahmed, A. U., & Saha, S. K. (2010). Post mortem outcome of organophosphorus compound poisoning cases at Mymensingh Medical College. *Mymensingh Medical Journal, 19*(2), 170–172.
Rahman, M., Kabir, M. H. M. I., Sultana, S., Abdullah, I., & Shimu, A. T. (2025). Suicidal behaviours and associated factors among Bangladeshi medical students: A systematic review and meta-analysis (2000-2024). *BMJ Open, 15*(3), e095573. https://doi.org/10.1136/bmjopen-2024-095573
Rahman, M. F., Islam, M. S., Uddin, N. M., Alam, M. S., Poly, T. B., & Nurunnabi, M. (2023). Epidemiological evaluation of suicidal deaths due to organophosphorus compound poisoning. *Journal of Monno Medical College, 9*(1), 20–23. https://doi.org/10.3329/jmomc.v9i1.69147
Rahman, M. S. (2018). Dowry, the oppression of women and femicide in Bangladesh. *Journal of Comparative Social Work, 13*(1), 103–123. https://doi.org/10.31265/jcsw.v13i1.161
Reza, A. S., Feroz, A. H. M., Islam, S. N., Karim, M. N., Rabbani, M. G., Shah Alam, M., Rahman, M. M., Rahman, M. R., Ahmed, H. U., Bhowmik, A. D., Khan, M. Z. R., Sarkar, M., Alam, M. T., & Jalal Uddin, M. M. (2014). Risk factors of suicide and para suicide in rural Bangladesh. *Journal of Medicine, 14*(2), 123–129. https://doi.org/10.3329/jom.v14i2.19653
Sharmin Salam, S., Alonge, O., Islam, M. I., Hoque, D., Wadhwaniya, S., UlBaset, M. K., Mashreky, S. R., & El Arifeen, S. (2017). The burden of suicide in rural Bangladesh: Magnitude and risk factors. *International Journal of Environmental Research and Public Health, 14*(9), 1032. https://doi.org/10.3390/ijerph14091032
Sharmin, M. F., & Saha, A. K. (2024). Gender disparities in suicide prevalence and risk factors in Bangladesh. *Asian Journal of Medical and Biological Research, 10*(3), 110–118. https://doi.org/10.3329/ajmbr.v10i3.72309
Shah, M., Ahmed, S., & Arafat, S. (2017). Demography and risk factors of suicide in Bangladesh: A six-month paper content analysis. *Psychiatry Journal, 2017*, 3047025. https://doi.org/10.1155/2017/3047025
Shuvo, T. A., Hossain, K., & Dey, D. R. (2025). Suicide attempts in Bangladesh: Prevalence, trends, and disparities. *Journal of Medicine, Surgery, and Public Health, 5*, 100170. https://doi.org/10.1016/j.glmedi.2024.100170
Soron, T. R. (2019). "I will kill myself" – The series of posts in Facebook and unnoticed departure of a life. *Asian Journal of Psychiatry, 44*, 55–57. https://doi.org/10.1016/j.ajp.2019.07.002
Selim, N. (2010). An extraordinary truth? The Ādam "suicide" notes from Bangladesh. *Mental Health, Religion & Culture, 13*(3), 223–244. https://doi.org/10.1080/13674670903061230
Sumon, S. R., Asha, M. T., Rahman, M. Z., Tabassum, R., Mollika, F. A., & Khan, B. H. (2021). An autopsy based study on socio-economical pattern of organophosphorus poisoning cases recorded from Sir Salimullah Medical College Morgue. *Mymensingh Medical Journal, 30*(1), 111–114.

Sultana, F., Ahmad, M., Islam, M. S., Hossain, M. A., & Nurunnabi, M. (2024). Epidemiological evaluation of suicidal deaths due to hanging: A retrospective medicolegal study in Sylhet. *IAHS Medical Journal, 7*(1), 13–16. https://doi.org/10.3329/iahsmj.v7i1.77483

Talukdar, S., Jahan, Z., Akter, S., Chowdhury, P., Talukder, S. K., & Mim, S. N. M. (2024). Autopsy of suicidal death analysis in 250 beaded general hospitals Sirajganj. *International Journal of Forensic Expert Alliance, 1*(2), 43–47. https://doi.org/10.70818/ijfea.v01i02.015

Talukder, M. A., Mansur, M. A., & Kadir, M. M. (2008). Incidence of typical and atypical hanging among 66 hanging cases. *Mymensingh Medical Journal, 17*(2), 149–151.

Uddin, M. J., Alim, S. M. A. H. M., Akhtar, R., Rahman, M., Ashikuzzaman, M., Rana, M., & Hossain, M. G. (2025). Psychiatric comorbidities among suicide attempters in Northern Bangladesh. *TAJ: Journal of Teachers Association, 38*(3), 53–59.

Verma, V., Paul, S., Ghose, A., Eddleston, M., & Konradsen, F. (2017). Treatment of self-poisoning at a tertiary-level hospital in Bangladesh: Cost to patients and government. *Tropical Medicine & International Health, 22*(12), 1551–1560. https://doi.org/10.1111/tmi.12991

World Health Organization. (2021a). *Suicide Worldwide in 2019: Global health estimates*. WHO. Accessed September 17, 2025, from https://www.who.int/publications/i/item/9789240026643

World Health Organization. (2021b). *Mental Health ATLAS 2020*. WHO. Accessed September 17, 2025, from https://www.who.int/publications/i/item/9789240036703

Yusuf, H. R., Akhter, H. H., Rahman, M. H., Chowdhury, M. E., & Rochat, R. W. (2000). Injury-related deaths among women aged 10-50 years in Bangladesh, 1996-97. *Lancet (London, England), 355*(9211), 1220–1224. https://doi.org/10.1016/S0140-6736(00)02088-2

Chapter 14
Suicide Prevention in Bangladesh

Mohima Benojir Hoque and S. M. Yasir Arafat

1 Introduction

Globally, more than 720,000 people died by suicide in 2021. It is a serious public health problem in high-income countries (HICs) as well as predominantly in lower- and middle-income (LMICs) countries, where 73% of the suicides occurred (World Health Organization [WHO], 2025). One person dies every 40 s because of suicide, and many more attempt suicide all over the world (WHO, 2014). It is one of the top 20 leading causes of death worldwide, which causes more deaths than malaria, breast cancer, war, and homicide (WHO, 2021a). It is the third leading cause of death among individuals aged 15–29 years (WHO, 2025). Although suicide is a sensitive issue, it is underreported in countries like Bangladesh, where there is a lack of good data records, and suicides have often been classified as accidents or other forms of unnatural deaths. Suicide registration is a difficult process comprising a number of different persons, including law enforcement authorities (Arafat, 2025a; WHO, 2025). This chapter begins with a global context of suicide and encompasses how suicide prevention gets global attention, strategic approaches of suicide prevention, the risk factors of suicide in Bangladesh, an overview of the current status of suicide prevention in Bangladesh, readiness of national suicide prevention strategies, challenges of suicide prevention in Bangladesh, and future ways out for suicide prevention in Bangladesh.

M. B. Hoque
BRAC James P Grant School of Public Health, BRAC University, Dhaka, Bangladesh

S. M. Y. Arafat (✉)
Department of Psychiatry, Bangladesh Specialized Hospital, Dhaka, Bangladesh

Faculty of Medicine and Health Sciences, Department of Public and Community Health, Frontier University Garowe, Garowe, Somalia

S. M. Y. Arafat (ed.), *Suicidal Behavior in Bangladesh*, Mental Health Systems and Policy in Low- and Middle-Income Countries,
https://doi.org/10.1007/978-981-95-8321-8_14

2 How Suicide Prevention Gets Global Attention

While considering global suicide prevention, the need for intersectoral collaboration, multidisciplinary approaches, and continued evaluation and review have been emphasized, and key elements have been identified as a necessary means of increasing the effectiveness of suicide prevention strategies (WHO, 2018). In 2014, WHO published its first-ever world suicide prevention report, "Preventing Suicide: A Global Imperative" (WHO, 2014), where WHO made a call to action for countries to employ a multisectoral approach that addresses suicide in a comprehensive manner. "Prevention of Suicide: Guidelines for the Formulation and Implementation of National Strategies" was published by the United Nations (UN) following consultation with a variety of experts and with technical support from WHO in 2018 (WHO, 2018). Currently, some 40 countries at every income level have incorporated a state suicide prevention policy, and only a few LMICs have accepted a national suicide prevention strategy (WHO, 2021a).

The WHO MiNDbank online platform was created to provide easy and rapid access to global resources, national- and regional-level strategies, services, and laws for improving mental health and related areas such as suicide, substance abuse, disability, general health, and human rights. Another global effort to address suicide is the creation of *World Suicide Prevention Day*, organized by the *International Association for Suicide Prevention (IASP)*. This day is observed worldwide on 10 September each year, providing a vital opportunity to raise awareness about suicide prevention (WHO, 2018).

The *WHO Mental Health Action Plan* 2013–2020 was approved by the *World Health Assembly* in 2013 (WHO, 2013). The action plan labels suicide prevention as a priority through reducing the suicide rate by 10% by 2020. It is also highlighting suicide as a serious public health problem worldwide, and it can be prevented with appropriate efforts. National responses to suicide with comprehensive multisectoral suicide prevention strategies are essential to achieving this target. In 2015, the *Sustainable Development Goals* (SDGs) also focused on the agenda adopted by the UN General Assembly. The third goal of the SDGs is to safeguard healthy lives and uphold well-being for people of all ages. Again, the target of SDG 3.4.2 is to decrease suicide by 33% through enhanced intervention and prevention in 2030 (Naghavi & Global Burden of Disease Self-Harm Collaborators, 2019; WHO, 2018; Khan et al., 2021).

3 Strategic Approaches for Suicide Prevention

Numerous strategic approaches are suggested for suicide prevention and classified as universal, selected, and indicated (WHO, 2014; Mann et al., 2005; Zalsman et al., 2016; Arafat & Kabir, 2017). Universal suicide prevention strategies are designed to reach the total population with a view to taking full advantage of health and reducing suicide risk by eliminating barriers to health care and increasing protective measures, for example, societal support and altering the environment (Table 14.1). Selective strategies mark vulnerable groups of people based on features such as age, occupation, sex, or family history. Indicated strategies target another vulnerable group of individuals who have displayed initial signs of suicide potential (WHO, 2014).

WHO launched a wide-ranging "Mental Health Action Plan 2013–2020" in 2013, which persuades the countries to work on the way of their own mental health policies. The plan highlighted points such as strengthening of effective leadership and mental health governance; providing complete, unified, and amicable mental health and participatory community care services; and implementing policies for prevention and promotion in mental health and support information systems and evidence-based research for mental health. WHO's Global Strategy published a policy and interventions to reduce harmful use of alcohol. And it also provides measures for effective suicide prevention through proper guidance, mindfulness and potentials, health services' response, community accomplishment, drunk-driving policies and countermeasures, marketing of alcoholic drinks, minimizing the negative consequences of harmful drinking and alcohol intoxication. Available treatment for mental and substance use disorders can reduce the risk of suicidal behavior, and executing health literacy policies and practices throughout health systems and institutions, especially at community health centers, is the main way to improve access to healthcare services in general and mental health care in particular. Pesticide self-poisoning is the most common method of suicide worldwide. So, to prevent suicide, limiting access to the means of suicide is effective. The main intervention is restricting access to the means of suicide, such as pesticides, firearms, bridges, buildings,

Table 14.1 Suicide prevention strategies (Adapted from WHO, 2014)

Name of the strategy	Category
Mental health policies	Universal
Policies to reduce harmful use of alcohol	
Access to health care	
Restriction of access to means	
Responsible media reporting	
Raising awareness about mental health, substance use disorders, and suicide	
Interventions for vulnerable groups	Selective
Gatekeeper training	
Crisis helplines	
Follow-up and community support	Indicated
Assessment and management of suicidal behaviors	
Assessment and management of mental and substance use disorders	

railroads, poisonous gases, and pharmacological agents. A study shows that responsible media reporting of suicide helps to reduce suicide rates. It may play a significant role by avoiding exaggeration and glamorization, using responsible language, avoiding detailed descriptions of suicidal acts, providing educational materials to the public, and mentioning information about suicide prevention services. Awareness raising on mental health, substance use disorders, and suicide may help to reduce stigma and negative attitudes among people with mental disorders. Selected strategic approach includes interventions for vulnerable groups, gatekeeper training, and crisis helplines. A number of vulnerable groups have been identified as having a higher risk of suicide, such as persons who have experienced abuse, trauma, conflict, or disaster; refugees and migrants; indigenous peoples; prisoners; and lesbian, gay, bisexual, transgender, and intersex persons. Sometimes people who are at risk of suicide may not seek help. A *gatekeeper* is anyone who is in a position to identify whether someone may be contemplating suicide, and the potential gatekeepers are primary mental and emergency health service providers, teachers and community leaders, other school staff, police officers, firefighters and other first responders, spiritual and religious leaders or traditional healers, and human resource staff and managers. Crisis helplines are a kind of public call centers that people can turn to when other social support or professional care is unavailable or not preferred. Indicated approach includes community support and follow-up, assessment and management of suicidal behaviors, and mental and substance use disorders (Zalsman et al., 2016; WHO, 2014; Mann et al., 2005; Arafat & Kabir, 2017).

In 2021, WHO declares an implementation guide for suicide prevention, which is known as LIVE LIFE where, LIVE stands for leadership, interventions, vision, and evaluation and builds the pillars of LIFE, that is, the core interventions, which are less means, communication with the media for accountable reporting, life skills development to the younger and primary identification, management and follow-up. The core pillars of LIVE LIFE are situation analysis, multisectoral collaboration, raising awareness and promotion, capacity-building, funding, investigation, monitoring, and assessment (WHO, 2021b).

4 Risk Factors for Suicide in Bangladesh

The foundation of any effective response to prevent suicide is to find out the appropriate risk factors and their mitigation by implementing appropriate interventions. Suicidal behaviors are multifaceted, and no single factor is adequate to elucidate a suicidal act. There are various contributing factors and underlying pathways to suicide and a range of options for its prevention. Protective factors are equally important and have been identified as improving resilience. Therefore, mitigating the identified risk factors is imperative for effective interventions. Consequently, enhancing protective factors is also an important aim of any comprehensive suicide prevention response (WHO, 2018). An ecological model is used to best describe both risk and protective factors of suicide, which can help to take effective measures

(WHO, 2014). It is multifactorial, driven by a series of sociocultural, psychological, economic, biological, and environmental issues, such as financial loss, interpersonal conflict, loneliness, chronic illness, mental health and substance abuse problems, discrimination, and difficulties accessing health care. Given the interplay of factors, multisectoral action is essential (WHO, 2014).

We discussed the risk factors for suicide in Bangladesh in Chap. 1 and the socio-ecological perspective in Chap. 5 of this book (Arafat & Saleem, 2026; Arafat & Kabir, 2026). In the country, the majority of the suicide cases are found in early adulthood, and the significant risk factors are psychiatric disorder, sexual abuse, previous attempt, immediate life event, unemployment, social isolation, physical abuse, and physical disorder. Other risk factors are emotional issues, relationship events, rape, eve-teasing, and sexual relationships. Study reveals that among the total respondents, 61% have psychiatric disorders such as Axis I disorders—major depressive disorder (MDD), personality disorders, schizophrenia, and substance misuse. A total 91% have experienced life events such as academic failure, arguments with family member, arguments with spouse, broken engagement, extramarital affair, taking a large loan, spousal extramarital affair, sexual assault, major personal physical illness, marital separation, business failure, child married, divorce, and moving to another city (Arafat, 2017, 2019; Arafat et al., 2021a, 2021b, 2024a).

Moreover, it is a customarily predominating issue among married women who are young, come from a subordinate socioeconomic division, and live in rural parts of the country (Feroz et al., 2012; Shahnaz et al., 2017; Sharmin Salam et al., 2017). Evidences from several studies reveal that the effects of patriarchal society, early marriage, forced marriage, lower socioeconomic status of women, lower female education, divorce, threat to divorce, conflicts with in-laws, forced childbearing, infertility, and various forms of exploitation and coercion are significantly linked with suicide and suicidal behaviors among women and girls in the country (Feroz et al., 2012; Arafat, 2019; Sharmin Salam et al., 2017; Khan et al., 2022). Again, people residing in the countryside, particularly in *Chuadanga*, *Jenaidah*, *Kustia*, *Meherpur*, *Jashore*, and *Chandpur*, were more vulnerable to suicide in Bangladesh (Feroz et al., 2012; Shahnaz et al., 2017; Chowdhury et al., 2018; Arafat, 2017, 2019). It is also found that in Bangladesh, the common approaches for suicide and attempts to suicide are hanging and pesticide ingestion (Mashreky et al., 2013; Shahnaz et al., 2017; Arafat et al., 2018; Arafat, 2019; Khan et al., 2020).

5 Current Status of Suicide Prevention in Bangladesh

Bangladesh is a densely populated South Asian country containing about 170 million inhabitants (Bangladesh Bureau of Statistics, 2024). Evidence suggests that the country lacks a comprehensive database on suicide, a national suicide surveillance system, a strategy for suicide prevention, and experimental study on suicide (Arafat, 2019, 2025b). Besides, suicide and self-harm are considered illegal, and social, religious, and legal consequences hamper the suicide disclosures (Arafat, 2017). In

Bangladesh, there are a few but sporadic activities on suicide prevention interventions initiated at different levels with limited resources following variable methods (Arafat, 2018, 2024a; Box 14.1).

5.1 *Mental Health Support: Suicide Prevention Clinics*

There were two *Suicide Prevention Clinics (SPCs)* in Bangladesh that have ceased their activities. In 2016, the first SPC was launched in Bangladesh Medical University (BMU), formerly Bangabandhu Sheikh Mujib Medical University (BSMMU), under the Department of Psychiatry. The clinic ran on Saturdays and provided psychotherapy for 2 h only (Arafat, 2018). It was the only public sector facility to provide treatment to patients with suicidal behavior (Arafat, 2018). But most of the people are unfamiliar with the existing facility due to insufficient promotional activities and media coverage. The website of BMU also did not deliver any message about the services of the clinic (Arafat, 2018). A recent study on the clinic data reveals that about 73% of the respondents were under the age of 25, and approximately 70% were females with depression, followed by personality disorder, which was the most common psychiatric disorder (Shah et al., 2018). The activities have ceased since the COVID-19 pandemic.

Another SPC was started in October 2021 under the Department of Psychiatry of Enam Medical College and Hospital (EMCH), a private medical college in Dhaka. There was provision of services from 9 am to 5 pm on every working day. There are no other specialized clinical services for suicide prevention in the country. The maximum patients who came to the SPC at BMU were referred by the psychiatry outpatient department, whereas in EMCH, the picture is different. At EMCH, patients received self-report awareness materials, banner with information of suicide and self-harm. The activities have ceased since December 2023. In the country, outpatient departments for mental health services exist in 72 hospitals, but it cannot go without question regarding the availability of any specialist on mental health in all centers apart from medical college hospitals (WHO, 2022). The general physicians who are trained in mental health are not available in all the centers at primary health care facilities of Bangladesh. Consequently, it is difficult to accept that these centers can efficiently handle suicidal behavior and suicide in the country. It is also to note that none of these individuals in the SPCs has any official training on suicide prevention, rather than their inadequate theoretical knowledge.

5.2 *Means Restriction: Category 1 Pesticides Ban*

Globally, approximately 15–20% of suicides, which are equivalent to 140,000 deaths, are due to intentional ingestion of acutely toxic pesticides (WHO, 2024). The main reason behind the decline of suicide rate globally is the reduction in access to exceedingly harmful pesticides (HHPs) by reducing agricultural use, harmless use, and packaging, and mainly due to legislation and prohibition of HHPs (Chowdhury et al., 2018). Bangladesh is an agrarian country where pesticide self-poisoning is extremely prevalent for both suicide deaths and attempts to suicide. The government of the country has proclaimed pesticide regulation and banned extremely hazardous pesticides (HHPs) from use in agriculture over the last two decades (Chowdhury et al., 2018). The regulatory body of the country partially or totally banned 21 hazardous pesticides (WHO class I) during the period from 1996 to 2007 and moved toward less harmful WHO toxicity class II, III, and U pesticides. By the year 2000, all kinds of WHO Class I toxicity HHPs were prohibited. During the postban period (2001–2014), suicides due to pesticides decreased to 35,071 in comparison with the preban period from 1996 to 2000. It was also evidenced that unnatural deaths after banning HHPs declined, and the number was 76,642. It was found that there is an impact of pesticide legislation on pesticide suicide and unnatural deaths without any detrimental consequence on agricultural output (Chowdhury et al., 2018). So, the country should consider extremely limited access to pesticides and other deadly means, as well as banning toxic pesticides used for suicidal ingestion (Chowdhury et al., 2018).

5.3 *Help Lines:* Kaan Pete Roi *and National Helpline (999)*

In Bangladesh, the only telephonic helpline *Kaan Pete Roi* (my ears wait to listen), for suicide prevention, was established in 2013. It is also known as Bangladesh–Befrienders, an initiative of IASP. Nonetheless, the services are available for 12 h (3 pm–3 am) and are unable to reach 24 h every day (Arafat et al., 2025a; Iqbal et al., 2019, 2024; Arafat, 2018).

The national crisis hotline (999) was launched in December 2017 (Arafat, 2025a) by the home ministry of Bangladesh and plays a significant role in suicide prevention by saving endangered individuals. Recent evidence shows promise in suicide prevention in the country (Arafat et al., 2025a). Enduring collaboration between the helpline is warranted to ensure 24/7 services.

5.4 *NGOs SOVA and BTF*

There are a few organizations that aim to work in preventing suicide in Bangladesh. *Society for Voluntary Activities* (SOVA), a nongovernment organization (NGO), is actively involved in suicide prevention activities in Jhenaidah, a suicide-prone district in Bangladesh (Khan et al., 2021). This organization extensively worked in mitigating and resolving causes related to suicide and attempt to suicide in Jhenaidah from 2005 to 2017 under direct financial backing of *Manuser Jonno Foundation* (foundation for man). In recognition of its highly impressive activities, SOVA achieved an international award (known as Lee Award) from the IASP. Currently, it is not functioning because of not able to assemble funds from any donor organization for being instrumental (Khan et al., 2021).

Brighter Tomorrow Foundation (BTF) is another NGO established in 2015 with a view to working for public mobilization against suicide, sensitization of reporting in media, and celebrating international suicidal prevention day and mental health day (Khan et al., 2021).

5.5 *Academic Society: SSPB*

The Society for Suicide Prevention Bangladesh (SSPB), an association, was founded in 2016 with the ambition to enhance suicide prevention in Bangladesh. Unfortunately, it is struggling to demonstrate noticeable suicide prevention activities. Also, it could not make any national and international collaboration for expanding its activities (Arafat, 2018).

6 Readiness of National Suicide Prevention Strategies

WHO widely explored the importance of developing a national suicide prevention strategy that has numerous benefits, such as helping to outline the scope and magnitude of the problem, as well as momentously recognizing that suicidal behavior is a major public health problem. It is also an indicator of the commitment of a government to addressing the issue. It recommends a structural framework incorporating various aspects of suicide prevention and provides authoritative guidance on key evidence-based suicide prevention activities. It helps to identify key stakeholders and allocates specific responsibilities to them. Moreover, it outlines necessary coordination among these various groups; identifies vital gaps in existing legislation, service provision, and data collection; and indicates the human and financial resources required for interventions. It shapes advocacy, awareness-raising, and media communications and proposes a robust framework of monitoring and evaluation, thereby instilling a sense of accountability among those in charge of interventions, as well as providing a context for a research agenda on suicidal behaviors (WHO, 2018).

According to Arafat (2021), Bangladesh has not formulated a central suicide database and national suicide prevention strategies until now. This section aims to focus on the current status of Bangladesh with regard to establishing national suicide prevention strategies based on 12 components suggested by WHO (Table 14.2).

Table 14.2 Readiness for national suicide prevention strategy. (WHO, 2014; Arafat, 2021, 2024a)

Sn.	Component	Status of Bangladesh
1	Sensible media reporting	Quality of media reporting is poor. There are no country-specific guidelines.
2	Raising awareness	There are sporadic activities by NGOs which are not planned and enduring. No national activity is available.
3	Training and education	Not available, low suicide literacy.
4	Treatment	Inadequate.
5	Economics (funds and political will)	Poor.
6	Crisis intervention	Kaan Pete Roi and National Emergency Service—999.
7	Oversight and coordination	Absent.
8	Means restriction	Class I pesticides banned.
9	Postvention	Not started yet.
10	Access to services	Not easily accessible.
11	Surveillance	Not started yet.
12	Stigma reduction	High stigma, suicide is a criminal offense.

Responsible media reporting is a key element of the national suicide prevention strategy, but it is poor in quality and unresponsive to Bangladesh. It has no concrete guidelines, which are obligatory to improve the current status. To sustain nationwide suicide prevention program and awareness raising is an important component. However, few periodic activities are done by some NGOs and at the government level. There is also lack of structured policies, which is necessary to raise awareness among the mass population at satisfactory level. Develop skilled manpower through training and education is key to articulating suicide prevention strategies, but it is not outlined yet in Bangladesh. The available treatment facilities for suicide patients are insufficient, and as it is an illegal offense, the individual with suicidal behavior laelled as police case. There is also lack of funding and political motivation for research on suicide and activities for suicide prevention. The services available for crisis intervention are inadequate according to demand. There is also lack institutional support to create leaders for the promotion and prevention of suicide. The government of Bangladesh has banned WHO class I pesticide, but policies regarding other methods of means restriction have been ignored. As an element of national suicide prevention strategies, it is recommended to take care of the postvention, which is challenging due to legal status of the society and stigma. Again, stigma, inadequate services, and avoidance of the providers may hinder the accessibility of individuals who are vulnerable. Establishing a national suicide surveillance is challenging for underreporting and poor quality of data. So, Bangladesh is far from the components of national suicide prevention strategies suggested by WHO.

Box 14.1 Suicide prevention activities in Bangladesh. (Adapted from Arafat, 2024a)

A. Clinical services (Suicide Prevention Clinic)

i. Bangladesh Medical University—ceased after the COVID-19 pandemic
ii. Enam Medical College and Hospital—ceased in late 2023

B. Crisis intervention (hotline)

i. Kaan Pete Roi—only dedicated helpline for suicide prevention
ii. National Emergency Service—999

C. NGO

i. SAJIDA Foundation
ii. Society for Voluntary Activities (SOVA)
iii. Brighter Tomorrow Foundation (BTF)
iv. Handicap International (humanity & inclusion)

D. Means restrictions

i. Category I pesticide ban

E. Society for Suicide Prevention, Bangladesh

7 Challenges of Suicide Prevention in Bangladesh

A well-designed suicide prevention strategy may threaten its success and sustainability due to barriers. So, overcoming barriers is crucial, and actions need to be well-defined and structured, taking into account the stakeholders involved, the resources available, and the characteristics of the national and local contexts. Considering this in advance may help to avoid barriers and reduce their consequences (WHO, 2018). According to WHO, potential barriers to implementing national suicide prevention strategies are related to management and logistics, stakeholders for leadership & management, teamwork & collaboration and legislation & policies, financial resources, human resources, multisectoral involvement, data and stigma (WHO, 2018).

From the previous section, it gives an impression that Bangladesh may not be rapidly moving forward toward suicide prevention because of the lack of effective and comprehensive policy measures to fight suicide and suicidal behavior (Arafat, 2025c). Again, the prevention interventions that are available are isolated, segmented, mostly underperforming, underfunded, or not funded. So, there is no visible societal impact. In such a circumstance, it is not surprising for LMICs like Bangladesh to have obstructing factors and challenges (Khan et al., 2021). The significant challenges for suicide prevention in Bangladesh are as follows:

7.1 *Data Is Silent*

Lack of national suicide data is the fundamental challenge for suicide prevention in Bangladesh (Arafat, 2025b). A reliable source of suicide information is a real challenge in the country, and the actual rate of suicide is yet to be estimated (Arafat, 2017, 2019). A countrywide epidemiological study has not been conducted in Bangladesh, and there is no publicly available data released periodically (Arafat, 2019).

7.2 *Criminal Legal Status*

According to Section 309 of the Penal Code (1860), suicide attempt is considered a criminal offence in Bangladesh. Any person who attempts suicide and activities related to it will be punishable through imprisonment and fine. The law enforcement agency has the right to arrest people who are attempting suicide. In addition, to avoid legal procedure and harassments, patient cannot complete treatment and leave the hospital without any prior notice. It is also a stigmatized and discriminated issue in the country (Bose & Arafat, 2026).

7.3 *Poor Quality of Media Reporting*

Accountable media reporting is key to a potential national suicide prevention strategy for the mass population (WHO, 2023a; Zalsman et al., 2016). Media plays a noteworthy role in raising awareness among the people and changing their attitude on suicide and the prevention of suicide. In Bangladesh, there is poor-quality media reporting for suicidal behavior (Arafat et al., 2019; Arafat & Anik, 2026). As suicide is a criminal offence in Bangladesh, media broadcasting of suicide events is undertaken by crime journalists (Arafat, 2019). A study conducted reveals that reports of suicide news are placed on the first page of the newspaper, and the majority reported the methods of suicide with details. About 50% of the articles provide a monocausal description of the suicide incidents. Few articles report the place of suicide and suicide note in detail, and also the impact of suicide on the bereaved persons. It also noted a lack of supportive reporting features on suicide and views of mental health experts (Arafat et al., 2020). Furthermore, media reports from online portals also deliver data in poor quality on suicidal behavior, such as mentioning the victim's name with details and methods of suicide, including the victim's image. There was no report noted with education and prevention approaches of suicide for mass population (Arafat et al., 2019). The detailed media reporting status has been discussed in Chap. 11 of this book (Arafat & Anik, 2026).

7.4 *Poor Awareness and Suicide Literacy Along with High Suicide Stigma*

Study reveals that suicide literacy among the university students of Bangladesh is inadequate, and they also have poor knowledge on suicidality and depression. The presence of stigma, legal status of suicide as a criminal offence, and lack of mass education among the people could be the key determinants of poor literacy of suicide that hamper help-seeking for suicide in the country (Arafat et al., 2021c, 2022; Arafat & Ali, 2026).

7.5 *Inadequate Mental Health Services*

In Bangladesh, the available mental health services are drastically inadequate according to need of the people. Currently, there are no specialized mental health services for persons with suicidal behavior (Arafat, 2024a). Moreover, as it is considered as criminal offense the patient with self-harm is supposed to police custody for judicial procedure. The extreme lack of mental health services is a significant challenge for the national suicide prevention strategy in the country (Arafat, 2018, 2024a; Arafat et al., 2019).

7.6 *Negligible Budget*

Fund availability for suicide prevention activities, research on suicide, and mental health services is undoubtedly inadequate. Normally, the budget for mental health is approximately 0.5% of health budgets. There is also lack of political motivation to introduce a suicide prevention policy, which is mandated for the country (Arafat, 2021).

8 Suicide Prevention in Bangladesh: Way Forward

The report "National suicide prevention strategies: progress, examples and indicators" was released by WHO in 2018 to support countries with their continued progress in suicide prevention, while inspiring others to establish or revise their national suicide prevention strategies. In this situation, Bangladesh should pay attention to the global call and formulate a national suicide prevention action plan (Khan et al., 2021). National suicide database and suicide surveillance are an imperative consideration of Bangladesh. Changes in the legal system to decriminalize suicide in the country should be considered as an instantaneous priority, which has already been done in some other parts of the world (Arafat, 2019, 2026). Decriminalization may help to destigmatize the problem and increase proper help-seeking behaviors for suicidality, as well as demolish the undue legal harassment (Arafat, 2019). It is an immediate obligation for the country to construct an appropriate prevention strategy to formulate, initiate, implement, and evaluate its effectiveness. Multisectoral collaborators such as clinicians, social scientists, researchers, funders, media professionals, social workers, voluntary organizations, nongovernmental organization, funders, and government and/or any organization connected with suicidality are also key actors for the country. International organizations should come forward to cooperate with the country in this regard (Arafat, 2019).

Bangladesh may consult with Bhutan and Sri Lanka as they have an effective national prevention strategy and have a similar socioeconomic and cultural context (Khan et al., 2021; WHO, 2018). In 2015, Bhutan adopted 3 years action plan from 2015 to 2018 for suicide prevention (Vijayakumar et al., 2020). This multifaceted action plan necessitates diverse cross-sectoral key stakeholders, sectors, and organizations. A Suicide Prevention Steering Committee (NSPSC) was created under the Ministry of Health to maintain governance and active operation of the plan (WHO, 2018).

8.1 Data

Bangladesh needs national suicide data for the prevention of suicidal behavior (Arafat, 2025b). National suicide database and suicide surveillance are an imperative consideration of Bangladesh. A national suicide surveillance system can provide data on suicide and self-harm to guide LIVE LIFE interventions and the source of data, such as civil registration and vital statistics, health and police records, verbal autopsies, and population-based surveys.

8.2 Media Monitoring

Responsible media reporting of suicide is one of the four pillars of the WHO's LIVE LIFE suicide prevention framework. Detrimental media reporting transmits contagion risks for people vulnerable to suicide. There is an opportunity to implement media reporting approaches that may have protective effects on the population (WHO, 2021b).

8.3 Intersectoral Collaboration

It is necessary since the risk factors for suicide are linked with many areas. A whole-of-society approach works across government sectors or departments and includes nongovernmental and community groups and facilitates knowledge-sharing, exchange of methodologies and lessons learned, and sharing of suicide-related data and research under the leadership of government (WHO, 2014). Intersectoral collaborators such as clinicians, social workers, researchers, media professionals, social scientists, voluntary organizations, and government and nongovernmental organizations connected with suicidality are key actors in the country. International organizations should come forward to cooperate with the country in this regard (Arafat, 2019).

8.4 More Funds in Suicide Research

Financing for suicide prevention is often inadequate because of factors such as poor economic conditions, lack of prioritization of suicide as a serious issue, and lack of recognition that suicides are preventable. So, requests for funds should include a focus on the development and implementation of policies, strategies, and plans (WHO, 2014).

8.5 Raising Awareness

It depends on targeting a public audience and an organized process of communication which draws people's attention to the facts, such as suicide is a serious public health issue. Advocacy aims to bring about changes such as decriminalization or a national suicide prevention strategy. Both strategies can range from a single community to nationwide public communication campaigns such as 'World Suicide Prevention Day'. It may also help to decrease stigma and negative attitudes among people with mental health disorders (WHO, 2014).

8.6 Gatekeeper Training

Sometimes people who are at risk of suicide may not seek help. A "gatekeeper" is anyone who is in a position to identify whether someone may be contemplating suicide, and the potential gatekeepers are primary, mental and emergency health providers, teachers and other school staff, community leaders, police officers, firefighters and other first responders, military officers, social welfare workers, spiritual and religious leaders or traditional healers, and human resource staff and managers (WHO, 2014).

8.7 Decriminalization

In many countries, decriminalization of suicide is considered a part of suicide prevention strategy (World Health Organization, 2023b). The issue is also raised by some other Asian countries (Arafat, 2026). At present, the legalization of suicide is a rising issue raised by scientists in Bangladesh. In the country, it is a vital prerequisite for confirming a suitable suicide prevention environment (Arafat, 2026). However, only decriminalization will not provide any positive impact on suicide prevention in Bangladesh without addressing the other vital issues related to suicide, such as trustworthy reporting of media on suicidal behavior, suicide surveillance system, national database of suicide, national suicide prevention strategies, and empirical research and appropriate policy implementation (World Health Organization, 2023b; Arafat & Khan, 2019). This may lead to changing the attitude of the masses to suicidality by reducing legal restrictions and social stigma and also increasing accessibility to health care.

On the contrary, the recently endorsed *Bangladesh Mental Health Act 2018* does not suggest any clear provision to approach decriminalization of suicide or attempt to suicide, but the matter of decriminalization must be prioritized so that suicidal populations can have access to treatment instead of punishment (Arafat, 2025c). Again, Bangladesh is on the way to articulate an inclusive suicide prevention policy or an essential database for suicide prevention in line with the call of WHO (Arafat, 2021). Bangladesh highly needs an inclusive and vigorous mental health strategy that integrates suicide prevention (Arafat, 2025c).

8.8 National Suicide Prevention Strategy

'National suicide prevention strategies: Progress' examples and indicators' a report launched by WHO in 2018 to support the countries in suicide prevention with their continued progress, whilst inspiring others to launch or revise their national suicide prevention strategies. In this situation, Bangladesh should pay attention to global call and articulate a national suicide prevention action plan (Khan et al., 2021). It is an immediate obligation for the country to construct appropriate prevention strategy to formulate, initiate, implement and evaluate its effectiveness.

8.9 Increased Psychiatric Services

Generally, in a primary care setting, depression and other forms of psychiatric disorders are undertreated and underpredictable. Studies from several developed countries revealed that there is a significant association between the education of primary care providers and reducing suicide by early identification of depression, substance abuse, and other risk factors for suicide. Subsequently, educating physicians of primary health care level for appropriate assessment of depression and evaluation of risk of suicide is an element of suicide prevention (Mann et al., 2005; Zalsman et al., 2016).

8.10 Religious or Spiritual Beliefs

Religious beliefs and spirituality give mental happiness. They inspire people to endure any kind of difficulties. Generally, people die by suicide when they cannot accept something contrary to their expectations. Islam prohibits suicide and considers it a great sin. Again, spirituality gives mental satisfaction, which is very important in abstaining from any kind of harm, including suicide. Thus, religion and spirituality can play a vital role in preventing all sorts of destruction, including oneself (Arafat et al., 2024b). So, by maintaining religious obligation and spirituality, a society can prevent suicide.

Additionally, engaging the religious leaders (Imams) in suicide prevention targeting the suicide literacy could be tested in the country as it has about 1.7 million Imams and Muazzins who are available at least five time a day for general population (Arafat, 2024b).

8.11 Restriction of Offending Medications

Use of sedatives like benzodiazepines is one of the leading methods of self-harm and suicidal behavior in Bangladesh (Arafat et al., 2024a, 2025b). One recent report noted rampant dispensing of sedatives by online orders, which results in suicide attempts (Arafat, 2025d). Attention from regulatory authorities are warranted, and dispensing of bendodiazepines could be restricted under "Means Restriction" category (Arafat, 2025c).

8.12 Policy Development

In Bangladesh, suicide and suicide prevention are not given enough attention (Arafat, 2025a). In this country, efforts to comprehend and effectively address suicide behavior are hampered by the lack of a national suicide database and surveillance system. It is also difficult to manage suicide by stigma, underreporting, and a lack of mental health resources (Iqbal et al., 2024). Studies conducted by Arafat et al. (2025b) and Iqbal et al. (2024), provide a foundation for policy development to manage and prevent suicide (Box 14.2).

Box 14.2 Important areas for policy development for suicide prevention in Bangladesh. (Adapted from Arafat et al., 2025a; Iqbal et al., 2024)

1. Establishment of a national suicide database and national suicide surveillance system
2. Publicly available quality data
3. Enduring and active collaboration among prominent stakeholders
4. Law enforcement agencies
5. The legislative body
6. The media
7. Mental health professionals
8. Public health professionals
9. Involvement of volunteers
10. Expansion of helpline services
11. Integration into national emergency frameworks
12. Increased public awareness to reduce stigma and encourage help-seeking behaviour.

9 Conclusion

In Bangladesh, suicide is a neglected public health issue. The key risk factors are located within the family, and the common methods are hanging and fall from height. The criminal legal status, poor quality, lack of awareness, actual suicide rate, poor quality media reporting, inadequate mental health services, social stigma, negligible budget, and poor coordination among the sectors are real challenges for this part. Preventive measures have been in progress but have yet to make tracks. Finally, empirical studies, increased psychiatric services through primary care physician education at different levels of health sector, decriminalization, and national suicide surveillance are the priority list for the country.

References

Arafat, S. M. Y. (2026). Law, policy, and strategies on suicide prevention in Bangladesh. In S. M. Y. Arafat (Ed.), *Suicidal behavior in Bangladesh*. Springer. https://doi.org/10.1007/978-981-95-8321-8_10

Arafat, S. M. Y., & Ali, S. A. Z. (2026). Literacy and stigma of suicidal behavior in Bangladesh. In S. M. Y. Arafat (Ed.), *Suicidal behavior in Bangladesh*. Springer. https://doi.org/10.1007/978-981-95-8321-8_12

Arafat, S. M. Y., & Anik, A. I. (2026). Media and suicidal behavior in Bangladesh. In S. M. Y. Arafat (Ed.), *Suicidal behavior in Bangladesh*. Springer. https://doi.org/10.1007/978-981-95-8321-8_11

Arafat, S. M. Y., & Kabir, R. (2026). Data is silent, epidemiology is blur: Suicidal behavior in Bangladesh-what is known and what needs to improve. In S. M. Y. Arafat (Ed.), *Suicidal behavior in Bangladesh*. Springer. https://doi.org/10.1007/978-981-95-8321-8_1

Arafat, S. M. Y., & Saleem, T. (2026). Suicidal behavior in Bangladesh: A socio-ecological analysis. In S. M. Y. Arafat (Ed.), *Suicidal behavior in Bangladesh*. Springer. https://doi.org/10.1007/978-981-95-8321-8_5

Arafat, S. M. Y. (2025a). Suicide prevention in Bangladesh: The role of police. *The Lancet. Psychiatry, 12*(3), 173. https://doi.org/10.1016/S2215-0366(24)00443-7

Arafat, S. Y. (2025b). Suicide is criminal, data is silent: Reimagining suicide surveillance in Bangladesh—from police reports to public health action. *International Journal of Mental Health and Addiction*, 1–3. https://doi.org/10.1007/s11469-025-01514-1

Arafat, S. M. Y. (2025c). Suicide prevention in Bangladesh: Critical analysis of mental health law, policy and strategy. *BJPsych International, 22*(4), 138–141. https://doi.org/10.1192/bji.2025.10042

Arafat, S. M. Y. (2025d). Online dispensing of benzodiazepines can be an emerging threat for suicide prevention in Bangladesh: A case and potential preventive measures. *Asian Journal of Psychiatry, 106*, 104446. https://doi.org/10.1016/j.ajp.2025.104446

Arafat, S. M. Y., Mourin, C., & Jahan, R. (2025a). Crisis help line and suicide prevention in Bangladesh: Challenges and ways ahead. *Asian Journal of Psychiatry, 109*, 104565. https://doi.org/10.1016/j.ajp.2025.104565

Arafat, S. M. Y., Mali, B., & Mazumder, A. H. (2025b). Nonsuicidal self-injury in Bangladesh: A narrative review. *Health Science Reports, 8*(5), e70790. https://doi.org/10.1002/hsr2.70790

Arafat, S. M. Y., Shormi, F. R., & Kibria, M. G. (2024a). Psychiatric disorder and life-event in self harm: A cross-sectional study among clinical population in Bangladesh. *Heliyon, 10*(19), e38627. https://doi.org/10.1016/j.heliyon.2024.e38627

Arafat, S. M. Y., Rezaeian, M., & Khan, M. M. (2024b). Suicidal behavior in islamic countries: An overview. In S. M. Y. Arafat, M. Rezaeian, & M. M. Khan (Eds.), *Suicidal behavior in muslim majority countries*. Springer. https://doi.org/10.1007/978-981-97-2519-9_1

Arafat, S. M. Y. (2024a). Suicidal behavior and suicide prevention in Bangladesh. In S. M. Y. Arafat (Ed.), *Mental health in Bangladesh*. Springer. https://doi.org/10.1007/978-981-97-0610-5_11

Arafat, S. M. Y. (2024b). Islamic religious leaders and mental health services in Bangladesh: An existing untapped area. *Mental Health, Religion & Culture, 27*(7), 740–741. https://doi.org/10.1080/13674676.2025.2507401

Arafat, S., Hussain, F., Hossain, M. F., Islam, M. A., & Menon, V. (2022). Literacy and stigma of suicide in Bangladesh: Scales validation and status assessment among university students. *Brain and Behavior, 12*(1), e2432. https://doi.org/10.1002/brb3.2432

Arafat, S. M. Y., Mohit, M. A., Mullick, M. S. I., Kabir, R., & Khan, M. M. (2021a). Risk factors for suicide in Bangladesh: Case–control psychological autopsy study. *BJPsych Open, 7*(1), e18. https://doi.org/10.1192/bjo.2020.152

Arafat, S., Khan, M., Knipe, D., & Khan, M. M. (2021b). Population attributable fractions of clinical and social risk factors for suicide in Bangladesh: Finding from a case-control psychological autopsy study. *Brain and Behavior, 11*(12), e2409. https://doi.org/10.1002/brb3.2409

Arafat, S., Menon, V., & Kar, S. K. (2021c). Media and suicide prevention in Southeast Asia: Challenges and directions. *Journal of Public Health (Oxford, England), 43*(1), e123–e124. https://doi.org/10.1093/pubmed/fdaa084

Arafat, S. M. Y. (2021). Formulation of national suicide prevention strategy of Bangladesh: The readiness assessment. *Journal of Public Health (Oxford, England), 43*(1), e131–e132. https://doi.org/10.1093/pubmed/fdaa117

Arafat, S. M. Y., Khan, M. M., Niederkrotenthaler, T., Ueda, M., & Armstrong, G. (2020). Assessing the quality of media reporting of suicide deaths in Bangladesh against world health organization guidelines. *Crisis, 41*(1), 47–53. https://doi.org/10.1027/0227-5910/a000603

Arafat, S. M. Y. (2019). Current challenges of suicide and future directions of management in Bangladesh: A systematic review. *Global Psychiatry, 2*(1), 9–20. https://doi.org/10.2478/gp-2019-0001

Arafat, S. M. Y., Mali, B., & Akter, H. (2019). Quality of online news reporting of suicidal behavior in Bangladesh against World Health Organization guidelines. *Asian Journal of Psychiatry, 40*, 126–129. https://doi.org/10.1016/j.ajp.2018.10.010

Arafat, S., & Khan, S. T. (2019). Suicide prevention in Bangladesh: Only decriminalization would not be beneficial in an expected fashion. *Asian Journal of Psychiatry, 42*, 22–23. https://doi.org/10.1016/j.ajp.2019.03.027

Arafat, S. M. Y. (2018). Suicide prevention activities in Bangladesh. *Asian Journal of Psychiatry, 36*, 38. https://doi.org/10.1016/j.ajp.2018.06.009

Arafat, S. M. Y., Mali, B., & Akter, H. (2018). Demography and risk factors of suicidal behavior in Bangladesh: A retrospective online news content analysis. *Asian Journal of Psychiatry, 36*(July), 96–99. https://doi.org/10.1016/j.ajp.2018.07.008

Arafat, S. M. Y., & Kabir, R. (2017). Suicide prevention strategies: Which one to consider? *South East Asia Journal of Public Health, 7*(1), 1–5. https://doi.org/10.3329/seajph.v7i1.34671

Arafat, S. M. Y. (2017). Suicide in Bangladesh: A mini review. *Journal of Behavioral Health, 6*(1), 66–69. https://doi.org/10.5455/jbh.20160904090206

Bangladesh Bureau of Statistics. (2024). *Population & Housing Census 2022*. Accessed June 30, 2025, from https://bbs.gov.bd/site/page/47856ad0-7e1c-4aab-bd78-892733bc06eb/Population-&-Housing

Bose, P. K., & Arafat, S. M. Y. (2026). Forensic medicine, post-mortem and suicide in Bangladesh. In S. Y. Arafat (Ed.), *Suicidal behavior in Bangladesh*. Springer. https://doi.org/10.1007/978-981-95-8321-8_2

Chowdhury, F. R., Dewan, G., Verma, V. R., Knipe, D. W., Isha, I. T., Faiz, M. A., Gunnell, D. J., & Eddleston, M. (2018). Bans of WHO class I pesticides in Bangladesh-suicide prevention without hampering agricultural output. *International Journal of Epidemiology, 47*(1), 175–184. https://doi.org/10.1093/ije/dyx157

Feroz, A., Islam, S. N., Reza, S., Rahman, A. M., Sen, J., Mowla, M., & Rahman, M. R. (2012). A community survey on the prevalence of suicidal attempts and deaths in a selected rural area of Bangladesh. *Journal of Medicine, 13*(1), 3–9. https://doi.org/10.3329/jom.v13i1.10042

Iqbal, Y., Jahan, R., & Das, A. (2024). Policy recommendations from ten years of suicide prevention through Bangladesh's only telephone-based suicide prevention helpline. *South East Asian Journal of Suicide Prevention, 1*(1) https://seajsp.qvjournal.com/index.php/about/article/view/6

Iqbal, Y., Jahan, R., & Matin, M. R. (2019). Descriptive characteristics of callers to an emotional support and suicide prevention helpline in Bangladesh (first five years). *Asian Journal of Psychiatry, 45*, 63–65. https://doi.org/10.1016/j.ajp.2019.09.005

Khan, A. R., Arendse, N., & Ratele, K. (2021). Suicide prevention in Bangladesh: The current state and the way forward. *Asian Social Work and Policy Review, 15*(1), 15–23. https://doi.org/10.1111/aswp.12214

Khan, A. R., Ratele, K., Helman, R., Dlamini, S., & Makama, R. (2022). Masculinity and suicide in Bangladesh. *Omega, 86*(1), 218–240. https://doi.org/10.1177/0030222820966239

Khan, A. R., Ratele, K., Arendse, N., Islam, M. Z., & Dery, I. (2020). Suicide and attempted suicide in Jhenaidah district, Bangladesh, 2010–2018. *Crisis, 41*(4), 304–312. https://doi.org/10.1027/0227-5910/a000631

Mann, J. J., Apter, A., Bertolote, J., Beautrais, A., Currier, D., Haas, A., Hegerl, U., Lonnqvist, J., Malone, K., Marusic, A., Mehlum, L., Patton, G., Phillips, M., Rutz, W., Rihmer, Z., Schmidtke, A., Shaffer, D., Silverman, M., Takahashi, Y., & Hendin, H. (2005). Suicide prevention strategies: A systematic review. *Journal of the American Medical Association, 294*, 2064–2074. https://doi.org/10.1001/jama.294.16.2064

Mashreky, S. R., Rahman, F., & Rahman, A. (2013). Suicide kills more than 10,000 people every year in Bangladesh. *Archives of Suicide Research, 17*, 387–396. https://doi.org/10.1080/13811118.2013.801809

Naghavi, M., & Global Burden of Disease Self-Harm Collaborators. (2019). Global, regional, and national burden of suicide mortality 1990 to 2016: Systematic analysis for the Global Burden of Disease Study 2016. *BMJ, 364*, l94. https://doi.org/10.1136/bmj.l94

Shah, M., Sajib, M., & Arafat, S. (2018). Demography and risk factor of suicidal behavior in Bangladesh: A cross-sectional observation from patients attending a suicide prevention clinic of Bangladesh. *Asian Journal of Psychiatry, 35*, 4–5. https://doi.org/10.1016/j.ajp.2018.04.035

Shahnaz, A., Bagley, C., Simkhada, P., & Kadri, S. (2017). Suicidal behavior in Bangladesh: A scoping literature review and a proposed public health prevention model. *Open Journal of Social Sciences, 5*, 254–282. https://doi.org/10.4236/jss.2017.57016

Sharmin Salam, S., Alonge, O., Islam, M. D., Hoque, D., Wadhwaniya, S., Ul Baset, M. D., Mashreky, S., & El Arifeen, S. (2017). The burden of suicide in rural Bangladesh: Magnitude and risk factors. *International Journal of Environmental Research and Public Health, 14*(9), 1032. https://doi.org/10.3390/ijerph14091032

Vijayakumar, L., Daly, C., Arafat, Y., & Arensman, E. (2020). Suicide prevention in the Southeast Asia region. *Crisis, 41*(Suppl 1), S21–S29. https://doi.org/10.1027/0227-5910/a000666

World Health Organization. (2025). *Suicide*. WHO. Accessed June 30, 2025, from https://www.who.int/news-room/fact-sheets/detail/suicide

World Health Organization. (2024). *Preventing suicide by phasing out highly hazardous pesticides*. WHO. Accessed September 02, 2025, from https://www.who.int/publications/m/item/preventing-suicide-by-phasing-out-highly-hazardous-pesticides

World Health Organization. (2023a). *Preventing suicide: a resource for media professionals: Update 2023*. Accessed June 30, 2025, from https://www.who.int/publications/i/item/9789240076846

World Health Organization. (2023b). *WHO policy brief on the health aspects of decriminalization of suicide and suicide attempts*. World Health Organization. Accessed August 31, 2025, from https://www.who.int/publications/i/item/9789240078796

WHO. (2022). *Mental Health Atlas 2020 country profile: Bangladesh*. Accessed July 15, 2022, from https://www.who.int/publications/m/item/mental-health-atlas-bgd-2020-country-profile

WHO. (2021a). *Suicide worldwide in 2019: Global health estimates*. World Health Organization. Accessed September 1, 2022.

WHO. (2021b). *LIVE LIFE: An implementation guide for suicide prevention in countries*. World Health Organization. Accessed September 5, 2022.

WHO. (2018). *National suicide prevention strategies: Progress, examples and indicators*. World Health Organization. Accessed September 05, 2022, from https://www.who.int/mental_health/suicide-prevention/national_strategies_2019/en/

WHO. (2014). *Preventing suicide: A global imperative*. World Health Organization. Accessed July 25, 2022, from https://www.who.int/mental_health/suicide-prevention/world_report_2014/en/

WHO. (2013). *Mental health action plan 2013–2020*. World Health Organization. Accessed July 25, 2022, from https://www.who.int/publications/i/item/9789241506021

Zalsman, G., Hawton, K., Wasserman, D., van Heeringen, K., Arensman, E., Sarchiapone, M., Carli, V., Höschl, C., Barzilay, R., Balazs, J., Purebl, G., Kahn, J. P., Sáiz, P. A., Lipsicas, C. B., Bobes, J., Cozman, D., Hegerl, U., & Zohar, J. (2016). Suicide prevention strategies revisited: 10-year systematic review. *The Lancet. Psychiatry, 3*(7), 646–659. https://doi.org/10.1016/S2215-0366(16)30030-X

Index

S. M. Y. Arafat (ed.), *Suicidal Behavior in Bangladesh*, Mental Health Systems and Policy in Low- and Middle-Income Countries,
https://doi.org/10.1007/978-981-95-8321-8